A COOKBOOK AND LIFESTYLE GUIDE FOR DIABETES AND FAMILY HEALTH

# Living
*into the 21st Century*
# with
# Diabetes
*Peggy Stacy*

### The West Australian

First published 1998 by West Australian Newspapers Limited, 50 Hasler Road, Osborne Park 6017. Reprinted 1999–2002.

Distributed by West Australian Newspapers

©Peggy Stacy 1998

All rights reserved. Except as provided by Australian copyright law, no part of this book may be reproduced without written permission of the publisher.

Printed by PK Print Pty Ltd, Hamilton Hill 6163

Edited and produced by Darlington Publishing Group, Darlington 6070

Cover design Mark Fisher

Photographs Jason Stacy; Allan Borushek, for providing additional photographs taken by Richard Meyers.

National Library of Australia cataloguing-in-publication data:

Stacy, Peggy.

Living into the 21st century with diabetes: a cookbook and lifestyle guide for diabetes and family health.

ISBN 0 909699 66 6

1. Diabetes - Diet therapy - Recipes. 2. Diabetes - Popular works. I. Title: II. Title: Living into the 21st century with diabetes.

641.56314

**Enjoy your favourite Hunsa Smallgoods with that *FAT FREE DIFFERENCE* and *GUILT FREE FEELING*.**

Ask for our products at your favourite Supermarket.

**the WA Fat Free Company.**

# Foreword

This cookbook for people with diabetes will make your kitchen workbench irresistible. You can begin weighing, chopping and peeling healthy ingredients immediately without the enthusiasm-sapping task of searching shops for hidden exotica found in most modern recipes but not in the cupboard.

Peggy Stacy is an experienced Australian medical dietitian and home cook. Here she shares more than 300 of her best easy recipes which look and taste a treat every time. She encourages the use of a wide variety of nutritious foods with plenty of complex carbohydrates and high fibre, low fat content, and permissable amounts of sugar, all carefully measured and weighed. An extensive introduction on diabetes includes dietary guidelines, Glycaemic Index and some complete day-to-day menus, and is an added bonus. There are practical cooking suggestions throughout.

Peggy's delicious foods plus the physical exercise she recommends will encourage health and happiness, particularly for those with today's common problems that include diabetes and obestiy. These recipes will make healthy eating a daily delight. Enjoy!

DR TIMOTHY WELBORN MBBS (WA), FRACP, PHD
Head of Diabetes Centre
Sir Charles Gairdner Hospital, Perth, Western Australia

# Introduction

The recommended diabetic diet is a healthy diet and this cook book and lifestyle guide shows how to follow a well-balanced, varied healthy eating plan with diabetes. It will help in the control of blood sugar and add to the enjoyment of a normal lifestyle. There are many cornerstones to the healthy diabetic diet. Food intake is low fat, high fibre, with sensible quantities of carbohydrate (sugar-producing food) at any one time.
It would be wise for everyone to follow such a regimen. In this book there are over 300 recipe ideas of which at least 50 are vegetarian.
The meal plans and menus will help in the selection of appropriate, interesting and varied meals on a daily basis.
There is also a complete nutritional analysis of each recipe which provides the means to measure and maintain the most suitable nutrient levels for each individual.
Readers are urged to refer to the **Recipe Analysis Explained** on p30 and the supportive charts at the back of the book.
Specific dietary advice covering diabetes, general nutrition, weight control, exercise, fat, Glycaemic Index and alcohol is also given.
This is the book that should be included
in your kitchen above all others.

# Diabetes monitoring made easy.

**ACCU-CHEK®**
Advantage

- Bold, easy to read display
- Unique comfort curve strip
- No cleaning required
- 100 test memory

**ACCU-CHEK®**
Active

The fastest meter on the Australian market

- 5 second test time
- Tiny drop of blood
- 200 test memory
- Auto start
- Infra-red download capability

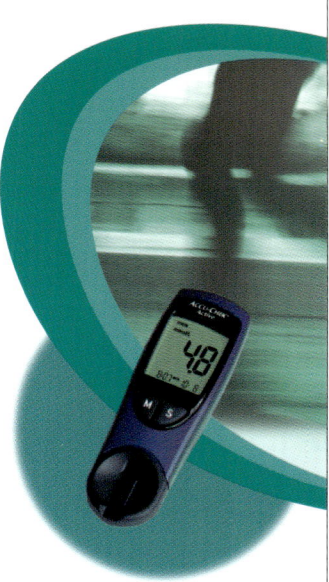

Roche

Enquiry Line: 1800 251 816
www.accu-chek.com

**ACCU-CHEK®**
Live life. We'll fit in.

# Contents

| | |
|---|---|
| Foreword | 3 |
| Introduction | 4 |
| Learning About Diabetes and Good Health | 7 |
| Choosing and Following a Balanced Diabetic Diet | 15 |
| Recipe Section | 29 |
|     Breakfast | 31 |
|     Luncheon | 34 |
|     First Course, Savouries and Dips | 37 |
|     Soups | 42 |
|     Main Meals | 47 |
|         Meat Alternatives | 47 |
|         Chicken | 62 |
|         Meat | 67 |
|         Fish and Seafood | 77 |
|     Vegetables and Grains | 84 |
|     Salads and Dressings | 95 |
|     Sauces | 104 |
|     Desserts | 109 |
|     Baking | 120 |
| Charts and Tables | 132 |
|     Healthy Food Choices Based on Glycaemic Index | 132 |
|     Mini Fat Counter Table | 133 |
|     Alcohol, Energy and Carbohydrate (CHO) Chart | 134 |
|     Carbohydrate, Kilojoule and Calorie Content of Common Foods | 135 |
|     Recipe Nutritional Analysis Summary | 140 |
|     Handy Abbreviation and Measurement Guide | 147 |
|     Index | 148 |

Dedicated to my youngest brother who has lived successfully with Insulin Dependent Diabetes Mellitus only to have to face a new battle with cancer. He has been an inspiration to me and has given me the impetus to complete this book.

## *Acknowledgments*

Diana Osler, dietitian, business partner and good friend for her support, contributions, proofreading and assistance in photography.
Ruth Foley, friend and dietitian who has given valuable advice and time in proofreading.
My son, Jason Stacy, for the main photographs and assistance in food presentation.
The staff at the Perth Diet Clinic, especially Margaret Rudderham, Susan Harris and Leigh Croxford in typing, nutrient analysis and support in the long hours that this book has taken. It wouldn't have been completed without them.
Allan and Helen Borushek for assistance and support.
Typesetting and design, Ross Haig with assistance from Keith Jones.
McGregor Ceramics, who provided pottery for photographs.
Bernie Ayers, Manager, Health Promotions Research, Diabetes Australia for support.
Rhys Jones, General Manager, Diabetes Australia for support.
Dr Tim Welborn for doing the Foreword.
Ross O'Dea for support and publishing.
Australian Diabetes Educators Association (ADEA) Quality Assurance subcommittee/Resource Approval for reviewing and endorsing the book for 1998 to 2001.
Ingrid Tigwell from ADEA for support in endorsing the book.
Sue Gough for reviewing the book for Diabetes Australia.

# Learning About Diabetes and Good Health

Diabetes is a condition in which there is little or no control of sugar levels in the blood. High blood sugar levels lead to sugar being excreted in the urine. An estimated 650,000 Australians have diabetes of which 350,000 know they have it and another 300,000 remain undiagnosed. A further significant number are in danger of developing diabetes, particularly those who are older and overweight.
Control of diabetes will help prevent long-term complications including heart disease, stroke, blindness, kidney failure, limb amputation and impotence.
A team of specialists comprising general practitioner, diabetes specialist, dietitian, diabetes educator and podiatrist work together to ensure that the individual has adequate care. Those with diabetes should be in control of their own health and have sufficient knowledge to seek further advice when and if required.

*Types of Diabetes 8*
*Diet and Diabetes 8*
*Diet and Blood Sugar Control 8*
*Blood Glucose Monitoring 9*
*Weight Control and Diabetes 9*
*Physical Activity, Exercise and Diabetes 10*
*Blood Fats and Diabetes 10*
*Vegetarian Eating 11*
*Alcohol 11*
*Artificial Sweeteners 11*
*Glycaemic Index 12*
*Diabetes Australia 13*
*Dietary Guidelines for Australians 13*
*How to Adapt Your Cooking Recipes 14*

## Types of Diabetes

*Impaired Glucose Tolerance*
This occurs before diabetes develops. Losing weight and following a diet for diabetes will help to delay or prevent the onset of diabetes and complications.

*Insulin Dependent Diabetes Mellitus (IDDM) or Type 1 Diabetes*
This mostly affects children and young adults but can occur at any age. Representing approximately 10% of people with diabetes, it is a life-threatening condition which necessitates insulin by injection. A careful eating plan and regular exercise is important.
Symptoms include thirst, frequency of passing urine and weight loss.

*Non Insulin Dependent Diabetes Mellitus (NIDDM) or Type 2 Diabetes*
This represents approximately 90% of people with diabetes and is more likely to be inherited. Mostly NIDDM affects those of older years, especially when overweight. It is usually treated by diet and exercise, sometimes with the addition of tablets or insulin. Symptoms occur gradually and may go unnoticed for many years. The most common indicators are thirst, frequency of passing urine and tiredness.

*Gestational Diabetes Mellitus (GDM)*
This occurs in 6% of women during pregnancy. It increases the risk of pregnancy complications and results in a higher risk of developing NIDDM in later life. Women who develop GDM should endeavour to keep to an ideal weight after pregnancy and to follow a good healthy eating plan that is low in fat and high in fibre. Refer to the **Healthy Food Pyramid** p16.

## Diet and Diabetes

*Diabetes and Control*
Whilst many medical advances have taken place in the care of people with diabetes, diet remains the cornerstone of maintaining good health. Understanding the relevance of weight and the role of exercise and carbohydrates (CHO), which are sugar producing foods, is important for management. Changes in recent years mean that the emphasis has moved away from simple versus complex CHO to their effect on blood glucose levels. Sugar need no longer be excluded but should be minimised to assist in CHO and weight control.

*The Glycaemic Index (GI)*
This is the amount a controlled quantity of CHO raises the blood sugars over a set amount of time. It has become important, as low glycaemic index (GI) foods help to stabilise blood sugars. Low GI foods have been used as frequently as possible throughout the book. Refer to the detailed section on **Glycaemic Index** p12 and the chart on **Healthy Food Choices Based on Glycaemic Index** p132.

*Meal Planning*
A well-planned diet for the person with diabetes should include meals the entire family can enjoy. A basic meal should incorporate the **Healthy Food Chart** p16 and the **Australian Dietary Guidelines** p13 to give nutritionally balanced eating. This will help prevent common diseases such as coronary heart disease, cancer and intestinal tract problems.

## Diet and Blood Sugar Control

*Distribution of Carbohydrate (CHO)*
Insulin is necessary to control blood sugar levels. As those with diabetes have a reduced amount, or no insulin in the pancreas, the quantity of carbohydrate (CHO) breaking down to sugar in the blood must be controlled at any one time. If too little CHO is consumed at one time (as from skipping meals or having meat and salad only) low blood sugars can result.
It is not advisable to consume extra CHO later as often there won't be enough insulin (unless it given by injection).
Too much CHO at one time will elevate blood sugars. This can be partially controlled with tablets, insulin or exercise. It is better for people with higher energy (kilojoule and calorie) requirements to have in-between meal snacks.
Having a controlled amount of CHO throughout the day to match your energy requirements is ideal and will give blood sugars within a healthy range.

*Snacks Between Meals*
Snacks between meals are an individual thing. Overweight people with diabetes who are not on diabetic medication may not need snacks unless the break between meals is exceptionally long. Those on medication and/or insulin may need snacks to maintain blood sugar levels between meals or before or during exercise. Discuss this with your general practitioner, dietitian or diabetes educator.

**UNWISE**
Eating Pattern

3 Large Meals
Uneven Carbohydrate
Distribution

**BLOOD SUGAR LEVELS**
Excess Variation

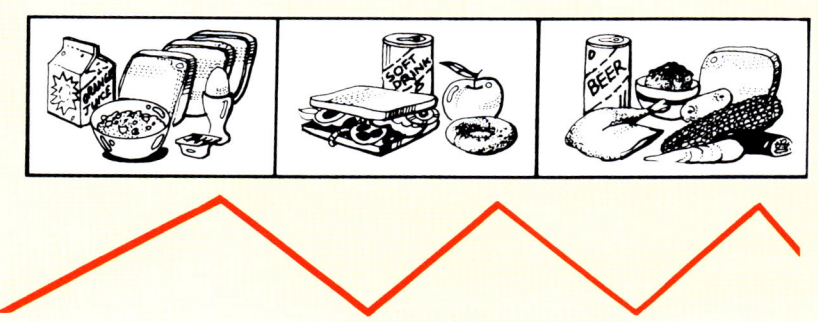

**WISE**
Eating Pattern

3 Medium Meals + 3 Snacks
Even Carbohydrate
Distribution

**BLOOD SUGAR LEVELS**
Minimum Variation

*Changing Insulin Requirements*
Insulin requirements for each individual will vary under different circumstances.

**Reduced Insulin Requirements**
Increased exercise
Reduction of food containing carbohydrate
Weight loss

**Increased Insulin Requirements**
Illness, fever
Trauma, stress
Surgery
Increased age
Reduced exercise
Increased carbohydrate intake
Weight gain

## Blood Glucose Monitoring

*Testing Blood Sugars*
Those with diabetes should be in control of their own health. The best way to regulate this is to test blood sugars at home.
Usually blood sugars are tested before breakfast (fasting) and/or 2 hours after a meal (non-fasting or random). A doctor, dietitian or diabetes educator will suggest the frequency and timing best suited to each individual.

*Good Control*
It is important to maintain blood sugars under 10mmol/litres. Ideally, blood sugars should range between 4 and 7 mmol/litre. Normal fasting blood sugars for non diabetics are 3.5 to 5.5 mmol/litre.
Better control will be facilitated with home glucose monitoring.

*Home Blood Glucose Monitors*
A glucose monitor is a small compact machine that gives a instant blood sugar reading when a drop of blood from the finger is placed on a testing strip that is inserted in the machine. There are a number of monitors or machines on the the market. Diabetes Australia, diabetes educators and some chemists will offer a range to choose from. Make sure to select one that is easy to use and read. Some machines with a computer hook-up will allow accumulated results to be printed as a graph or table. There is usually a rebate available from health funds provided a doctor's referral is obtained.

## Weight Control and Diabetes

Control of overweight reduces the risk of diabetes, heart disease and hypertension (blood pressure). To lose weight one should have sensible, controlled eating with reduced fat and increased exercise. If the kilojoules and carbohydrate (CHO) are reduced then the insulin or hypoglycaemic medication must also be reduced to avoid low blood sugars or insulin reactions. Check with your general practitioner for advice on reducing medication.

## LEARNING ABOUT DIABETES

*Hints for Weight Control*
- Reduce or eliminate high fat take-away and fatty foods.
- Eat a diet high in fibre and in slow absorbing CHO and low glycaemic index foods (GI) such as beans, lentils, whole grain breads, cereals, fruit and vegetables. In this book recipes include low GI foods as much as possible. Refer to the section on **Glycaemic Index** p12 and the chart on **Healthy Food Choices Based on Glycaemic Index** p132.
- Reduce fat content by removing the fat and skin from meat and chicken and use low fat dairy products. Use less fat when cooking.
- Spread bread with ricotta, cottage cheese or **Hommos** p39 instead of butter or margarine.
- Refer to the **Mini Fat Counter Table** p133 and **How to Adapt Your Cooking and Recipes** p14.

*Acceptable Weekly Weight Loss*
An acceptable rate of loss is 1/2 to 1kg per week. Even less is still quite acceptable if it is maintained over a period of time. Avoid gaining if at all possible. It is better to change your eating habits to ones you can follow indefinitely and thereby lose weight slowly.

*Crash Dieting Doesn't Work — Exercise and Controlled Eating Does*
It is wise to match the amount of food with the amount of exercise or physical activity to avoid slowing the metabolism. Cutting down on kilojoules too drastically causes the body to compensate by slowing the metabolism and long-term weight loss becomes more difficult. Increasing exercise and physical activity will stimulate the metabolism to work better. This requires a permanent change in lifestyle.

*How to Lose Weight Without Dieting*
Check your eating habits
- Do you eat too quickly?
- Do you chew your food poorly?
- Are you the first one finished?
- Do you eat when you are not hungry?
- Do you eat because you are bored or stressed?
- Do you shop when you are hungry?

If 'yes' to any of the above applies, and you are unable to solve these problems yourself, seek the help of a dietitian or psychologist.

## Physical Activity, Exercise and Diabetes

Active recreational habits, social sport, gardening and housework are all important to include in the regular routine as they will help to control weight. Be as active in your everyday lifestyle as possible.

Exerting yourself to the point of puffing will improve your aerobic fitness and speed up the metabolism. Any active sport or exercise is good but sustained activity for 35 minutes or more will help to reduce your insulin requirement and help control blood sugars for 24 hours or more.

Choose walking, swimming, cycling, rowing or an exercise bicycle. Start slowly and build up as you become fitter.

Discuss your programme with your general practitioner beforehand.

Refer to the National Heart Foundation in your state for further information and one of their *Be Active Everyday* leaflets.

Exercise reduces insulin requirements in people with NIDDM and IDDM. It also brings down blood sugar levels when adequate insulin is available.

However exercise is not recommended for people with IDDM with blood sugars above 15mmol/litre. If this is not understood, discuss this with a dietitian or a diabetic educator.

## Blood Fats and Diabetes

Coronary heart disease is a major concern for many people with diabetes. It is important to watch total fat. Refer to **Mini Fat Counter Table** p133 in the chart section.

Restrict saturated fat which is found in foods such as fatty meats, cheese, full cream milk, butter, coconut and palm oil. These foods can contribute to high cholesterol and triglycerides. High cholesterol in the blood is caused either from consuming too much saturated fat and cholesterol-rich foods, or because the body makes too much.

Fat, sugar, alcohol and excess weight often adversely affect triglycerides. With diabetes, poor diet and high blood sugar are additional factors which can also contribute to this problem.

If you have a high cholesterol or triglycerides, it is desirable to receive advice from a doctor or an accredited dietitian.

The bar analysis at the end of each recipe includes the saturated fat and total fat. (A detailed explanation of this analysis can be found at the start of the **Recipe Section** p30). All recipes have been designed to be low in fat and saturated fat.

## Vegetarian Eating

A well-balanced vegetarian diet can be healthy. A little more care and knowledge is required to ensure that the diet is adequate in all essential nutrients.
In a Vegan Diet all animal products are excluded which leaves no sources of B12 and only marginal levels of calcium, iron, zinc and riboflavin.
A Lacto-Vegetarian Diet includes dairy products. In this case only B12, iron and zinc may be marginal or inadequate.
In a Lacto-Ovo-Vegetarian Diet only meat, poultry and fish are excluded. This is the least restrictive regime and should be adequate in all nutrients if wholegrain cereals, breads, beans and lentils are included with cheese, milk and eggs.
Always try and have a combination of cereals, seeds and nuts with legumes to give complete protein.
This book recommends the inclusion of vegetarian recipes as a part of everyday eating. They complement many meat dishes and add a great deal of variety and flavour. Milk products, beans, lentils and wholegrain cereals all have a low glycaemic index which aids the control of diabetes. Refer to **Glycaemic Index** p12 and to the **Healthy Food Choices Based on Glycaemic Index** p132.
There is a wide selection of recipes in the Main Section under Main Meal Dishes Based on Meat Alternatives. There are 25 recipes that are vegetarian and more that may be adapted.
Don't forget the Soups and Salads and First Course sections which give a further 15 recipes to choose from. There are many ideas in the Luncheon and Sandwich Section that can also be used.
Refer to the **Vegetarian Menus on** p22 for more ideas.

## Alcohol

Alcohol is a concentrated source of energy (almost as high as fat). It is wise to limit the amount of alcohol, which lowers blood sugars initially and raises them later. It is the alcohol and not the sugar in alcoholic drinks that is potentially detrimental to health, particularly in excessive amounts. Always make sure that alcohol is consumed with food so a severe hypoglycaemic reaction (low blood sugar) does not occur. Limit your intake of alcohol as it requires extra B vitamins to be metabolised. It takes approximately 1 hour to break down 10g of alcohol (e.g. 1 standard drink). 1g of alcohol provides 29 kilojoules (7 calories). Alcohol results in increased fat storage, especially abdominal fat. It is used as energy before fat. No more than 1 to 2 standard drinks a day should be consumed for women and 3 to 4 for men!
Refer to **Alcohol, Energy and Carbohydrate Chart** p134 in the charts section.

*Handy Hints*
- It is unwise to include alcohol in preference to a nutritionally well-balanced diet.
- Use light beers in preference to regular beer, but be aware that the light beers contain more carbohydrate. They still must be controlled in quantity. Check the **Alcohol, Energy and Carbohydrate Chart** p134.
- Wines may be diluted with soda.
- Make sure to have water on your table and drink water interspersed with alcohol.
- Spirits are a good choice but again must be watched for quantity and should be mixed with soda, water or low kilojoule mixer.
- Sweet sherry, vermouth, liqueurs and port are enriched with extra sugar and alcohol. They are best avoided or used in very limited quantities.
- Try to consume 3 litres of fluid daily, of which 6 - 8 glasses should be water.
- Soda water and unflavoured mineral water have no kilojoules and can contribute to the 3 litres of fluid a day.
- Low kilojoule soft drinks are without significant kilojoules but have many additives.
- Refer to the **Alcohol, Energy and Carbohydrate Chart** p134.

## Artificial Sweeteners

Artificial sweeteners are suitable for those who find it difficult to wean themselves off sweet foods.
**Tablets** (eg. Equal, Hemesetas) do not contribute kilojoules and are more suitable for adding to coffee and tea. If possible reduce sugar and learn to enjoy a more natural flavour.

| Sugar | Grams | KJ | Cal | CHO |
|---|---|---|---|---|
| 1 tsp | 4.5 | 73.5 | 18 | 4.5 |
| 1 tabsp | 18 | 301 | 72 | 18 |
| ¼ cup | 55 | 921 | 220 | 55 |
| ½ cup | 110 | 1842 | 440 | 110 |
| 1 cup | 220 | 3685 | 880 | 220 |

| Sugar substitute | KJ | Cal | CHO |
|---|---|---|---|
| 1 tsp | 8.1 | 1.90 | 0.5 |
| 1 tabsp | 32 | 7.6 | 2 |
| ¼ cup | 96 | 22.8 | 6 |
| ½ cup | 192 | 45.6 | 12 |
| 1 cup | 384 | 91.2 | 24 |

Try a herbal tea or use non fat or low fat milk which is sweeter in tea and coffee.
**Granulated (powdered) sweeteners** - These contain lactose or maltodextrin which is much sweeter than sugar. One teaspoon is usually equal to about 8 Kilojoules or 2 calories in comparison to about 70 Kilojoules or 18 calories for equivalent sugar. Granulated sweeteners can work well in cooking, particularly if added near the end. We have tested all recipes labelled **NS (No added sugar)** using powdered sugar substitutes such as Splenda™ or Equal™ and have found them satisfactory. Sometimes there is not a significant saving in carbohydrate or kilojoules.

The new approach is to reduce and/or limit sugar and develop a more savoury taste. Cutting down on added sugar in all forms will result in a more nutritious diet and when combined with an exercise programme will promote control of weight.

Adding fruit juice or using a small quantity of honey as a substitute may remove the need for sugar or sweetener. Try **Fruity Loaf** p126. Honey will allow you to reduce the fat content as well as it keeps muffins and cakes moist. Try **Oatmeal Fruit Slice** p126, **Carrot Cake** p121 and **Banana Date Muffins** p127. Fresh and dried fruit give natural sweetness as in **Fruity Loaf** and **Fresh Fruit Lemon Jelly** p112. Low joule soft drinks and cordial and low joule jelly are artificially sweetened products that are suitable for inclusion in your diet. Low joule jelly can be used to sweeten yoghurt or rhubarb or other acidic fruit. Artificial sweeteners are not recommended for gestational diabetes.

## Glycaemic Index (GI)

The effects of different Carbohydrate (CHO) foods on blood glucose level (BGL) have been tested and compared with the effect of glucose. All foods tested contain the same amount of CHO. Those foods which result in a large increase in BGL over 2 hours have a high Glycaemic Index (GI). Foods which cause a slower rise in BGL have a low GI e.g. glucose itself has the highest GI of 100.
Lentils have a GI of 30. Foods with a low GI eaten regularly as part of a mixed diet give improved control of BGL. It is advised that a low GI food be included frequently in meals. Factors which influence the GI of food are -
- The type of sugar or starch in the food.
- The degree of processing or cooking (mashing or puréeing increases GI).
- The presence of substances in the food which may interfere with digestion and absorption.
- Fat in food lowers the GI. However high fat foods are not recommended for general nutrition reasons so they should be avoided even if they do have a low GI.

Choose foods which have a low GI and which are also nutrient rich, low in fat, low in sugar and high in fibre.

The total amount of CHO eaten at the meal is still important, regardless of the GI of the CHO foods. Refer to **Food Groups** p16-17 to check on reasonable quantities. For example one potato has the same CHO as ½ cup of cooked pasta, but pasta, which gives a smaller increase in blood sugar levels, has a lower GI. If ½ cup of pasta is substituted for one potato at the meal, blood sugar will not rise as much. However if 2 cups of pasta are substituted for one potato the BGL will be expected to rise more rapidly. Low joule vegetables are highly recommended as they are low in kilojoules and high in fibre and it would be difficult to get a high blood sugar even with substantial amounts.

Glycaemic Index is only a guide to assist in understanding and improving blood sugars and weight control. Refer to the chart **Healthy Food Choices Based on Glycaemic Index** p132. It has been modified to include low glycaemic index foods which satisfy the criteria for good nutrition. Straight glycaemic index charts may differ from this.

Foods high in fat, sugar and salt have not been given a 'Best Choice' rating as they are not recommended.
'Best Choice' has a Glycaemic Index of usually less than 50% in comparison to glucose.
'Good Choice' is about 50 to 70%.
'Fair Choice' is about 70 to 100%.

LEARNING ABOUT DIABETES

## Diabetes Australia

Diabetes Australia has branches in each State where support and further information may be obtained. For all inquiries phone 1800 640 862 or contact the relevant State branch as per the addresses below.

*National Office*
1st Floor Churchill House
218 Northbourne Ave
BRADDON ACT 2612

*ACT*
The Grant Cameron Community Centre
Mulley Street
HOLDER ACT 2611

*NSW*
PO Box 9824
SYDNEY NSW 2001

*Northern Territory*
2 Tiwi Place
TIWI NT 0810

*Queensland*
corner Ernest and Merival Streets
SOUTH BRISBANE QLD 4101

*South Australia*
159 Burbridge Road
HILTON SA 5033

*Tasmania*
79 Davey Street
HOBART TAS 7000

*Victoria*
3rd Floor, 100 Collins Street
MELBOURNE VIC 3000

*Western Australia*
48 Wickam Street
EAST PERTH WA 6000

## Dietary Guidelines for Australians

- Enjoy a wide variety of nutritious foods.

- Eat plenty of breads and cereals (preferably wholegrain), vegetables (including legumes), and fruits.

- Eat a diet low in fat and, in particular, low in saturated fat.

- Maintain a healthy body weight by balancing physical activity and food intake.

- If you drink alcohol, limit your intake.

- Eat only moderate amounts of sugar and foods containing added sugar.

- Choose low salt foods and use salt sparingly.

- Encourage and support breast feeding.

- Eat foods containing calcium. This is particularly important for girls and women.

- Eat foods containing iron. This is particularly important for girls, women, vegetarians and athletes.

# HOW TO ADAPT YOUR COOKING AND RECIPES

### How to Lower Fat and Cholesterol

| Ingredient | Adaptation |
|---|---|
| Full cream milk | Non fat milk |
| Full cream evaporated milk | Low fat evaporated milk (1.6%) |
| Yoghurt | Low fat yoghurt or diet yoghurt |
| Cream | Low fat evaporated milk (4% fat) |
| Sour cream | Low fat yoghurt |
| Coconut cream | Low fat evaporated milk plus coconut essence |
| Cream cheese | Ricotta or cottage cheese |
| Regular cheese | Less than 10% fat cheese |
| Eggs | Low cholesterol egg substitute |
| Butter or table margarine | Mono/polyunsaturated margarine |
| Vegetable oil or lard | Mono/polyunsaturated oil |
| Cooked chicken | Remove chicken skin, prefer breast |
| Fatty meats | Lean meat, remove all fat |
| Streaky bacon | Middles eye rasher or turkey bacon |
| Fried food | Grill or microwave food |
| Luncheon meat | 97% fat free ham or turkey products |
| Tuna or salmon in oil | Tuna or salmon in brine or spring water |
| Cakes, biscuits and slices, commercial varieties | Homemade or low fat commercial varieties |
| Puff and regular pastry | Filo pastry and spray with oil |
| Salad dressing | No oil or home-made salad dressings |

### How to Lower Salt or Sodium

| Ingredient | Adaptation |
|---|---|
| Regular salt | Lite salt |
| Salt in cooking | Lemon juice, curry powder, spices |
| Canned sauces | Home-made sauces |
| Canned vegetables | No added salt varieties, fresh or frozen |
| Canned or smoked fish | Fresh fish or canned in spring water |
| Savoury biscuits | Reduced salt biscuits |
| Commercial salad dressings | Home-made salad dressings |
| Corned meats | Fresh meats |
| Bacon & ham | Substitute fresh vegetables such as mushrooms and add seasoning |
| Stock cubes | Low sodium stock powder e.g. Massel™ |
| Soy sauce | Lite soy sauce |
| Tomato sauce | Lite tomato sauce |
| Canned vegetables or juices | Fresh or frozen vegetables or juices |

### How To Lower Sugar

| Ingredient | Adaptation |
|---|---|
| Sugar | Reduce quantity of sugar |
|  | Use honey as it is sweeter |
|  | Use a liquid or powdered equivalent substitute |
|  | Add fruit juice instead of sugar |
|  | Use fresh or dried fruit instead of sugar |

### How to Increase Fibre

| Ingredient | Adaptation |
|---|---|
| White flour | Wholegrain or wholemeal flour |
| Refined cereal (cornflakes) | Wholegrain and bran types |
| White rice | Basmati, Mahatma or long grain rice |
| Plain pasta | Wholemeal pasta |
| Peeled or boiled vegetables | Unpeeled or raw vegetables |
| White bread crumbs | Wholemeal bread crumbs |

# Choosing and Following a Balanced Diabetic Diet

The Food Groups referred to in the following pages relate to the **Healthy Diet Chart**. In order to have a balanced healthy diet, foods should be chosen daily from each group. To assist, examples of different carbohydrate and Kilojoule meal plans have been given. Choose according to your particular requirement e.g. a moderate intake would be 5000 KJ (1200 calories) to 8400 KJ (1500 calories) There are Sample Menus to assist in spreading the carbohydrate intake throughout the day.
This is followed by menus for Breakfast, Lunch, Vegetarian, Dinner and Special Menus. These relate to the recipe section and will assist you in choosing a varied diet. Plan your own menus by referring to the easy reference **Recipe Nutritional Analysis Summary** p140 in the chart and table section and **How To Adapt Your Cooking and Recipes** (facing page).

*Healthy Diet Chart 16*
*Food Groups 16*
*Balanced Meal Plans for Different*
  *Energy Requirements 18*
*Sample Menus 18*
*Breakfast Menus 21*
*Vegetarian Menus 22*
*Lunch Menus 23*
*Dinner Menus 25*
*Special Menus 27*
  *Buffet 27*
  *Special Lunch 27*
  *Barbecue 27*
  *Christmas 27*
  *Cocktail Party 28*
  *Dinner 28*

**A BALANCED DIABETIC DIET**

# HEALTHY FOOD CHART

### Recommended Serves Per Day

**EAT LEAST**
- Limit Indulgences
  Sugar, Fat,
  Alcohol

**EAT MODERATELY**
- Milk and Milk Products
  2 - 3 Serves such as Milk,
  Yoghurt, Cheese

- Meat and Meat Alternatives
  3 - 4 Serves such as Meat,
  Chicken, Fish, Lentils,
  Beans and Nuts

**EAT AND DRINK MOST**
- Fruit
  2 - 3 Serves such as Citrus,
  Fresh, canned or stewed without
  sugar and dried

- Low Joule Vegetables
  2 - 3 Cups or 5 Serves such as
  Green, Yellow and
  Red choices

- Breads, Cereals, Grains and
  Starchy Vegetables
  4 or More Serves such as
  Oatmeal, Whole grains, Pasta,
  Potato and Long grain rice

- Water
  3 Litres of fluid daily made up
  from Water, Tea, Coffee, Juice
  and Low joule soft drinks

## Food Groups

Choose foods from the food groups in the Healthy Food Chart. Because of the difference in GI, serves that have equivalent carbohydrate will have a different effect on blood sugar levels.

Slightly larger serves may be consumed of low glycaemic index (GI) food in a mixed meal. Quantities needed will vary depending on exercise, energy expenditure and the type of carbohydrate selected. The evidence is that low GI foods satisfy the appetite better.

# A BALANCED DIABETIC DIET

## Indulgences
Limit indulgences to 1 to 2 a day or less.

*Sugar* - avoid added sugar. Check **Carbohydrate, Kilojoule and Calorie Content of Common Foods** p135 under charts and tables. Use sugar substitutes - refer to section on **Artificial Sweeteners** p11.

*Fat* - avoid added fat (butter, margarine, oil, mayonnaise). Fat contains no significant carbohydrate. Sufficient fat will be available naturally in food to meet needs (refer **Mini Fat Counter Table** p133).

*Alcohol* - alcohol (refer to **Alcohol, Energy and Carbohydrate Chart** p134)

## Milk and Milk Products Group
Include 2 to 3 milk and milk product serves a day such as milk, yoghurt and cheese. They are good sources of carbohydrate, calcium and protein.
1 serve has 10 grams carbohydrate.
- 1 glass of milk (preferred low fat).
- 200 gram carton of yoghurt (preferred diet or natural with no added sugar).
- 1 scoop of ice cream (preferred low fat).

or

1 serve has no significant carbohydrate.
- 1/2 cup cottage or ricotta cheese.
- 1 slice cheese (preferred reduced fat).

## Meat and Meat Alternatives Group
Include 3 to 4 serves or 90 to 120 grams or more of Meat and Meat Products such as meat, fish, chicken, beans, lentils and nuts.
Meat, fish and chicken are good sources of protein, vitamins and minerals.
Beans, lentils and nuts are good sources of protein, carbohydrate and fibre.
1 serve has no significant carbohydrate
- 30 grams of meat or chicken (lean no skin or fat).
- 60 grams of fish (white flesh).
- 30 grams salmon or tuna (preferred spring water or brine).
- 1 egg.

or

Meat Alternatives
- 1/2 cup soya beans, 100 grams tofu, 1 tabsp peanut butter, 1/4 cup hommos has 2.5 gram carbohydrate.
- 1/2 cup (75g) brazil nuts, almonds, hazelnuts has 3 grams carbohydrate.
- 1/2 cup lentils and split peas has 7 grams carbohydrate.
- 1/2 cup (75g) mixed nuts or peanuts has 10 grams carbohydrate.
- 1/2 cup cooked kidney beans, baked beans, cannelloni beans, haricot beans, Lima beans, mixed beans, chick peas has 15 grams carbohydrate.
- 1/2 cup (75 g) cashew nuts has 20 grams carbohydrate.

## Fruit Group
Include 2 to 3 serves of fruit a day, 1 citrus and fresh fruit with skins. They are good sources of carbohydrate, vitamins, fibre and antioxidants.
1 serve has 15 grams carbohydrate.
- 1 medium apple, orange, peach, nectarine, mandarin, unripe banana, pear.
- 2 apricots, plums, kiwi fruit.
- 1/2 cup stewed fruit or fruit salad.
- 15 to 20 grapes, strawberries or cherries.
- 1/2 grapefruit or mango.
- 1 cup stewed rhubarb, no sugar.
- 2 tabsp dried fruit e.g. sultanas, apricots, currants.

## Low Joule Vegetables Group
Include 2 to 3 cups (or 5 serves) of vegetables a day for a good source of carbohydrate, fibre, vitamins and antioxidants.
Insignificant carbohydrate, eat as much as you like in salads, casseroles and as vegetables -
- asparagus, bean sprouts, beetroot, broccoli, brussel sprouts, cabbage, capsicum, carrot, cauliflower, celery, Chinese greens, chokos, cucumber, eggplant, green beans, Italian greens, lettuce, mushrooms, onion, pumpkin, radish, sauerkraut, silverbeet, spinach, swedes, tomato, turnip, zucchini.

## Breads, Cereals, Grains and Starchy Vegetables Group
Include 4 or more breads and cereals, pasta, rice, potatoes, peas and corn. They are good sources of carbohydrate energy, fibre and vitamins.
1 serve has 15 grams of carbohydrate.
- 1 slice bread (prefer whole grain).
- 1/4 slice Lebanese bread.
- 2/3 cup cooked porridge or other cereal (prefer low fat, low sugar and high fibre).
- 2 rye vita or wholemeal saltine crackers (prefer low fat and high fibre).
- 1 small potato.
- 1/2 cup cooked pasta.
- 1/2 cup cooked rice (preferred long grain e.g. Basmati or Mahatma).
- 1/2 cup peas, parsnips, corn or sweet potato.

## Water - no significant carbohydrate
Have 3 litres or 12 cups of total fluid daily as water, tea, coffee, low kilojoule soft drink, low kilojoule cordial or soda.

# A BALANCED DIABETIC DIET

## Balanced Meal Plans for Different Energy Requirements

For balanced nutrition and recommended quantities of carbohydrate per day, select the suggested number of serves from each food group according to individual energy requirements. Carbohydrate should form 50 to 60% of total daily kilojoule intake.

| MEAL PLAN | 4200KJ | 5000KJ | 6300KJ | 8400KJ | 12600KJ | Gestational 8400KG |
|---|---|---|---|---|---|---|
|  | 1000 Cal | 1200 Cal | 1500 Cal | 2000 Cal | 3000 Cal | 2000 Cal |
| Milk & Milk Products | 2 | 2 | 2 | 2 | 3 | 4 |
| Meat & Alternatives | 4 | 5 | 6 | 6 | 8 | 6 |
| Breads Grains Vegies | 4 | 5 | 7 | 12 | 20 | 10 |
| Low Joule Vegies | 4 | 5 | 6 | 6 | 8 | 6 |
| Fruits | 2 | 3 | 3 | 4 | 6 | 4 |
| Fats | 1 | 1 | 2 | 3 | 5 | 3 |
| Total CHO | 130g | 165g | 200g | 290 | 460g | 280g |
| Range | 100-150 | 150-200 | 200-250 | 250-300 | 400-500 | 250-300 |

## Menu 4200 KJ (1000 Calories)

| MENU | | FOOD GROUPS | CARBOHYDRATE |
|---|---|---|---|
| BREAKFAST | | | |
| | 1 orange | 1 Fruit | |
| | 2/3 cup porridge with | 1 Bread | 35 g |
| | 1/2 cup non fat milk | 1/2 Milk & Milk Products | |
| LUNCH | | | |
| | 1 multigrain sandwich with | 2 Bread | |
| | 1 teaspoon mono or | 1 Fat | |
| | polyunsaturated margarine and | 1 Low Joule Vegetable | 35 g |
| | 1 slice of low fat cheese and | 1 Milk & Milk Products | |
| | 1/2 cup shredded lettuce | | |
| AFTERNOON TEA | | | |
| | 1 small apple | 1 Fruit | 15g |
| DINNER | | | |
| | 120 grams lean steak | 4 Meat and Alternatives | 30g |
| | as a stir fry with | | |
| | 1/2 cup each beans, | 3 Low Joule Vegetables | |
| | carrots, cauliflower | | |
| | 1/2 cup Basmati rice | 1 Bread | |
| SUPPER | | | |
| | 1/2 glass low fat milk for | 1/2 Milk & Milk Products | 10g |
| | coffee or to drink | | |
| | | **TOTAL:** | **125g** |

# A BALANCED DIABETIC DIET

## Menu 5000 KJ (1200 Calories)

| MENU | | FOOD GROUPS | CARBOHYDRATE |
|---|---|---|---|
| **BREAKFAST** | | | |
| | ½ glass of apple juice | 1 Fruit | 47g |
| | 1 English Multigrain muffin with 1 tsp margarine and **Strawberry Fruit Spread** p32 | 2 Bread<br>1 Fat | |
| **MORNING TEA** | | | |
| | 1 small apple | 1 Fruit | 15g |
| **LUNCH** | | | |
| | 1 Lavash bread with lean shaved ham and low fat grated cheese with 1 cup grated carrot, shredded lettuce, sliced tomato, cucumber and sprouts and 1 teaspoon low fat mayonnaise | 2 Bread<br>1 Meat and Alternatives<br>1 Milk and Products<br>2 Low Joule Vegetable<br>1 Fat | 40g |
| **AFTERNOON TEA** | | | |
| | 1 small pear | 1 Fruit | 15g |
| **DINNER** | | | |
| | 120 g grilled chicken with ½ cup pasta with **Fresh Tomato Sauce** p105 and ½ cup zucchini/ ½ cup carrot | 4 Meat and Alternatives<br>1 Bread<br>3 Low Joule Vegetables | 30g |
| **SUPPER** | | | |
| | 1 glass low fat milk for coffee or to drink | 1 Milk and Products | 10g |
| | | **TOTAL:** | **157g** |

**Note** If milk was used at lunch rather than cheese, total CHO would be 168g

## A BALANCED DIABETIC DIET

### Menu 8400 KJ (1500 Calories)

| MENU | FOOD GROUPS | CARBOHYDRATE |
|---|---|---|
| **BREAKFAST** <br> 1 cup of All-Bran™ with <br> 1 small sliced banana and <br> 1 cup non fat milk | 1 Fruit <br> 2 Bread <br> 1 Milk and Products | 55g |
| **MORNING TEA** <br> 1 orange | 1 Fruit | 15g |
| **LUNCH** <br> 1 cup **Cauliflower Soup** p42 <br> 1 large ham and salad <br> wholegrain roll with <br> 2 teaspoons of margarine and <br> 1 cup salad | 3 Bread <br> 2 Fat <br> 1 Meat and Alternatives <br> 3 Low Joule Vegetables | 60g |
| **AFTERNOON TEA** <br> 1 fresh peach | 1 Fruit | 15g |
| **DINNER** <br> 150 g lean chicken with <br> 1 cup **Grilled Fine Polenta** p92 <br> ½ cup each of spinach, <br> carrots and brussel sprouts | 5 Meat and Alternatives <br> 2 Bread <br> 3 Low Joule Vegetables | 47g |
| **SUPPER** <br> 1 cup low fat milk in tea <br> and coffee | 1 Milk and Milk Products | 10g |
| | **TOTAL:** | **202g** |

**Note Cauliflower Soup** is counted as a Low KJ Vegetable

### Balanced Eating

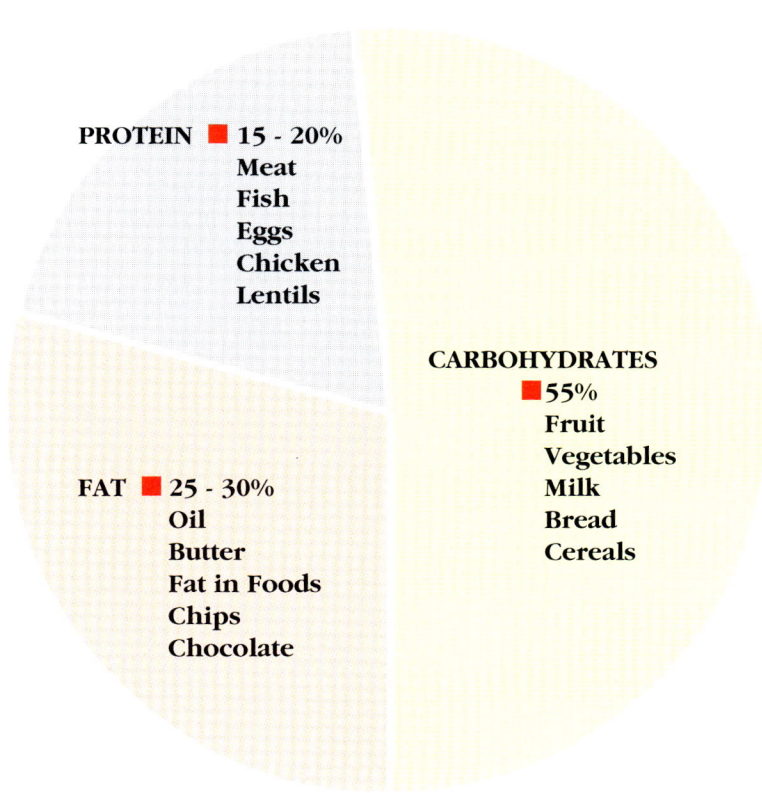

# Breakfast Menus

## Light breakfasts
### 25 and 45 grams of CHO

1 Small Banana
2/3 Cup Porridge
with
1/2 cup Low Fat Milk

∽

100ml Apple Juice
2 slices Multigrain Toast
Vegemite

∽

1 Medium Peach
1 slice Multigrain Toast
Peanut Butter

∽

2 Slices Wholegrain Toast
**Savoury Corn Spread** p32

∽

1/2 Medium Grapefruit
1/2 cup All Bran™
1/2 cup Low Fat Milk

∽

1/2 cup **Untoasted Muesli** p32
1/2 cup Low Fat Milk

∽

1 Multigrain Muffin
**Strawberry Fruit Spread** p32

∽

1 Slice Multigrain Toast
**Savoury Baked Beans** p33
1 Scrambled Egg

∽

1 English Muffin
**Yoghurt Cheese** p39
**Strawberry Fruit Spread** p32

∽

**Oatmeal Apple Porridge** p32
1/2 cup Low Fat Milk

## High kilojoule breakfasts
### 45 to 60 grams of CHO

1 1/2 cups of Porridge
1 cup Low Fat Milk

∽

120ml Apple Juice
2 Slices Wholegrain Toast
**Cooked Tomato Savoury** p105

∽

100ml Unsweetened Pineapple Juice
1 Large Roll
1 tabsp Peanut Paste

∽

2 Slices Wholegrain Toast
1/2 cup **Savoury Baked Beans** p33

∽

1 cup All Bran™
1 cup Low Fat Milk
100ml Grapefruit Juice

∽

3/4 cup **Untoasted Muesli** p32
3/4 cup Low Fat Milk

∽

2 Wholegrain English Muffins
60 g Low Fat Ham

∽

1 Orange
1 Poached Egg
1 Grilled Tomato
2 Slices Wholegrain Toast

∽

1/2 cup Stewed Plums
2 Slices Wholegrain French Toast
Milk Coffee with 1/2 cup Milk

# A BALANCED DIABETIC DIET

## Vegetarian Menus Suitable for Lunch or Dinner

### Low Carbohydrate
### 25 to 45 grams

**Lentil Bean Goulash** p49
½ cup Pasta

∽

**Lentil Bean Pie** p49
Tossed Salad
Low Joule Dressing

∽

**Broccoli Soufflé** p52
**Roast Vegetable Salad** p101
1 Slice Watermelon

∽

**Eggplant Soup** p43
**Savoury Corn Spread** p32
with
1 Slice Wholegrain Toast

∽

**Red Lentil Soup** p46
**Damper with Beer** p130

∽

**Baked Frittata** p52
**Spinach Tomato Salad** p100

∽

**Macaroni Cheese** p56
Coleslaw

∽

**Cauliflower Soup** p42
**Vegetable Lasagne** p59

∽

3 **Soya Bean Patties** p51
**Chinese Mixed Vegetable Salad** p102
1 Mandarin

∽

**Cheesy Pumpkin Ricotta Bake** p54
**Red Cabbage Salad** p101

### High Carbohydrate
### 45 to 60 grams

**Kidney Bean Rice Medley** p48
NS* **Burgundy Pears** p113

∽

**West Meets East Soup** p45
1 **Potato Muffin** p128
1 Small Banana

∽

**Lentil Sauce** p105
1 cup **Cous Cous** p90
Tossed Salad
**Compote of Fruit** p112

∽

**Baked Ratatouille** p60
1 cup **Rich Coarse Polenta** p92
NS* **Gingered Rockmelon** p111

∽

**Gnocchi** p58
**Vegetable Curry** p61
Broccoli
½ cup Fruit Salad

∽

**Vegetable Pasta** p55
**Grilled Eggplant** p88
Fresh Asparagus

∽

**Vegetable Parcels** p60
**Crunchy Cajun Chips** p94
Coleslaw

∽

**Leek and Pear Soup** p44
2 **Wholemeal Crêpes** p129
filled with
Mashed Pumpkin
Fetta, Spinach
**Apple Cottage Pudding** p117

*NS = No Added sugar

# Lunch Menus

### Low Carbohydrate content 25 to 45 grams carbohydrate per meal

**Lombok Fish Soup** p45
1 Chicken/Lettuce Sandwich
on
Rye Bread

∽

**Chilli Beans** p48
on
1 Slice Wholegrain Toast
with
Sliced Tomato and Shredded Lettuce

∽

**Bruschetta** p40
1 Small Banana

∽

**Zucchini Slice** p55
Tossed Salad
with
**Mustard Herb Dressing** p97

∽

**Baked Frittata** p52
**Low Joule Caesar Salad** p101

∽

**Stuffed Artichokes** p87
1 Small Wholemeal Roll
with
**Hommos** p39

∽

**Chick Peas with Tomato and Macaroni** p56

**Cauliflower Soup** p42
1 Sandwich
made with
2 Slices Multigrain Bread
and
97% Fat Free Ham and Salad

∽

**Clam Chowder** p45
1 Slice Multigrain Bread
with
Salad of
Tomato/Onion Sliced in Vinegar

∽

**Macaroni Bean Salad** p99
Sliced Cucumber
Grated Carrot
60g Shaved Roast Beef

∽

**Lentil Sauce** p105
over
1 cup Pasta

∽

**Crispy Lavash Bread** p125
spread with
Cottage Cheese, Avocado
45g Sliced Chicken Breast
**Honey Orange Dressing** p96
Snow Pea Sprouts

∽

**Quiche** p54
3 Spears Tinned Pickled Asparagus
Mixed Lettuce
2 Nine Grain Vita Wheat™ Biscuits

## Lunch Menus

### High Carbohydrate content 45 to 60 grams carbohydrate per meal

**Tuna Hot Pot** p82
Tossed Salad
1 Slice Rockmelon

∽

**Pasta with Low Fat Pesto Sauce** p56
Tossed Salad
with
**Balsamic French Dressing** p95
½ cup Fruit Salad

∽

**Pumpkin and Ginger Soup** p44
1 Horseshoe Grain Roll
with
60g Shaved Pork, Apple Sauce
and
Alfalfa Sprouts

∽

60g Cold Roast Beef
**German Potato Salad** p100
**Red Cabbage Salad** p101
with
**Honey Orange Dressing** p96
**Strawberry Pie** p114

∽

**Broccoli Soufflé** p52
**Damper with Beer** p130
**Roast Vegetable Salad** p101
Fruit Platter (equal 1 Fruit)

**Lasagne** p68
1 Slice French Bread
Coleslaw
with
**Creamy Mustard Dressing** p96

∽

60g Focaccia Bread
with
Mashed Pumpkin
**Grilled Eggplant** p88
**Peeled Red Capsicum** p86
Fetta Cheese
plus
1 cup Tossed Salad
with
Low Joule Dressing

∽

**Cauliflower Soup** p42
**Cornish Pasties** p70
**Low Joule Caesar Salad** p101
with
**Low Joule Caesar Salad Dressing** p97
1 Fresh Pear

∽

**Mediterranean Pie** p61
Tossed Salad
with
**Balsamic French Dressing** p95
1 **Plain Scone** p121
1 Small Pear

## Dinner Menus

### Low Carbohydrate content 25 to 45 grams per meal

120g Grilled Rump Steak
**Pasta Verde Primavera** p58
Carrots Julienne

∽

**Vegetable Lasagne** p59
Fresh Asparagus

∽

**Lamb and Mushroom Curry** p74
1 cup Brown Rice
Green Beans

∽

**Savoury Mince** p70
1/2 cup Mashed Potato
Carrots and Broccoli

∽

**Satay Chicken Kebabs** p63
1 cup Pasta
Spinach

∽

**Grilled Tandoori Chicken** p66
1/2 cup **Cous Cous** p90
Beans and Grilled Tomato
**Chocolate Mousse** p111

∽

**Steak Diane** p72
Spinach and Carrots
1 Medium Baked Potato

**Curried Fish** p80
**Armadillo Potatoes** p93
Pumpkin and Cabbage

∽

**Pan Fried Fish with Fresh Tomato Salsa** p78
3/4 cup Mashed Potatoes
Grilled Tomato and Silverbeet

∽

**Stir Fry Scallops** p79
3/4 cup Long Grain Rice

∽

**Pork Tenderloin Teriyaki** p75
**Baked Ratatouille** p60
**Scalloped Potatoes** p93
Beans

∽

100g Roast Chicken
2 Small Roast Potatoes
1/2 cup Roast Pumpkin
Bok Choy

∽

**Chilli Con Carne** p71
Small Wholegrain Dinner Roll
Green Salad

∽

**Lemon Fish Rolls** p80
10 Oven Chips
Stir Fry Vegetables

## Dinner Menus

### High Carbohydrate content 45 to 60 grams per meal

**Paella** p57
Mixed Green Salad

∽

**Moussaka** p71
**Sunflower Rice** p94
Tossed Salad
**Fresh Fruit Lemon Jelly** p112

∽

**Spaghetti Bolognaise** p70
Tossed Salad
**Balsamic French Dressing** p95

∽

**Barramundi Almondine** p81
**Rich Coarse Polenta** p92
**Cauliflower Cheese** p86
½ cup Peas
**Spanish Cream** p116

∽

**Hungarian Chicken** p62
½ cup **Cous Cous** p90
Brussel Sprouts
Beans
NS* **Apricot Whip** p110

∽

**Chicken Dahl Curry** p65
½ cup Brown Rice
Grilled Tomato
NS* **Lemon Sponge** p111

∽

**Laksa** p46
1 Small Wholegrain Roll
NS* **Strawberry Whirl** p113


*NS = No Added Sugar

**Cabbage Rolls** p69
Beans
NS* **Bread Pudding** p119

∽

**Lamb Shank and Dumpling Ragout** p74
½ cup Mashed Potato
Fresh Asparagus
**Lemon Delicious** p119

∽

**Salmon Steaks** p78
1 Large Potato
Stir Fry Vegetables
NS* **Summer Pudding** p116

∽

**Tropical Crown Lamb Roast** p73
1 cup **Grilled Fine Polenta** p92
**Savoury Spinach** p88
Baby Squash
**Strawberry Mousse** p111

∽

150g Grilled Chicken Breast
with
**Plum Sauce** p106
**Vegetable Curry** p61
**Green Bean Bundles** p85
1 cup Mashed Potato

∽

**Chilli Mussels** p79
**Steak with Green Capsicum** p72
1 cup Basmati Rice
Carrot Coins

*Note*
Quantities are given for breads, cereals, grains, starchy vegetables and fruit but not for low kilojoule vegetables which may be eaten freely. For main courses and desserts, quantities are those specified in the recipe unless otherwise indicated.

## Special Menus

Small quantities of a variety of dishes may be consumed for a special occasion

### BUFFET MEAL

*Savouries*
COLD
**Hommos** p39 and **Mexican Dip** p38 with
**Crispy Lavash Bread** p125
HOT
**Spring Rolls** p40
**Savoury Meat Balls** p41

*plus*

HOT
**Cheesy Pumpkin Ricotta Bake** p54
**Sunflower Rice** p94
**Baked Ratatouille** p60
**Grilled Tandoori Chicken** p66
COLD
**Rare Roast Beef Salad** p98
**Spinach Tomato Salad** p100
Coleslaw

*plus*

*Dessert*

**Strawberry Pie** p114
NS* **Burgundy Pears** p113
**Carrot Cake** p121


### SPECIAL LUNCH

**Eggplant Soup** p43
**Mango Chicken Salad** p99
Fresh Wholemeal Rolls
**Compote of Fruit** p112

*NS = No Added Sugar

### BARBECUES

**Barbecue Spare Ribs** p76
**Cous Cous** p90
**Spinach Tomato Salad** p100
NS* **Chocolate Mousse** p111

∽

**Satay Chicken Kebabs** p63
Basmati Rice
**Low Joule Caesar Salad** p101
**Tulip Fruits** p115

∽

Barbecue Steak
**Roast Vegetable Salad** p101
Coleslaw
**Spanish Cream** p116
with Fresh Raspberries

### CHRISTMAS

HOT
Roast Turkey
**Plum Sauce** p106
Roast Potatoes and Sweet Potatoes
**Baked Cauliflower Cheese** p86
Beans
**Brussel Sprouts with Baby Corn** p85
**Summer Pudding** p116

∽

COLD
Seafood Platter
with
**Seafood Sauce** p107
Cold Roast Ham
Cold Roast Beef
**Chinese Mixed Vegetable Salad** p102
**German Potato Salad** p100
**Tropical Sicilian Salad** p102
Fresh Fruit Platter
Trifle
**Stained Glass Window Cake** p122

## Special Menus

### COCKTAIL PARTY

Wholegrain Circles of Bread with
Pickled Asparagus

*or*

Fresh Prawns and Fresh Coriander

*or*

Shaved Beef and **Sundried Tomatoes** p89

*plus*

Toasted Wholegrain Triangles with
**Yoghurt Cheese** p39 and
Smoked Salmon and Caper Berries

*or*

Sliced Hard Cooked Egg and Dill Pickles

*plus*

**Spinach Dip** p37 in Fresh Wholegrain Loaf

*plus*

**Seafood Avocado Dip** p41 with
Low Fat Dry Biscuits or
**Crispy Lavash Bread** p125

*plus*

**Savoury Meat Balls** p41 with **Fresh Tomato
Savoury Sauce** p105

*plus*

**Spring Roll** p40 with **Plum Sauce** p106

*plus*

**Bruschetta** p40
(using thin French Sticks to keep them small)

*plus*

**Ribbon Sandwiches** p35
with
Ham, Mustard and Sprouts
Curried Egg and Shredded Lettuce

### DINNER
*Summer*

**Red Capsicum Dip** p38
with
Vegetable Crudites

**Avocado Salmon Mousse** p41

**Pork Tenderloin Teriyaki** p75

**Grilled Fine Polenta** p92

**Low Joule Caesar Salad** p101

**Strawberry Pie** p114

*Winter*

**Lombok Fish Soup** p45

**Beef Stroganoff** p68

**Sunflower Rice** p94

Broccoli

**Peeled Capsicum** p86

Mashed Pumpkin with Ginger

**Lemon Delicious** p119

# Recipe Section

The recipes that follow combined with the menus make it easy for readers to choose a wide variety of meals for many occasions that will suit most tastes.
Ideas for breakfast and lunch through a large main meal section together with soups, sauces, salads and dressings will give infinite variety to meals.
Desserts and baking suggestions will give confidence in choosing snacks and something special to end a meal. All recipes are suitable for the person with diabetes.
Refer to the previous section on **Choosing and Following a Balanced Diabetic Diet** p15 for extensive meal plans and menus ideas.
The **Recipe Analysis Explained** overpage will assist in understanding the nutritional analysis given at the bottom of each recipe.
Refer to **Recipe Nutritional Analysis Summary** p140 for a quick reference of the kilojoules, calories and carbohydrate content of each recipe.
Remember to read the introductions at the beginning of each section. There are ideas for lunches, salads and vegetables dishes as well as actual recipes.
Do enjoy the recipes in this book as eating should be a pleasure.

| | | | |
|---|---|---|---|
| *Breakfast* | *31* | *Vegetables and Grains* | *84* |
| *Luncheon* | *34* | *Low Joule Low Carbohydrate* | |
| *First Course, Savouries and Dips* | *37* | *Vegetables* | *84* |
| *Soups* | *42* | *High Joule High Carbohydrate* | |
| *Main Meals* | *47* | *Vegetables and Grains* | *90* |
| *Main Meal Dishes Based on* | | *Salads and Dressings* | *95* |
| *Meat Alternatives* | *47* | *Salad Maker Chart* | *103* |
| *Bean Dishes* | *48* | *Dressings* | *95* |
| *Soya Bean Dishes* | *50* | *Salads* | *98* |
| *Egg and Cheese Dishes* | *52* | *Main Meal Salads* | *98* |
| *Pasta and Grain Dishes* | *55* | *Side Salads* | *100* |
| *Vegetable Dishes* | *60* | *Sauces* | *104* |
| *Chicken* | *62* | *Desserts* | *109* |
| *Meat* | *67* | *Fresh Fruit Ideas* | *109* |
| *Beef* | *68* | *Cold Desserts* | *109* |
| *Lamb* | *73* | *Hot Desserts* | *117* |
| *Pork* | *75* | *Baking* | *120* |
| *Fish and Seafood* | *77* | | |

## The Recipe Analysis Explained

Each recipe has been computer analysed for its nutritional composition, using the Australian Commonwealth Government NUTTAB database with computer package "Serve".

Nutrients per serve analysis includes:

| | |
|---|---|
| Kilojoules | KJ |
| Calories | Cal |
| Protein - grams (g) | Pro |
| Carbohydrate - grams (g) | CHO |
| Total Fibre - grams (g) | Fibre |
| Total Fat - grams (g) | T. fat |
| Saturated Fat -grams (g) | S. fat |
| Cholesterol - milligrams (mg) | Chol |
| Sodium - milligrams (mg) | Na |

Note: The analysis for Kilojoules, Calories and Protein is given to support control of weight and balanced nutrition. Recipes can be chosen that are low in energy value to promote weight loss or that are high for people with large energy needs. It is important to have adequate protein for body building, particularly in growing years.

**Carbohydrate (CHO):**
It is recommended that 50 to 60% of the energy come from CHO.
For example on an intake of 6300KJ or 1500 calories, 200gms of carbohydrate would be required per day. The total carbohydrate rather than the sugar content is important. All carbohydrate breaks down to sugar. When reading labels in recipes, judge a product on the type and quantity of carbohydrate. Low glycaemic index foods are preferred and are used frequently throughout the recipes.

**Fat:**
It is recommended that no more than 30% of energy come from fat.
For example on an intake of 6300 kilojoule or 1500 calories no more than 50 grams of fat should be consumed per day. Total fat is important in controlling weight. All recipes have been prepared with minimum fat using low fat cooking methods.

**Saturated Fat (S. fat):**
Saturated fat will clog the arteries and may lead to atherosclerosis and heart disease. Recipes have used mono or polyunsaturated oils and margarine for this reason. Try to restrict saturated fat to no more than 1/3 of the total fat.

**Cholesterol (Chol):**
Total cholesterol is of concern so low cholesterol egg mix has been suggested and tested in recipes. Include this product as desired. Analysis has been done using eggs only. Often 1 to 2 eggs in a recipe will not give a significant amount of cholesterol per serve. Try to limit Cholesterol to 200mg per day. One egg yolk equals 220mg of cholesterol so you can easily work out the saving by using low cholesterol egg substitute.

**Sodium (Na)**
An acceptable low sodium intake is no more than 2000 mg in a day.
Sodium or salt contributes to hypertension. In order to have a healthy diet and lifestyle it is wise to limit high salt or sodium foods. We have taken this into consideration in choosing recipes and have used products such as light soy sauce and low sodium stock powder rather than the regular products.

## Readers Guide

*Crudits* - raw vegetables, cut up and used in dips.
*Julienne* - to cut into fine strips. Usually refers to vegetables.
*Zest* - is the rind without the pith on oranges and lemons. Use a lemon zester to achieve long fine strips. A grater is a good substitute. Try to only get the skin.
*Low Sodium Stock Powder* - Commercial stock cubes, powders and stock are all high sodium. Try and buy low sodium brands or make your own.
Italian Soup Mix - A commercial mix of different lentils and beans.
Remember that KJ = kilojoules, g = grams, tsp = teaspoon, tabsp = tablespoon and Na is sodium. Check the **Measurement Guide** p147 for more information.
NS - refers to the analysis of a recipe made with a sugar substitute.
All **recipe** references in book are in **bold**.
GI = Glycaemic Index.

# BREAKFAST RECIPES

## Breakfast

Breakfast can be the most important meal of the day. If you miss breakfast, there will be a loss of energy late in the morning and you may be tempted into eating inappropriate food later. As you will find in this section, breakfast need not be too heavy and could be as light as a **Fruit Smoothie** p33.

*French Toast 31*
*Fruit Smoothie 33*
*Oatmeal Apple Porridge 32*
*Savoury Baked Beans 33*
*Savoury Corn Spread 32*
*Strawberry Fruit Spread 32*
*Untoasted Muesli 32*

**Untoasted Muesli**

Check some of our **Breakfast Menus** p21 for ideas and choose according to your energy requirements.
The **Light Breakfasts Menus** p21 are for people with low energy requirements and those also weight-watching. They range in carbohydrate from 25 to 45 grams. Breakfast need not be boring — try different combinations. A small glass of fruit juice, preferably unsweetened, may be consumed. Apple and grapefruit are best choices. Grainbread with fruit spread, vegemite or peanut paste is recommended.
As milk is a low glycaemic food this is ideal with a high bran cereal. Yoghurt is another good choice. You can buy the low fat natural and add fresh fruit such as peaches, apples or strawberries. Make your own **Muesli** p32, or dress up porridge by making **Oatmeal Apple Porridge** p32.
Low glycaemic foods such as baked beans and corn are ideal on toast. These can be dressed up as in our recipes **Savoury Baked Beans** p33, **Savoury Corn Spread** p32 or **Cooked Tomato Savoury** p105.
More substantial **High Kilojoule Breakfast Menus** p21 are for people with high energy needs or who are underweight. Try some of our combinations that range from 45 to 60 grams of carbohydrate. If you have a large appetite or requirement make sure to have something for morning tea.

## FRENCH TOAST

*1 egg or low cholesterol egg mix (50g)*
*1 cup non fat milk (250ml)*
*Pepper to taste*
*4 slices thick wholemeal or fibre bread (100g)*
*2 tsp mono/polyunsaturated margarine (10g)*

- Beat egg, milk and pepper in a flat square pan or pie dish.
- Add bread and allow to soak up all liquid. Move the bottom slices of bread to the top and keep on swapping around until all liquid is equally absorbed into all slices.
- Cook covered in a lightly greased frying pan for 2 or 3 minutes or until puffy.
- Serve plain or with a scrape of honey and cinnamon or with **Strawberry Fruit Spread** p32.

**Serves 4**

*Variations*
- Make a sandwich by putting ham or cheese between and reheating for 1 minute.
- Top with **Cooked Tomato Savoury** p105 or **Savoury Corn Spread** p32.

*Handy Hint*
Teach children to cook by starting with easy recipes. The experience gained will be invaluable in later life.

NUTRIENTS PER SERVE

| KJ | Cal | Pro (g) | CHO (g) | Fibre (g) | T.fat (g) | S.fat (g) | Chol (mg) | Na (mg) |
|---|---|---|---|---|---|---|---|---|
| 487 | 118 | 7 | 15 | 1.4 | 3 | 0.7 | 49 | 190 |

## UNTOASTED MUESLI

*5 cups traditional oatmeal (500g)*
*3 cups natural bran (150g)*
*1½ cups wheatgerm (120g)*
*1 cup lecithin meal (100g)*
*1½ cups Four Bran mix (250g)*
*¾ cup dried chopped apricots (100g)*
*1 cup chopped pecans (100g)*
*⅓ cup sunflower seeds (50g)*
*⅓ cup sesame seeds (50g)*
*⅔ cup sultanas (100g)*
*½ cup sugar (110g) or equivalent substitute (optional)*

- Mix oatmeal, bran, wheatgerm, lecithin meal, bran mix, apricots, pecans, sunflower seeds, sesame seeds and sultanas together.
- Mix in sugar if desired.
- Store in an airtight container.

**Serves 50 x ¼ cups**

*Variation*
For **Toasted Muesli** mix together all ingredients except apricots and sultanas. Add ½ cup mono/polyunsaturated oil. Bake in 150°C oven for 1½ hours, stirring to prevent browning on edges. Mix in apricots and sultanas. Store in an airtight container. Kilojoules and fat will be higher with increased oil.

NUTRIENTS PER SERVE

| KJ | Cal | Pro (g) | CHO (g) | Fibre (g) | T.fat (g) | S.fat (g) | Chol (mg) | Na (mg) |
|---|---|---|---|---|---|---|---|---|
| 506 | 122 | 4 | 13 | 4 | 6 | 0.8 | 0 | 3 |

(Excluding sugar or oil)

## STRAWBERRY FRUIT SPREAD

*½ tsp gelatine (1.5g)*
*2 tabsp cold water (40ml)*
*1 cup mashed strawberries (200g)*
*1 tabsp sugar (18g) or equivalent substitute*
*½ tsp lemon juice (3ml)*

- Mix gelatine and cold water in a saucepan.
- Stir and heat until melted.
- Add strawberries, sugar and lemon juice and stir and cook for 5 minutes.
- Chill and serve as a fresh fruit preserve.
- Refrigerate.

**Serves 12 x 1 tabsp serves (Total 1 cup)**

*Variation*
Substitute apricots, plums, raspberries, blueberries or peaches. Adjust sugar if necessary. Use seasonal, inexpensive fruit.

*Note*
A fat free low sugar fresh fruit spread to use on toast, hot cakes or pikelets.

*Handy Hint*
Make this quick and easy spread when fruit is in season. It keeps well for about 10 days in the refrigerator and is much better than jam.

NUTRIENTS PER SERVE

| KJ | Cal | Pro (g) | CHO (g) | Fibre (g) | T.fat (g) | S.fat (g) | Chol (mg) | Na (mg) |
|---|---|---|---|---|---|---|---|---|
| 44 | 10 | 0.4 | 2 | 0.4 | 0.02 | 0 | 0 | 1 |

## OATMEAL APPLE PORRIDGE

*1 cup traditional oatmeal (90g)*
*¼ cup natural unprocessed bran (25g)*
*½ tsp cinnamon*
*1 medium peeled, cored and chopped apple (100g)*
*2 tabsp sultanas (30g)*
*3½ cups water (825ml)*
*Salt to taste*

- Mix oatmeal, bran, cinnamon, apple and sultanas together in a large bowl.
- Add water and salt to taste.
- Cook in the microwave at 70% power for 10 minutes or in a heavy based saucepan for 10 minutes.

**Serves 4 x 1 cup**

*Note*
A hot, nutritious, low glycaemic breakfast for cold mornings. No need for a sweetener or sugar with the natural sweetness from apple and sultanas.

NUTRIENTS PER SERVE

| KJ | Cal | Pro (g) | CHO (g) | Fibre (g) | T.fat (g) | S.fat (g) | Chol (mg) | Na (mg) |
|---|---|---|---|---|---|---|---|---|
| 537 | 129 | 4 | 23 | 5 | 2 | 0.4 | 0 | 5 |

## SAVOURY CORN SPREAD

*2 tabsp finely chopped spring onion (10g)*
*½ small red or green finely chopped capsicum (50g)*
*1 tsp mono/polyunsaturated oil (5ml)*
*1 tabsp water (20ml)*
*1 can creamed corn (310g)*

- Stir-fry onion and capsicum in oil and water in a heavy based saucepan or frying pan for 3 to 5 minutes.
- Stir in corn. Reheat and serve.

**Serves 4 x 1/4 cup**

*Note*
An easy quick spread ideal for use over toast, hotcakes or split English muffins. Excellent in a baked potato with cheese sprinkled on top. Corn is a low glycaemic index food.

*Handy Hint*
The use of savoury spreads such as this removes the need for margarine, thus reducing fat and increasing the vegetable intake.

NUTRIENTS PER SERVE

| KJ | Cal | Pro (g) | CHO (g) | Fibre (g) | T.fat (g) | S.fat (g) | Chol (mg) | Na (mg) |
|---|---|---|---|---|---|---|---|---|
| 320 | 77 | 2 | 13 | 3 | 2 | 0.2 | 0 | 241 |

## FRUIT SMOOTHIE

3 tabsp of skim milk powder (25g)
1 small banana, mashed (100g)
2 tsp honey (10ml)
2/3 cup water (165ml)

- Combine powdered milk, banana, honey and water in a bowl or blender.
- Whisk or blend until smooth.

**Serves 1**

*Variation*
Add a scoop of low fat ice cream or vary flavours by using strawberries or peaches or other available fruit.

*Note*
An excellent breakfast when time is short or for those that feel the normal breakfast is too heavy. Milk and banana are low glycaemic foods.

*Handy Hint*
Milk is a good source of calcium for those who like to drink milk. Calcium is particularly necessary for boys and girls in their teens, and women and men over the age of 50 to prevent osteoporosis. Two or three serves a day are recommended.

NUTRIENTS PER SERVE

| KJ | Cal | Pro (g) | CHO (g) | Fibre (g) | T.fat (g) | S.fat (g) | Chol (mg) | Na (mg) |
|---|---|---|---|---|---|---|---|---|
| 858 | 206 | 11 | 41 | 2 | 0.3 | 0.1 | 8 | 109 |

## SAVOURY BAKED BEANS

1 medium finely chopped onion (100g)
1 tsp mono/polyunsaturated oil (5ml)
2 tsp water (10ml)
1 medium finely chopped unpeeled apple (100g)
1 tsp lemon juice (5ml)
440g can baked beans (440g)

- Stir-fry onion with oil and water until onion is golden.
- Add apple and lemon juice and stir-fry for 2 minutes more.
- Stir in baked beans and cook until hot.
- Serve over wholemeal or wholegrain toast.

**Serves 4 x 1/2 cup**

*Note*
A hearty breakfast on a Saturday or Sunday morning or during the week for people with higher energy requirements. Use it as a luncheon dish over toast or split English muffins. There is no need to add margarine. A very good low glycaemic index food.

*Handy Hint*
Baked beans are high in fibre and low in fat while making a good contribution of protein.

NUTRIENTS PER SERVE

| KJ | Cal | Pro (g) | CHO (g) | Fibre (g) | T.fat (g) | S.fat (g) | Chol (mg) | Na (mg) |
|---|---|---|---|---|---|---|---|---|
| 439 | 106 | 5.5 | 17 | 6 | 2 | 0.3 | 0 | 444 |

## Commercial Breakfast Cereals

Commercial breakfast cereals are quick and easy. Choose ones with less than 8g of fat and less than 18g of sugar per 100g of cereal. Fibre greater than 6g per 100g is preferred. Some good choices are All-Bran™, Guardian™, BranBix™, Oat Flakes™ and Weet-Bix™.

## LUNCHEON RECIPES

# Luncheon

There are many recipes suitable for light or substantial lunches — hot or cold. Recipes have been grouped under types such as Vegetarian, Pasta, Chicken or Fish to encourage you to use them for either lunch or dinner. Some of the breakfast recipes will adapt for lunch or brunch. A variety of menus have also been included to used or to help plan your own menus. The kilojoules, carbohydrate and fat content of each recipe is also given to help you plan the quantities needed.

*Spinach Pinenut Roulade p53*

### Cold Choices
Some cold ideas are salads such as **Rare Roast Beef Salad** p98 or **Mango Chicken Salad** p99. Try some of the Luncheon and Sandwich ideas and use the **Sandwich Ingredients** chart overpage.
**Baked Frittata** p52, **Quiche** p54 or **Cornish Pasties** p70 are all suitable hot or cold. They could be consumed for an evening meal and then used cold the next day.

### Hot Choices
In winter hot soups such as **Red Lentil Soup** p46, **Laksa** p46 or **Clam Chowder** p45 will be a substantial meal. Combine with fresh bread, **Plain Scones** p121 or **Damper with Beer** p130. Ideal lighter soups are **Cauliflower** p42 or **Pumpkin and Ginger** p44.
These may be consumed at home or taken to work and reheated in a microwave.
**Tuna Hotpot** p82, **Lasagne** p68 or **Spinach Pinenut Roulade** p53 would all be excellent for weekend meals.

### Entertaining
If you are entertaining for lunch try **Polenta Pie** p58 or **Mediterranean Pie** p61.
Special dishes such as **Chilli Mussels** p79 or **Moussaka** p71 plus many other dishes will be suitable for lunch or dinner, adapting well to special occasions.

### Vegetarian Choices
Vegetarian dishes are suitable on their own or in combination. Often there is one guest or family member who is vegetarian, and a particular dish prepared for them can provide an alternative for everyone else to enjoy.

**Cheesy Pumpkin Ricotta Bake** p54 or **Broccoli Soufflé** p52 would be popular choices using eggs.
Try **Vegetable Parcels** p60 or **Tofu Vegetable Stir Fry** p51. Remember to include beans as often as possible as in **Chilli Beans** p48.

## Luncheon and Sandwich Ideas

Refer to the **Sandwich Ingredients** chart overpage. This will give you the basis to develop endless combinations of sandwich and luncheon ideas. To help, here are a few ideas to get you started.
Remember you can mix and match breads, meats, cheeses, fruits and vegetables, sauces, spreads and condiments.

### Bagels
These are heavy so be careful of quantity.
Prepare **Ham and Bocconcini Cheese Bagel** p55 or spread bagels with **Hommos** p39 and top with shaved pork, apple sauce and alfalfa sprouts.

### Bread
Prefer wholegrain or soya linseed loaf. Use cottage, ricotta, **Yoghurt Cheese** p39 as a spread instead of butter or margarine.
Spread bread with cooked sweet potato, low fat ham with chutney and shredded lettuce.

### Crêpes
Increase fibre by making **Wholemeal Crêpes** p129 They may be prepared ahead and refrigerated or frozen.

34

## LUNCHEON RECIPES

Refer to **Savoury Stuffed Crêpes** p38 or fill with mashed pumpkin, low fat fetta and snow pea sprouts.

### Focaccia
Split and treat like rolls but remember that they are heavier so restrict size of serve. They lend themselves well to being served warm.
Fill Focaccia with grated low fat cheese, **Peeled Capsicum** p86, finely sliced chicken breast and **Thai Dressing** p97.

### Lavash Bread, Mountain Bread
Take to school or work with fillings separate so they don't go soggy. Spread with tabbouleh, shaved roast beef and finely shredded spinach.

### Oatcakes
Freeze well. Refer **Oatcakes** p124. Use in combination with salad, soup or with cheese. Spread oatcakes with **Hommos** p39 and combine with soup.

### Pita Bread
Fill with a savoury filling at home or take the filling in a separate container and fill just before eating.
Try **Lentil Sauce** p105 with **Grilled Eggplant** p88 and **Peeled Capsicum** p86.

### Polenta
Prepare **Grilled Fine Polenta** p92 and spread with savoury fillings for lunch or as savouries at a party. Spread with chutney and top with finely chopped chicken mixed with low fat mayonnaise, curry powder and chopped green grapes.

### Rice Crackers
Adapt well as open sandwiches with a variety of fillings such as low fat mayonnaise topped with grated carrot and sultanas.

### Ribbon Sandwiches
Make sandwiches by using 2 slices of wholegrain bread with one slice of white in between. Spread the wholegrain bread with the first filling, top with white bread and cover with the second filling. Remove crusts and cut into 2 or 3 sandwiches depending on the size desired.
Suggested fillings:
- ❑ Salmon with capers and curried egg with shredded lettuce.
- ❑ Cottage cheese and chopped dates and lean ham with **Creamy Mustard Dressing** p96.

### Rolls
Be aware of size as 25 grams equal 1 slice of bread. Choose whole grain or wholemeal if possible. Use low fat spreads and large quantities of vegetables to give moisture and bulk.
Spread rolls with **Savoury Baked Beans** p33 with mixed lettuce and sliced cucumber.

### Savoury Biscuits, Saos, Vita Wheat
Choose biscuits that are wholegrain and low fat. They may form open or closed sandwiches. Cover biscuits with thinly sliced roast beef with **Horse Radish Dressing** p96 and finely shredded red cabbage.

### Savoury Cases
Prepare **Savoury Cases** p130. Make ahead and freeze. Fill with moist fillings for at home lunches or when entertaining.
Fill with fresh seafood such as prawns, crab or crayfish or a calamari mixture and top with **Seafood Sauce** p107.

**Mediterranean Pie p61**

### Scones
Prepare **Plain Scones** p121 and combine with soup or salad or spread with cheese or other protein.
Spread with **Yoghurt Cheese** p39 flavoured with dill and top with smoke salmon and sprouts.

### Thick Slices French Loaf
Use a low fat spread and top with a combination of protein, condiments and garnish.
Use a base of cottage, ricotta, **Yoghurt Cheese** p39 or **Hommo**s p39 and top with a combination of sliced salmon or lean ham, and garnish with pickled asparagus, capsicum, sliced olives or sliced avocado.

# SANDWICH INGREDIENTS CHART

### BREAD

Bagel
Bread, wholemeal or grain, rye, soy linseed
**Damper with Beer**
English Muffins
Focaccia
Lavash Bread
Mountain Bread
**Oatcakes**
Pikelets
Pita bread
**Polenta, Grilled Fine**
Rice Crackers
Rolls
Savoury Biscuits
**Savoury Cases**
Saos
**Scones, Plain**
Thick Slices French Loaf
Vita Wheat
**Wholemeal Crêpes**

### MEATS, CHEESES AND ALTERNATIVES

**Baked Beans, Savoury**
Cheese, low fat, sliced, grated
Chicken, chopped
Cottage Cheese
Egg, curried or plain
Ham (97%) lean
**Hommos**
Meat Loaf
Nuts
Peanut Butter
Ricotta Cheese
Roast Meat, sliced cold
Salmon, tinned
Salmon, smoked
Tuna
Tuna & Cheese, low fat, grated
**Yoghurt Cheese**

### FRUIT AND VEGETABLES

Alfalfa
Asparagus, tinned or fresh
Avocado
Banana
Beetroot, grated or pickled
Cabbage, english shredded
**Capsicum, grilled, red or green**
Carrot, grated or sticks
Celery, sticks or chopped
Coleslaw
**Corn, Savoury Creamed**
Cucumber
Dates
**Eggplant, grilled**
Grapes
Lettuce, leaves or shredded
Mushrooms, raw or cooked
Pumpkin, cooked or mashed
Red Cabbage, shredded
Spinach
Sprouts, all types
Sweet Potato
**Tabbouleh**
Tomato
**Fresh Tomato Basil Salsa**

### SAUCES, SPREADS AND CONDIMENTS

Bread & Butter Pickles
Chutney
Cottage Cheese, plain, flavoured
**Creamy Mustard Dressing**
**Fresh Strawberry Spread**
Herbs e.g. Basil, Oregano, Coriander
**Horseradish Dressing**
Mayonnaise, light
Mustard
Mustard Sauce
Ricotta Cheese
Sultanas
**Thai Dressing**
Tomato Purée
**Cooked Tomato Savoury**
**Yoghurt Cheese**

**Bold** entries are recipes appearing in this book

# FIRST COURSE, SAVOURIES AND DIPS

## First Course, Savouries and Dips

*Avocado Salmon Mousse 41*
*Bruschetta 40*
*Hommos 39*
*Mediterranean Spread 40*
*Mexican Dip 38*
*Red Capsicum Dip 38*
*Savoury Meat Balls 41*
*Savoury Stuffed Crêpes 38*
*Seafood Avocado Dip 41*
*Spinach Dip 37*
*Spring Rolls 40*
*Yoghurt Cheese 39*

*Spinach Dip*

A wide variety of simple dips and savouries have been included to help with entertaining. Try to plan a combination of low joule, low carbohydrate dishes with more substantial ones. Refer to **Special Menus** p27 for further ideas. For example spread **Hommos** p39, **Mediterranean Spread** p40 or **Yoghurt Cheese** p39 on dry biscuits, **Crispy Lavash Bread** p125 or fresh or toasted wholegrain bread. Top with prawns, smoked salmon, pickled asparagus, shaved ham or drained **Sundried Tomatoes** p89.

There are low joule and low fat dips such as **Red Capsicum Dip** p38 or **Spinach Dip** p37. Combine this with a more substantial choice such as **Mexican Dip** p38 or **Seafood Avocado Dip** p41.

Pass **Spring Rolls** p40 and **Savoury Meat Balls** p41 around as hot savouries at a party.

For a dinner party try **Avocado Salmon Mousse** p41 or **Savoury Stuffed Crêpes** p38 as a well-presented first course. To save time the crepes may be made ahead and refrigerated. The **Avocado Salmon Mousse** p41 may be made the day before.

If you want just a light snack before a meal, use **Red Capsicum Dip** p38 with crudites (fresh bite size pieces of vegetables) or low fat dry biscuits. Serve a variety of sandwiches. Refer to the **Luncheon and Sandwich Ideas** p34 and note especially the **Ribbon Sandwiches.** See the **Sandwich Ingredients Chart** p36 for more options.

## SPINACH DIP

*1 pkt frozen thawed spinach (165g)*
*1 pkt spring vegetable soup*
*½ cup non fat yoghurt (125ml)*
*½ cup light (97% fat free) mayonnaise (125ml)*
*1 large round wholegrain loaf of bread (400g)*

❑ Drain spinach well.
❑ Mix with soup mix, yoghurt and mayonnaise.
❑ Using a bread knife cut the top off the bread and hollow out. Cut the bread that is removed into bite size pieces and lightly toast under griller.
❑ Fill the hollow with the spinach mixture and place toasted bread on a platter around it. Cover with top of bread as a lid.
❑ To serve, dip the bread in the spinach mixture.
❑ The bread bowl may be cut into bite size pieces as required after the dip has been finished.

**Serves 10**

*Note*
Leftovers as sliced bread is delicious next day.

NUTRIENTS PER SERVE

| KJ | Cal | Pro (g) | CHO (g) | Fibre (g) | T.fat (g) | S.fat (g) | Chol (mg) | Na (mg) |
|---|---|---|---|---|---|---|---|---|
| 536 | 129 | 5.8 | 22 | 4.3 | 1.7 | 0.6 | 3.6 | 673 |

## MEXICAN DIP

½ cup cottage cheese or reduced fat cream cheese (120g)
1 tsp garlic salt (5g)
¼ cup non fat yoghurt (65ml)
1 medium avocado, flesh only (200g)
½ tsp lemon juice (3ml)
1 small finely chopped tomato (75g)
Finely chopped green chillies (50g)
1 cup canned drained kidney beans (200g)
2 finely chopped spring onions (28g)
½ cup finely chopped stuffed green olives (80g)
½ cup medium commercial salsa sauce (125ml)
½ cup grated less than 10% fat cheese (60g)

- Mix cheese, garlic salt and yoghurt together.
- Place in the bottom of a flat dish.
- Mix avocado, lemon juice, tomato and chillies together.
- Spread on top of yoghurt and cheese.
- Mash kidney beans and spring onions together and microwave on **High** for 4 minutes.
- Add olives on top of avocado mixture.
- Top with salsa and grated cheese.
- Serve with corn chips or low fat biscuits.

**Serves 15**

*Variation*
Reduce kidney beans to ½ cup and add 50g finely chopped lean ham.

*Nutritional Tip*
The use of cottage cheese increases the calcium while reducing the fat content. The analysis is done on cottage cheese, not reduced fat cream cheese. Reduce sodium to 217mg using no added salt kidney beans.

NUTRIENTS PER SERVE

| KJ | Cal | Pro (g) | CHO (g) | Fibre (g) | T.fat (g) | S.fat (g) | Chol (mg) | Na (mg) |
|---|---|---|---|---|---|---|---|---|
| 214 | 51 | 4 | 3 | 2 | 2.4 | 0.6 | 3 | 342 |

## RED CAPSICUM DIP

1 large peeled and seeded red capsicum (300g)
2 crushed cloves garlic (6g)
½ cup beef stock (125ml)
2 tsp balsamic vinegar (10ml)

- Remove the seeds and stem from capsicum and cut into 8ths.
- Grill with skin side up until blackened, place in a plastic bag to sweat for 5 minutes.
- Peel capsicum and blend with garlic and stock until a smooth consistency is achieved.
- Serve with raw vegetables, crudites, savoury biscuits, **Crispy Lavash Bread** p125 or **Grilled Fine Polenta** p92.

*Note*
A savoury, very low kilojoule dip which also looks attractive.

**Serves 12 x 1 tabsp (Total 1 cup)**

NUTRIENTS PER SERVE

| KJ | Cal | Pro (g) | CHO (g) | Fibre (g) | T.fat (g) | S.fat (g) | Chol (mg) | Na (mg) |
|---|---|---|---|---|---|---|---|---|
| 32 | 8 | 0.5 | 1 | 0.3 | 0.1 | 0.03 | 0.06 | 10 |

## SAVOURY STUFFED CRÊPES

6 **Wholemeal Crêpes** p129
12 fresh asparagus spears (100g)
8 large spinach leaves (100g)
1 large flesh only avocado (200g)
2 tsp fresh lemon juice (10ml)
1 small red capsicum (100g)
1 small yellow capsicum (100g)
Black pepper

- Prepare **Wholemeal Crêpes** according to directions.
- Cook asparagus in plastic bag in microwave on **High** for 3 minutes or until just bright green and slightly soft.
- Take large spinach leaves, wash, place in plastic bag and microwave on **High** for 1 minute or until soft.
- Cool asparagus and spinach.
- Take each crêpe, cover with spinach leaves.
- Top with strips of avocado dipped in lemon juice, fine strips of red and yellow capsicum and fresh asparagus cut to the proper length.
- Season with freshly ground black pepper.
- Roll firmly, wrap in plastic wrap and chill.
- Just before serving remove plastic wrap and slice diagonally for presentation.
- May use fresh **Plum Sauce** recipe p106 or commercial plum sauce.
- Other vegetables may be substituted as desired.

**Serves 6**

NUTRIENTS PER SERVE

| KJ | Cal | Pro (g) | CHO (g) | Fibre (g) | T.fat (g) | S.fat (g) | Chol (mg) | Na (mg) |
|---|---|---|---|---|---|---|---|---|
| 672 | 163 | 7 | 10 | 3 | 11 | 2 | 48 | 37 |

# FIRST COURSE, SAVOURIES AND DIPS

*Savoury Stuffed Crêpes*

## HOMMOS

*425g can chick peas (300g) plus liquid*
*¼ cup sesame seeds (30g)*
*1 tabsp mono/polyunsaturated oil (20ml)*
*1cm piece crushed ginger (5g)*
*2 crushed cloves garlic (6g)*
*¼ cup lemon juice or to taste (65ml)*
*Salt and pepper to taste*

❑ Drain and reserve liquid from chick peas.
❑ Rinse chick peas and place in blender or food processor with sesame seeds, oil, ginger, garlic and lemon juice.
❑ Add ⅓ cup of reserved liquid.
❑ Blend until smooth.
❑ Taste and adjust seasoning as required with a little bit more of lemon juice, pepper or salt.
❑ Add more liquid to desired consistency.

**Serves 20 x 1 tabsp**

*Note*
A low fat, high protein spread to use with **Crispy Lavash Bread** p125, as a dip, in sandwiches or as a spread on toast for snacks in between meals. Good Glycaemic Index.

NUTRIENTS PER SERVE

| KJ | Cal | Pro (g) | CHO (g) | Fibre (g) | T.fat (g) | S.fat (g) | Chol (mg) | Na (mg) |
|---|---|---|---|---|---|---|---|---|
| 140 | 34 | 1.3 | 2 | 0.9 | 2 | 0.3 | 0 | 38 |

## YOGHURT CHEESE

*1 cup non fat natural yoghurt (250g)*

❑ Take a 40cm x 20cm piece of cheesecloth, fold in half and place on a dish.
❑ Pour 1 cup of yoghurt on top and tie up with a rubber band.
❑ Hang and leave to drip in the kitchen for 4, 6 or 8 hours. The longer it hangs the more firm it is.

**Serves 6 x 1 tabsp (Total ½ cup)**

*Uses*
**Yoghurt Cheese** may be spread instead of butter or margarine on bread or rolls, and be used as the basis of a dip. Combine it with capers and fill smoked salmon rolled into horns for something special. Store in sealed container in the refrigerator on kitchen paper to keep dry. Will keep up to one week.

*Note*
This is similar to a low fat Quark or a cheese called Fromage Blanche; it is to be noted the fat content is insignificant. One cup non fat yoghurt yields ½ cup of yoghurt cheese.

NUTRIENTS PER SERVE

| KJ | Cal | Pro (g) | CHO (g) | Fibre (g) | T.fat (g) | S.fat (g) | Chol (mg) | Na (mg) |
|---|---|---|---|---|---|---|---|---|
| 93 | 22 | 2.5 | 2.4 | 0 | 0.08 | 0.03 | 2 | 29 |

## MEDITERRANEAN SPREAD

¼ cup pitted chopped Kalamata olives (50g)
¼ cup sundried tomatoes (30g)
2 sliced, seeded and chopped chillies (hot)
2 crushed cloves garlic (6g)
2 tabsp olive oil (40ml)

- Place olives, sundried tomatoes, chillies, garlic and oil in a food processor and blend until smooth.
- Use as a spread on fresh bread as an appetiser for a party.

**Serves 16 x 2 tsp**

*Variation*
2 anchovies may be added for extra flavour. This will increase sodium.

NUTRIENTS PER SERVE

| KJ | Cal | Pro (g) | CHO (g) | Fibre (g) | T.fat (g) | S.fat (g) | Chol (mg) | Na (mg) |
|---|---|---|---|---|---|---|---|---|
| 107 | 26 | 0.2 | 0.35 | 0.3 | 2.6 | 0.4 | 0 | 126 |

## BRUSCHETTA

¼ cup finely chopped parsley
¼ cup finely chopped basil
2 anchovies (15g)
2 tsp capers
3 tsp lemon juice (15ml)
2 crushed cloves garlic (6g)
1 tabsp olive oil (20ml)
6 thick slices of toasted Italian bread, French Stick or English muffin (180g)
4 peeled, seeded and chopped Roman or pear shaped tomatoes (360g)
1 medium finely chopped onion (100g)
2 tabsp of parmesan cheese or 12 thin slices of Romano cheese (40g)

- Place parsley, basil, anchovies, capers, lemon juice, garlic and oil in a food processor and blend until smooth.
- Spread on 6 thick slices of toasted Italian bread or other suitable bases.
- Place tomato and onion on top and sprinkle with parmesan cheese or put thin slices of Romano cheese on top.
- Place under grill and heat through and melt cheese.

**Serves 6**

*Note*
This may be served as two slices as a luncheon or one as an entrée dish. Analysis is for 1 slice.

*Handy Hint*
The Romano cheese may be sliced very thinly using a potato peeler. This will increase the kilojoules slightly as more cheese will be used.

NUTRIENTS PER SERVE

| KJ | Cal | Pro (g) | CHO (g) | Fibre (g) | T.fat (g) | S.fat (g) | Chol (mg) | Na (mg) |
|---|---|---|---|---|---|---|---|---|
| 638 | 154 | 7 | 17 | 2 | 6.5 | 2 | 8 | 387 |

## SPRING ROLLS

½ cup raw rice vermicelli (50g)
1 medium finely chopped onion (100g)
1 crushed clove garlic (3g)
7 finely sliced mushrooms with stalk (50g)
Lean minced veal (400g)
Freshly ground black pepper
1 tabsp low sodium soy sauce (20ml)
¼ cup finely chopped spring onions (25g)
1 cup finely chopped cabbage (100g)
Bean sprouts (50g)
1 tsp cornflour (2.5g)
2 tabsp water (40ml)
36 spring roll wrappers (12cm x 12cm) (144g)
Mono/polyunsaturated cooking spray

- Cook vermicelli by pouring boiling water over it, leave for 5 minutes and drain.
- Stir-fry onion, garlic, mushrooms and mince in a non-stick pan until brown. Cool.
- Combine with vermicelli, pepper, soy sauce, spring onions, cabbage and bean sprouts.
- Mix cornflour and water together to form a smooth paste.
- Lay out six spring roll wrappers, place 1 heaped tablespoon on the corner of each, fold in bottom and sides and roll up. Seal with cornflour paste and turn under and place on greased baking tray. Spray with oil.
- Bake in 180°C oven for 30 minutes.

**Serves 36 rolls**

*Note*
These may be made, placed on a baking tray, frozen and then put into a plastic bag and baked as required.

NUTRIENTS PER SERVE

| KJ | Cal | Pro (g) | CHO (g) | Fibre (g) | T.fat (g) | S.fat (g) | Chol (mg) | Na (mg) |
|---|---|---|---|---|---|---|---|---|
| 112 | 27 | 3 | 3 | 0.3 | 0.3 | 0.06 | 9 | 60 |

## AVOCADO SALMON MOUSSE

**Bottom Layer**
3 tsp gelatine (9g)
¼ cup water (65ml)
1 tabsp lemon juice (20ml)
1 finely chopped spring onion (10g)
Few drops chilli sauce
½ tsp dried or 1 tabsp fresh oregano
1 large avocado, peeled and seeded (200g)

**Top Layer**
220g can of drained red salmon (185g)
3 tsp gelatine (9g)
¼ cup water (65ml)
Non fat natural yoghurt (100g)
½ cup low sodium tomato sauce (125ml)
½ cup light (97% fat free) mayonnaise (125ml)
½ cup finely chopped spring onion (50g)
1 stick finely chopped celery (75g)
Chilli sauce to taste

**Bottom Layer**
- Dissolve gelatine in hot water.
- Blend lemon juice, 3 tsp gelatine, spring onion, chilli sauce, oregano and avocado together.
- Place in a large greased mould or in 6 small ones and refrigerate for at least two hours to set bottom layer.

**Top Layer**
- Blend salmon with 3 tsp gelatine dissolved in hot water plus yoghurt, tomato sauce, mayonnaise, spring onion and celery together for top layer.
- Adjust seasoning with chilli sauce.
- When bottom layer is partially set, add top layer, cover with plastic wrap and refrigerate until firm.
- Unmould onto a bed of lettuce.
- Serve with caviar and sliced stuffed olives or prawns, or smoked salmon and a spoon of non fat yoghurt as a garnish.

**Serves 6**

*Note*
Excellent for a dinner party or special occasion.

NUTRIENTS PER SERVE

| KJ | Cal | Pro (g) | CHO (g) | Fibre (g) | T.fat (g) | S.fat (g) | Chol (mg) | Na (mg) |
|---|---|---|---|---|---|---|---|---|
| 841 | 202 | 12 | 12 | 1.5 | 12 | 3 | 28 | 409 |

## SAVOURY MEAT BALLS

Lean mince (500g)
1 medium grated carrot (100g)
1 medium finely chopped onion (100g)
1 egg (50g) or low cholesterol egg mix
Freshly ground black pepper
1 tsp curry powder
1 tsp cumin
2 tabsp fresh or 1 tsp dried tarragon leaves
2 tabsp finely chopped parsley
4 tabsp cornflour (45g)
2 tabsp mono/polyunsaturated oil (40ml)

- Blend mince, carrot, onion, egg, black pepper, curry powder, cumin, tarragon and parsley together.
- Form into 36 small firm balls and dip in cornflour.
- Cook in two batches, heating 1 tabsp of oil at a time in a non-stick pan, turning carefully to brown evenly.
- Drain on absorbent kitchen paper.
- Serve hot or cold.

**Serves 36 meat balls**

*Note*
These may be made ahead and reheated in the microwave on **Medium High** for 5 to 7 minutes. They freeze well.

NUTRIENTS PER MEAT BALL

| KJ | Cal | Pro (g) | CHO (g) | Fibre (g) | T.fat (g) | S.fat (g) | Chol (mg) | Na (mg) |
|---|---|---|---|---|---|---|---|---|
| 122 | 37 | 3 | 1.4 | 0.1 | 2 | 0.6 | 14 | 17 |

## SEAFOOD AVOCADO DIP

½ large ripe peeled and seeded avocado (100g)
125g reduced fat cream cheese (17% fat)
½ x 170g can of drained crab meat (65g)
½ x 200g can drained prawns (70g)
½ cup **Seafood Sauce** p107 (125ml)

- Mash avocado and mix with cream cheese.
- Place in a bowl and top with crab and then prawns.
- Pour over seafood sauce.
- Garnish with parsley and serve

**Serves 8**

NUTRIENTS PER SERVE

| KJ | Cal | Pro (g) | CHO (g) | Fibre (g) | T.fat (g) | S.fat (g) | Chol (mg) | Na (mg) |
|---|---|---|---|---|---|---|---|---|
| 399 | 97 | 4 | 4 | 0.4 | 7.3 | 2.5 | 40 | 272 |

# SOUP RECIPES

## Soups

When the chill winter sets in soups are the ideal culinary fare. Those chosen here are low joule or more substantial with a low Glycaemic Index.

Soups lend themselves well to freezing so you can have a selection on hand to dress up a meal or use as a quick main one. Label it well and use within three months. Enjoy the blend of exotic flavours we have offered you.

*Light*
*Cauliflower Soup 42*
   *Choko Soup 43*
   *Zucchini Soup 43*
   *Broccoli Soup 43*
   *'CCC' Soup 43*
*Eggplant Soup 43*
*Leek and Pear Soup 44*
   *Two Tone Soup 44*
*Pumpkin and Ginger Soup 44*

*Substantial*
*Clam Chowder 45*
*Laksa 46*
   *Seafood Laksa 46*
   *Vegetarian Laksa 46*
*Lombok Fish Soup 45*
*Red Lentil Soup 46*
*West Meets East Soup 45*

*Light Soups* A light addition to a meal with insignificant carbohydrate would be **Cauliflower Soup** p42 or the variations such as **Choko**, **Zucchini**, **Broccoli** or **'CCC'**. These could even substitute as a snack. Any low joule vegetables may be combined to make interesting soups. Chop the vegetables and serve as is or purée for a smoother finish.

Good filling soups which could be used in combination for a light luncheon are **Eggplant Soup** p43, **Leek and Pear Soup** p44 or **Pumpkin and Ginger Soup** p44.

*Substantial Soups* **Clam Chowder** p45, **Laksa** p46 and **Lombok Fish Soup** p45 will be a meal on their own as they contain protein as fish, beans or lentils, plus pasta or rice. **Red Lentil Soup** p46 and **West Meets East Soup** p45 are based on beans and lentils so are excellent in controlled amounts for people with diabetes. Be careful how much bread accompanies them or blood sugars could rise.

# LIGHT SOUPS

## CAULIFLOWER SOUP

5 cups water (1250ml)
4 tsp low sodium chicken stock (10g)
1 large well trimmed chopped cauliflower (1000g)
1 medium coarsely chopped onion (100g)
1 large coarsely chopped carrot (150g)
1 bay leaf
2 tsp fresh or $^1/_2$ tsp dry thyme
Freshly ground black pepper
$^1/_4$ cup finely chopped parsley

- ❑ Bring the water and stock powder to the boil in a large saucepan.
- ❑ Add cauliflower, onion and carrot.
- ❑ Season with bay leaf, thyme, black pepper.
- ❑ Simmer for 12 minutes or until vegetables are soft.

*Top to bottom: Cauliflower Soup, 'CCC' Soup, Zucchini Soup*

*Broccoli Soup*

❑ Purée in a blender, return to saucepan and stir in parsley.
❑ Use ½ tsp parmesan cheese per bowl if desired.
**Serves 8**

*Variation*
**Choko Soup** Substitute chokos for cauliflower and season with garlic and basil.
**Zucchini Soup** Substitute zucchini for cauliflower and season with tarragon and garlic.
**Broccoli Soup** Substitute broccoli for cauliflower and season with garlic, basil, black pepper, 2 tsp lemon juice and the zest of ½ a lemon.
**'CCC' Soup** Substitute vegetables with a mixture of 1 large capsicum, 2 - 3 cups of finely chopped cabbage plus 2 carrots. Season with herbs, parsley and fresh ground pepper as desired.

*Note*
Watch sodium. Low sodium stock powder is low in sodium compared with regular stock powder or cubes. Make fresh stock from bones in chicken carcass and season with fresh herbs.

NUTRIENTS PER SERVE

| KJ | Cal | Pro (g) | CHO (g) | Fibre (g) | T.fat (g) | S.fat (g) | Chol (mg) | Na (mg) |
|---|---|---|---|---|---|---|---|---|
| 184 | 44 | 4 | 5 | 3 | 0.6 | 0.2 | 0.4 | 85 |

# EGGPLANT SOUP

1 medium finely chopped onion (100g)
1½ slices finely chopped middle eye rasher bacon (50g)
1 crushed clove garlic (3g)
1 tsp ground coriander
2 tsp mono/polyunsaturated oil (10ml)
1 tabsp water (20ml)
4 cups beef stock (1000ml)
2 medium peeled eggplant (600g)
Finely chopped parsley

❑ Sauté onion, bacon, garlic and coriander in oil and water for 3 to 4 minutes.
❑ Slice eggplant, add to onion mixture and cook for a further 5 minutes.
❑ Add beef stock, cover and simmer for 1 hour or 30 minutes at **Medium** in microwave.
❑ Purée, adjust seasoning and reheat.
❑ Serve hot with chopped parsley as garnish.
**Serves 6**

*Note*
May use low sodium stock powder and water if stock not available.

NUTRIENTS PER SERVE

| KJ | Cal | Pro (g) | CHO (g) | Fibre (g) | T.fat (g) | S.fat (g) | Chol (mg) | Na (mg) |
|---|---|---|---|---|---|---|---|---|
| 271 | 64 | 4 | 5 | 3 | 3 | 0.6 | 5 | 207 |

## LEEK AND PEAR SOUP

*1 tabsp mono/polyunsaturated margarine (20g)*
*2 medium leeks (750g)*
*2 tabsp water (40ml)*
*4 medium peeled and cored green pears (400g)*
*4 cups chicken stock (1000ml)*
*2 cups water (500ml)*
*Pepper to taste*
*¼ cup non fat yoghurt as a garnish (65g)*

- ❏ Melt margarine in a microwave dish or saucepan.
- ❏ Wash leeks well, slice thinly using a little of the green and then rewash to make sure to remove all sand.
- ❏ Stir-fry leeks with water and margarine until they soften but are not brown.
- ❏ Slice pears and add to pan. Cook for 5 minutes.
- ❏ Add chicken stock and simmer gently until pears are quite soft.
- ❏ Sieve or blend until smooth.
- ❏ Adjust seasoning with pepper.
- ❏ Serve hot with a swirl of yoghurt.

**Serves 10**

### Variation
**Two Tone Soup** Serve equal portions of **Leek and Pear Soup** and **Broccoli Soup** p43 with a swirl of yoghurt. Other pleasing combinations could be **Pumpkin and Ginger Soup** with **Cauliflower Soup**, and **Eggplant Soup** plus **'CCC' Soup**. It is best with a variation in colour and flavour.

### Handy Hint
Put each soup in a jug and pour in to soup bowl from opposite sides at once.

NUTRIENTS PER SERVE

| KJ | Cal | Pro (g) | CHO (g) | Fibre (g) | T.fat (g) | S.fat (g) | Chol (mg) | Na (mg) |
|---|---|---|---|---|---|---|---|---|
| 285 | 68 | 2 | 9 | 3 | 2 | 0.4 | 0.6 | 63 |

*Two Tone Soup*

## PUMPKIN AND GINGER SOUP

*2 tsp mono/polyunsaturated margarine (10g)*
*1 tabsp water (20ml)*
*½ medium finely chopped onion (50g)*
*1 tsp finely chopped green or ¼ tsp dried ginger*
*1 tabsp wholemeal flour (10g)*
*2 cups puréed cooked pumpkin (600g raw)*
*2 cups chicken stock (500ml)*
*2 cups non fat milk (500ml)*
*Salt to taste*

- ❏ Melt margarine and water in a saucepan.
- ❏ Add onion, green ginger and sauté until transparent.
- ❏ Stir in flour.
- ❏ Add pumpkin and cook for 5 minutes.
- ❏ Gradually add chicken stock and milk.
- ❏ Gently simmer for 5 minutes.
- ❏ Rub through a sieve or purée in a blender.
- ❏ Serve hot or cold, garnished with spring onion or chopped parsley.

**Serves 6**

### Note
If using your own stock, always set it in the refrigerator and remove all fat. Save time by using low sodium chicken stock powder and water.

NUTRIENTS PER SERVE

| KJ | Cal | Pro (g) | CHO (g) | Fibre (g) | T.fat (g) | S.fat (g) | Chol (mg) | Na (mg) |
|---|---|---|---|---|---|---|---|---|
| 395 | 95 | 6 | 12 | 2 | 2 | 0.7 | 3 | 76 |

### Nutritional Hint
Boil up chicken carcass or meat bones with an onion, carrot, a little celery plus herbs from the garden. Let it set and strain. An inexpensive low sodium stock to use in any of the recipes.

# SUBSTANTIAL SOUPS

## LOMBOK FISH SOUP

1 small leek (75g)
2 crushed cloves garlic (6g)
1 tsp mono/polyunsaturated oil (5ml)
½ tsp sesame oil (2.5ml)
1 tabsp water (20ml)
White fleshed fish cubed (250g)
8 cups water (2 litres)
4 tsp low sodium vegetable stock powder (10g)
1 coarsely grated carrot (100g)
1 medium seeded and finely chopped tomato (100g)
Thick rice noodles (100g)
2 tsp lemon juice (10ml)
Salt to taste

- Wash leeks, finely slice the bottom ⅔ and discard the very green tough tops.
- Rewash to remove all sand.
- Stir-fry leeks and garlic in oils and 1 tabsp water until leeks are soft.
- Add fish and gently stir-fry for 2 - 3 minutes.
- Gently heat mixture in saucepan with 8 cups of water, stock powder, carrot and tomato.
- Pour boiling water over rice noodles in a large saucepan and leave for 10 minutes.
- Drain noodles and add to soup.
- Adjust seasoning with lemon juice and salt and serve.

**Serves 8**

*Note*
A light nourishing soup.

NUTRIENTS PER SERVE

| KJ | Cal | Pro (g) | CHO (g) | Fibre (g) | T.fat (g) | S.fat (g) | Chol (mg) | Na (mg) |
|---|---|---|---|---|---|---|---|---|
| 316 | 75 | 8 | 5 | 1 | 2.3 | 0.6 | 22 | 93 |

## CLAM CHOWDER

1 large finely chopped onion (150g)
1½ slices finely chopped middle eye rasher or turkey bacon (50g)
1 tabsp mono/polyunsaturated oil (20ml)
2 tabsp plain flour (20g)
2 cups water (500ml)
4 medium potatoes, peeled and cubed (400g)
2 x 220g tins of baby clams plus juice (440g)
1 can low fat evaporated milk (375ml)
Pepper to taste

- Stir-fry onion and bacon in oil.
- Thicken with flour and then slowly add water, stirring to make a smooth paste.
- Add cubed potato.
- Cook until potato is soft.
- Stir in clams, juice and milk.
- Check seasoning, reheat and serve.

**Serves 8**

*Handy Hint*
If time is short pre-cook potato in microwave while stir-frying bacon and onion. Use turkey bacon which is about 5% fat.

NUTRIENTS PER SERVE

| KJ | Cal | Pro (g) | CHO (g) | Fibre (g) | T.fat (g) | S.fat (g) | Chol (mg) | Na (mg) |
|---|---|---|---|---|---|---|---|---|
| 655 | 158 | 14 | 15 | 1 | 4 | 1 | 110 | 509 |

## WEST MEETS EAST SOUP

1 pkt Italian soup mix (375g) - refer p30
3 cups water (750ml)
2 large finely chopped onions (300g)
3 finely cubed potatoes (300g)
2 stalks of thinly sliced celery (150g)
8 tsp low sodium chicken stock powder (18g)
8 cups water (2 litres)
1 tsp finely sliced lemon grass
1½ tsp ginger or 2cm piece of ginger
½ tsp cumin
2 tsp curry powder
1 tsp Cajun seasoning (may be omitted)
2 crushed cloves of garlic (6g)
Salt to taste
1 cup of frozen mixed or fresh vegetables (150g)

- Place Italian soup mix in a saucepan with 3 cups of boiling water, leave for one hour, drain and rinse.
- Add onions, potato, celery, stock powder and 8 cups of water.
- Season with lemon grass, ginger, cumin, curry powder, Cajun seasoning and garlic.
- Cook slowly for about 3 to 4 hours until soft or for 35 to 40 minutes in a pressure cooker.
- Remove lid, check seasoning, add salt to taste and fresh or frozen vegetables, reheat and serve as a main meal soup.

**Serves 10**

NUTRIENTS PER SERVE

| KJ | Cal | Pro (g) | CHO (g) | Fibre (g) | T.fat (g) | S.fat (g) | Chol (mg) | Na (mg) |
|---|---|---|---|---|---|---|---|---|
| 662 | 160 | 11 | 21 | 9 | 2.5 | 0.5 | 0.6 | 115 |

## LAKSA

*4 small skinned, boned chicken breasts (400g)*
*Mixed noodles e.g. thin and thick vermicelli and egg noodles (200g)*
*2 medium julienne carrots (200g)*
*1 medium finely sliced onion (100g)*
*1 tsp mono/polyunsaturated oil (5ml)*
*1 tabsp water (20ml)*
*1/2 tsp chilli powder or fresh chilli to taste*
*2 tsp low sodium stock powder (5g)*
*1 tabsp curry powder (10g)*
*3 cups water (750ml)*
*1 can low fat evaporated milk (375ml)*
*2 heads finely sliced bok choy (400g)*
*Coconut essence to taste*
*Finely chopped coriander (optional)*
*Fresh chopped chilli to taste*
*2 tabsp chopped roasted peanuts (25g)*

- Grill chicken, cool and cut into thin strips.
- Pour boiling water over a mixture of noodles in a bowl and leave for 5 minutes.
- Drain and put aside to keep warm.
- Stir-fry carrot and onion in oil and 1 tabsp water in a saucepan for 5 minutes.
- Season with chilli, stock powder and curry powder.
- Add 3 cups of water and simmer for 3 to 4 minutes.
- Add evaporated milk and bok choy and cook for 2 minutes more.
- Season to taste with coconut essence.
- Place hot noodles in one large bowl or individual bowls.
- Ladle milk stock and vegetables over noodles.
- Garnish with sliced chicken, coriander, chilli and peanuts.
- Serve as a main meal.

**Serves 6**

### Variation

**Seafood Laksa** Substitute prawns and squid for chicken.
**Vegetarian Laksa** Substitute tofu and additional vegetables for chicken.

NUTRIENTS PER SERVE

| KJ | Cal | Pro (g) | CHO (g) | Fibre (g) | T.fat (g) | S.fat (g) | Chol (mg) | Na (mg) |
|---|---|---|---|---|---|---|---|---|
| 919 | 221 | 11 | 34 | 4 | 4.5 | 1.13 | 3 | 126 |

## RED LENTIL SOUP

*1 cup red lentils (220g)*
*2 cups water (500ml)*
*1 tsp mono/polyunsaturated oil (5ml)*
*2 tabsp water (40ml)*
*1 large finely chopped onion (150g)*
*2 crushed cloves garlic (6g)*
*2 finely chopped carrots (200g)*
*2 medium finely sliced stalks of celery (150g)*
*3 cups water (750 ml)*
*3 tsp low sodium stock powder (7.5g)*
*Freshly ground black pepper*
*Salt to taste*
*2 tabsp finely chopped fresh coriander or parsley*

- Bring lentils to the boil with 2 cups of water in a large saucepan.
- Simmer for 2 minutes, cover and leave for 1 hour and drain.
- Place oil, 2 tabsp of water, onion and garlic in a non-stick or heavy based frying pan.
- Stir-fry onion and garlic until soft and beginning to yellow.
- Add lentils with carrot, celery, 3 cups of water, stock powder and black pepper.
- Simmer for 1 hour.
- Purée in a blender or mash in saucepan.
- Just before serving check seasoning, add salt to taste and coriander or parsley.

**Serves 4**

### Note

A flavoursome low fat, high protein soup with lentils for a weekend meal. Combine with crusty bread or with **Damper with Beer** p130 for a complete meal. Freezes well. Substitute any low fat, low sodium stock for water and stock powder if available.

NUTRIENTS PER SERVE

| KJ | Cal | Pro (g) | CHO (g) | Fibre (g) | T.fat (g) | S.fat (g) | Chol (mg) | Na (mg) |
|---|---|---|---|---|---|---|---|---|
| 839 | 201 | 15 | 26 | 10.5 | 3 | 0.6 | 0.5 | 147 |

**MAIN MEALS: MEAT ALTERNATIVES**

# Main Meals

*Pasta Verde Primavera p58*

The main section includes a variety of recipes to cover every taste and requirement. It includes an excellent selection of vegetarian type recipes along with a comprehensive range of meat, fish and chicken dishes — light ones for lunch, or more substantial ones for dinner. Refer to the **Menus** p21 for ideas on how to use them, and to the **Luncheon** section p34.

This initial section of **Main Meals** begins with some 30 recipes based on meat alternatives — largely vegetarian and utilising beans, eggs and cheese, pasta and grains and various vegetables. After perusing the various recipes readers will come to realise the importance of choosing dishes that give adequate protein as supplied by the foodstuffs that recur in the next few pages.

## Main Meal Dishes Based on Meat Alternatives

*Bean Dishes 48 - 50*
*Soya Bean Dishes 50 - 51*
*Egg and Cheese Dishes 52 - 55*
*Pasta and Grain Dishes 55 - 59*
*Main Vegetable Dishes 60 - 61*

### Bean Dishes
Bean dishes are low in fat with high levels of protein. When combined with other vegetables and grains they make a complete meal. Make extra and freeze some for later. They are important in a vegetarian diet. Try **Red Lentil Bean Capsicum Stew** p50 which is a complete meal and can be made ahead.

### Soya Bean Dishes
Soya beans are rich in natural oestrogens called phytoestrogens which helps to protect against heart disease and cancer. Tofu is a particularly rich source of calcium. Soya beans are used to make soy milk. Make sure to choose soy milk that is calcium enriched.
**Asparagus and Tofu Stir Fry** p51 is quick and easy for one of those busy evenings.

### Eggs and Cheese Dishes
Egg and cheese dishes give variety in the diet and are economical.

If cholesterol is of concern, then low cholesterol egg mix may be used instead of fresh eggs. One egg yolk has 220 mg of cholesterol and the low cholesterol egg mix has no significant amount. It works well in mixed dishes such as **Cheesy Pumpkin Ricotta Bake** p54. Substituting 2 egg whites for 1 whole egg will also reduce fat and cholesterol.

Make use of low fat cheeses and milk in cooking for quality dishes that are low in fat and help prevent heart disease. Dairy products are important to prevent osteoporosis. Two to three serves per day should be included. **Zucchini Slice** p55 is excellent hot or cold and it freezes well.

MAIN MEALS: MEAT ALTERNATIVES

*Pasta, Rice and Polenta*
Pasta and grains give variety for lunch and dinner meals. They may be vegetarian meals as in **Gnocchi** p58 or **Macaroni Cheese** p56, or mixed dishes such as in **Paella** p57. They can be based on pasta, rice, cous cous or polenta. Often recipes are interchangeable and come from many ethnic groups.

*Main Vegetable Dishes*
Vegetables can either be combined with meat or with meat alternatives. When they combine with beans or cheese they are more nutritionally balanced. **Mediterranean Pie** p61 is a complete meal and ideal for a special occasion.

*Kidney Bean Rice Medley*

## BEAN DISHES

### KIDNEY BEAN RICE MEDLEY

½ cup of raw brown rice (100g)
Salt to taste
1 medium finely chopped onion (100g)
2 cm piece crushed ginger
1 tabsp mono/polyunsaturated oil (20ml)
½ small thinly sliced red capsicum (50g)
½ small thinly sliced green capsicum (50g)
1 medium coarsely chopped carrot (100g)
2 sticks finely sliced celery (150g)
440g can drained unsweetened pineapple (250g)
1 cup sultanas (170g)
¼ cup unsweetened pineapple juice drained from canned pineapple (65ml)
½ cup drained and washed canned kidney beans 100g)

❑ Cook rice in boiling salted water for about 35 minutes or until tender, drain and cool.
❑ Stir-fry onion and ginger in oil for 2 - 3 minutes in a heavy based fry pan.
❑ Add red and green capsicum, carrot, celery, pineapple, sultanas and pineapple juice.
❑ Stir-fry for 5 minutes or until heated through.
❑ Add kidney beans and rice and reheat.
**Serves 6 (Total 6 cups)**

*Note*
Salt can be added according to individual tastes. None is calculated in the recipe.

NUTRIENTS PER SERVE

| KJ | Cal | Pro (g) | CHO (g) | Fibre (g) | T.fat (g) | S.fat (g) | Chol (mg) | Na (mg) |
|---|---|---|---|---|---|---|---|---|
| 962 | 229 | 4 | 45 | 5 | 4 | 0.48 | 0 | 158 |

### CHILLI BEANS

6 chopped spring onions (70g)
1 medium finely chopped capsicum (150g)
8 small chopped mushrooms (50g)
2 tsp mono/polyunsaturated oil (10ml)
Commercial salsa (mild, medium or hot) (240 ml)
440g can drained kidney beans (300g)
Chopped coriander

❑ Sauté spring onions, capsicum and mushrooms in oil until tender.
❑ Stir in salsa and beans and cook until heated through.
❑ Garnish with chopped coriander.
❑ Serve with **Crispy Lavash Bread** p125 and a tossed salad.
**Serves 3**

*Note*
This is a quick and easy low fat recipe which is ideal for a light weekend meal.

NUTRIENTS PER SERVE

| KJ | Cal | Pro (g) | CHO (g) | Fibre (g) | T.fat (g) | S.fat (g) | Chol (mg) | Na (mg) |
|---|---|---|---|---|---|---|---|---|
| 652 | 156 | 9.2 | 20 | 9 | 4 | 1 | 0 | 536 |

MAIN MEALS: MEAT ALTERNATIVES

## LENTIL BEAN GOULASH

*1/3 cup dried yellow split peas (75g)*
*1/3 cup red lentils (75g)*
*1/3 cup green lentils (75g)*
*4 cups boiling water (1000ml)*
*2 medium finely chopped onions (200g)*
*2 crushed cloves garlic (6g)*
*2 tsp mono/polyunsaturated oil (10ml)*
*2 tabsp water (40ml)*
*1 tabsp fresh or 1 tsp dried oregano*
*1 tabsp fresh or 1 tsp dried thyme*
*1 tsp caraway seeds*
*1 cup canned, drained and washed kidney beans (200g)*
*1 can chopped tomatoes (400g)*
*1/2 cup water (125ml)*

- Place split peas and red and green lentils in a saucepan with 4 cups of boiling water, return to the boil and cook for 2 minutes.
- Cover and leave for 1 hour then drain and put aside until required.
- Place onion, garlic, oil and 2 tabsp water in a heavy based saucepan with oregano, thyme and caraway seeds.
- Stir-fry for 5 minutes.
- Add prepared peas, lentils plus kidney beans, tomatoes and 1/2 cup water.
- Bring to the boil and simmer over a low heat for 1 hour, stirring occasionally.

**Serves 5 (Total 5 cups)**

*Note*
Use in **Lentil Bean Pie** p49. You may vary the beans and lentils as desired but keep to the same total weight.
This recipe can be made in bulk and frozen in small quantities for individual meals which is ideal if you only have one vegetarian in the family or you are cooking for one.
Sodium can be reduced to 60g by using beans with no added salt.

*Handy Hint*
Use kitchen scissors to chop tomatoes in the can.

NUTRIENTS PER SERVE

| KJ | Cal | Pro (g) | CHO (g) | Fibre (g) | T.fat (g) | S.fat (g) | Chol (mg) | Na (mg) |
|---|---|---|---|---|---|---|---|---|
| 838 | 201 | 15 | 27 | 10 | 3.3 | 0.4 | 0 | 185 |

*Lentil Bean Pie*

## LENTIL BEAN PIE

*5 cups **Lentil Bean Goulash** p49*
*1 cup **Low Fat Fibre Pastry** p131*
*6 medium peeled potatoes (600g)*
*1/4 cup non fat milk (65ml)*
*2 tsp mono/polyunsaturated margarine (10g)*
*1/2 cup finely grated less than 10% fat cheese (60g)*

- Have goulash mixture on hand and prepare the pastry.
- Roll out pastry to fit the bottom of a large pie plate.
- Finish edges and prick well. Bake in a 200°C oven for 10 minutes or until puffed and lightly browned.
- Cube potatoes and boil or microwave until tender.
- Remove, drain and mash with milk, margarine and finely grated cheese.
- Place cooled goulash mixture in cooked pie shell and top with mashed potato.
- Bake in a 180°C oven for a further 30 minutes or until potato is browned and is heated through.

**Serves 8**

NUTRIENTS PER SERVE

| KJ | Cal | Pro (g) | CHO (g) | Fibre (g) | T.fat (g) | S.fat (g) | Chol (mg) | Na (mg) |
|---|---|---|---|---|---|---|---|---|
| 1318 | 318 | 16 | 35 | 9 | 12 | 2 | 5 | 170 |

## RED LENTIL BEAN CAPSICUM STEW

*½ cup red lentils (110g)*
*2 large chopped onions (300g)*
*2 tsp mono/polyunsaturated margarine (10g)*
*3 medium thinly sliced red capsicums (300g)*
*1 cup canned drained and washed red kidney beans (200g)*
*1 can chopped tomatoes (400g)*
*2 to 3 cups water (500 - 750ml)*

- Soak lentils in boiling water for 1 hour. Drain.
- Microwave onions and margarine for 3 minutes on **High** or stir-fry in a non-stick pan.
- Add red capsicum and microwave or cook a further 2 - 3 minutes.
- Add lentils, red kidney beans, canned tomatoes and 2 cups water if cooking in the microwave.
- Cook on **High** for 10 minutes then **Medium Low** for 40 minutes in the microwave or simmer on stove.
- More liquid may be needed for cooking on the stove.
- Serve as a main dish with extra vegetables.

**Serves 4**

*Note*
By using fresh kidney beans, sodium will be lower. Soak 100g of dried beans overnight, drain and cook for about 1 hour or until soft. This will be equivalent to 200g of canned beans. Prepare extra and have on hand in the freezer. To reduce the effects of wind add 1 tsp of mustard seed while cooking.

NUTRIENTS PER SERVE

| KJ | Cal | Pro (g) | CHO (g) | Fibre (g) | T.fat (g) | S.fat (g) | Chol (mg) | Na (mg) |
|---|---|---|---|---|---|---|---|---|
| 789 | 189 | 13 | 26 | 10 | 3 | 0.5 | 0 | 232 |

# SOYA BEAN DISHES

## ASPARAGUS AND TOFU STIR FRY

*1 tsp mono/polyunsaturated oil (5ml)*
*4 x 5cm squares fresh tofu (360g)*
*Fresh asparagus spears (500g)*
*½ cup finely chopped spring onions (50g)*
*⅓ cup pinenuts (60g)*
*2 tabsp Lite soy sauce (40ml)*
*⅓ cup water (85ml)*
*2 tabsp sherry (40ml)*
*2 tsp cornflour (5g)*
*1 tsp dry ginger (3g)*
*Freshly ground black pepper*

- Heat the oil in a non-stick frying pan.
- Add the tofu which has been blotted dry with kitchen paper and cut into cubes.
- Stir-fry for 5 minutes or until lightly brown.
- Cut asparagus spears diagonally into 1cm pieces.
- Add asparagus, spring onions and pinenuts to the tofu and continue to stir-fry.
- Mix together soy sauce, water, sherry, cornflour, dry ginger and black pepper to form a smooth paste.
- Add to tofu mixture and stir-fry for 1 to 2 minutes or until cornflour is thick and clear.
- Serve immediately.

**Serves 4**

*Note*
Lite rather than regular soy sauce reduces the sodium by 50%.

NUTRIENTS PER SERVE

| KJ | Cal | Pro (g) | CHO (g) | Fibre (g) | T.fat (g) | S.fat (g) | Chol (mg) | Na (mg) |
|---|---|---|---|---|---|---|---|---|
| 933 | 225 | 18 | 7 | 3 | 16 | 1 | 0 | 375 |

## MARINADE BAKED TOFU

*Tofu (150g)*
*2 tabsp Lite soy sauce (40ml)*
*½ cup apple juice (125ml)*
*1cm piece crushed ginger*
*1 crushed clove garlic (3g)*
*¼ tsp sesame oil (2.5ml)*
*1 tabsp balsamic vinegar (20ml)*

- Cut 2 pieces of tofu horizontally to make 4 flat pieces.

## MAIN MEALS: MEAT ALTERNATIVES

- Place in marinade of soy sauce, apple juice, ginger, garlic, oil and vinegar and leave for 1 to 2 days, turning occasionally.
- Drain and place on greased oven sheet.
- Bake at 200°C for 20 to 30 minutes or until it is puffed and golden brown. The time will vary according to the thickness and size of the tofu.

**Serves 4**

*Note*

Firm tofu as purchased in Asian and health food shops is preferred. Silken tofu will break apart when marinated. Use firm tofu in stir fries and soups or as indicated in individual recipes. Silken tofu is ideal in baking cakes or as a substitute for cream cheese. Tofu vary in size.

NUTRIENTS PER SERVE

| KJ | Cal | Pro (g) | CHO (g) | Fibre (g) | T.fat (g) | S.fat (g) | Chol (mg) | Na (mg) |
|---|---|---|---|---|---|---|---|---|
| 209 | 50 | 6 | 4 | 0.1 | 2 | 0.2 | 0 | 366 |

## SOYA BEAN PATTIES

½ cup dried (100g) or 1 cup of cooked soya beans (200g)
1 medium finely chopped carrot (100g)
1 medium finely chopped onion (100g)
2 chopped sticks celery (150g)
2 crushed cloves garlic (6g)
½ cup plain wholemeal flour (70g)
1½ tsp curry powder
¼ cup dried bread crumbs (30g)
2 extra tabsp of dried bread crumbs (20g)
2 tabsp mono/polyunsaturated oil (40ml)

- Prepare cooked soya beans by bringing to the boil, letting stand for 1 hour, drain and then recook until soft. Otherwise use canned, drained, washed soya beans.
- Mash or blend soya beans with carrot, onion, celery and garlic.
- Mix in flour, curry powder and bread crumbs.
- Form into 12 patties and dip in bread crumbs.
- Shallow fry in minimum of oil for about 5 minutes on each side.
- Serve hot or cold.

**Serves 12 patties**

NUTRIENTS PER SERVE

| KJ | Cal | Pro (g) | CHO (g) | Fibre (g) | T.fat (g) | S.fat (g) | Chol (mg) | Na (mg) |
|---|---|---|---|---|---|---|---|---|
| 265 | 64 | 1.7 | 6 | 1.8 | 3.6 | 0.4 | 0 | 88 |

*Soya Bean Patties*

## TOFU VEGETABLE STIR FRY

1 firm cubed piece of tofu (300g)
1 medium finely chopped onion (100g)
1 crushed clove garlic (3g)
2cm finely chopped ginger (5g)
1 tsp mono/polyunsaturated oil (5ml)
1 tabsp water (20ml)
2 medium julienne carrots (200g)
½ bunch of bite size broccoli florets (150g)
20 medium finely sliced mushrooms (150g)
1 tsp honey (5ml)
2 tabsp low sodium soy sauce (40ml)
¼ cup water (125ml)
2 tsp cornflour (5g)

- Spray a non-stick pan lightly with mono-unsaturated oil. Cut tofu into 1cm pieces.
- Stir-fry until brown.
- Place in serving dish to keep warm.
- Stir-fry onion, garlic and ginger in oil and water until soft.
- Add carrot, broccoli and mushrooms and stir-fry until beginning to soften.
- Add to tofu.
- Mix honey, soy sauce, water and cornflour in a pan, stir to form a smooth paste and cook for 2 to 3 minutes.
- Add to vegetables and tofu.
- Reheat and serve.

**Serves 4**

NUTRIENTS PER SERVE

| KJ | Cal | Pro (g) | CHO (g) | Fibre (g) | T.fat (g) | S.fat (g) | Chol (mg) | Na (mg) |
|---|---|---|---|---|---|---|---|---|
| 472 | 113 | 15 | 8 | 4.5 | 4.5 | 0.5 | 0 | 404 |

# EGG AND CHEESE DISHES

## BAKED FRITATTA

*1 cup cooked, peeled, sliced potato or sweet potato (200g)*
*1 cup peeled, sliced pumpkin (200g)*
*1 medium finely sliced white or red onion (100g)*
*1 cup blanched bite size pieces broccoli (200g)*
*1 bunch spinach (125g)*
*2 tabsp finely chopped chives (8g)*
*1 tabsp finely chopped parsley (10g)*
*6 eggs or low cholesterol egg mix (300g)*
*1 cup non fat milk (250ml)*
*2 crushed cloves garlic (6g)*
*Freshly ground black pepper*
*2 tabsp parmesan cheese (18g)*

- ❏ Cook potato, pumpkin and onion until just tender.
- ❏ Steam or microwave broccoli for 3 minutes.
- ❏ Wash spinach, finely slice and steam for 3 to 4 minutes to soften.
- ❏ Grease a large (25cm square) baking dish.
- ❏ Layer vegetables in the dish, sprinkling with chives and parsley as you go.
- ❏ Finish by spreading spinach over the top.
- ❏ Press down firmly to remove large spaces.
- ❏ Heat vegetables in 180°C oven for 10 minutes.
- ❏ Beat eggs and milk with crushed garlic and pepper until frothy.
- ❏ Pour over vegetable mixture in dish.
- ❏ Sprinkle parmesan cheese on top.
- ❏ Bake in a 180°C oven for 40 to 50 minutes or until egg is set.
- ❏ Serve as a main meal with salad.
- ❏ Ideal in lunches, hot or cold.

**Serves 6**

*Variation*
Make use of leftover or seasonal vegetables. Cabbage, mushrooms, carrots, grilled eggplant, zucchini, tomato or any vegetables to hand may be substituted and layered in this dish. Pasta or rice could replace some or all of potato or sweet potato.

NUTRIENTS PER SERVE

| KJ | Cal | Pro (g) | CHO (g) | Fibre (g) | T.fat (g) | S.fat (g) | Chol (mg) | Na (mg) |
|---|---|---|---|---|---|---|---|---|
| 1032 | 249 | 15 | 27 | 6.5 | 8.5 | 3.4 | 192 | 448 |

## BROCCOLI SOUFFLÉ

*1 small bunch trimmed broccoli florets (300g)*
*2 tabsp mono/polyunsaturated margarine (40g)*
*3 tabsp plain flour (30g)*
*½ tsp dry mustard*
*1 tsp fresh or ¼ tsp dried oregano*
*Freshly ground black pepper*
*1 cup non fat milk (250g)*
*4 eggs or low cholesterol egg mix (200g)*

- ❏ Cook broccoli florets until just tender.
- ❏ Melt margarine in a saucepan over low heat or in the microwave for 30 seconds.
- ❏ Stir in flour to form a smooth paste.
- ❏ Season with mustard, oregano and black pepper.
- ❏ Slowly add milk while stirring.
- ❏ Cook and stir over low heat or microwave until sauce is thick and smooth.
- ❏ Remove from heat and put aside.
- ❏ Separate eggs. Beat egg whites until stiff but not dry.
- ❏ Place broccoli in a blender or food processor, blend until smooth.
- ❏ Add egg yolks and white sauce and blend thoroughly.
- ❏ Fold egg whites into broccoli mixture.
- ❏ Place in a greased 1½ litre soufflé dish. Place dish in a shallow pan of water and bake in a 180°C oven for 1 hour.

## MAIN MEALS: MEAT ALTERNATIVES

**Broccoli Soufflé**

❏ Serve with salad and wholemeal bread.
**Serves 4**

*Variation*
Substitute salmon, tuna or chopped asparagus for broccoli in soufflé.

*Note*
Use 1 sachet low cholesterol egg mix plus 4 egg whites and reduce cholesterol by 180mg. Grated cheese may be added.

NUTRIENTS PER SERVE

| KJ | Cal | Pro (g) | CHO (g) | Fibre (g) | T.fat (g) | S.fat (g) | Chol (mg) | Na (mg) |
|---|---|---|---|---|---|---|---|---|
| 731 | 176 | 13 | 9 | 3 | 10 | 2 | 189 | 110 |

## SPINACH PINENUT ROULADE

*2 tabsp mono/polyunsaturated margarine (40g)*
*4 tabsp flour (40g)*
*2 tabsp fresh basil or 2 tsp dried*
*¼ tsp dry mustard*
*¼ tsp saffron or ½ tsp turmeric*
*1 cup non fat milk (250ml)*
*4 eggs separated (200g)*

**Roulade**
❏ Melt margarine on stove top or in microwave.
❏ Stir in flour, basil, mustard, saffron or turmeric to form a smooth paste.
❏ Slowly add milk whilst stirring.
❏ Cook and stir over low heat until smooth.
❏ Remove from heat and beat in egg yolks one at a time.
❏ Beat egg whites until stiff but not dry.
❏ Fold egg whites into sauce mixture.
❏ Grease or line a Swiss roll sized tray (23cm x 34cm) with baking paper.
❏ Spread mixture evenly.
❏ Bake at 200°C for 12 minutes or until lightly browned. Do not overcook.
❏ Turn out onto a rack which is covered with a clean tea towel.
❏ Spread with filling, roll up and keep warm to serve.

**Filling**
*1 bunch fresh washed spinach*
*1 tsp olive oil (5g)*
*2 tabsp pinenuts (30g)*
*½ cup finely grated less than 10% fat cheese (60g)*

❏ Wash and remove stems from spinach.
❏ Stir-fry in a non stick pan with oil until soft.
❏ Drain and spread spinach mixture on top of the cooked roulade.
❏ Top with grated cheese.
❏ Roll up and serve plain or with **Cheese Sauce** p108.

**Serves 4**

*Variation*
**Creamy Corn Roulade** Substitute creamed corn for spinach pinenut filling. Topped with **Cheese Sauce**.

*Note*
You may use 100g of low cholesterol egg mix for yolk plus 4 egg whites.
Low fat cheese is recommended but higher fat cheeses may be used if desired. Nutritional analysis is based on less than 10% fat cheese.

*Handy Hint*
White sauce may be easily prepared in the microwave in a glass measuring jug. There are less lumps and there is no chance of burning.

NUTRIENTS PER SERVE

| KJ | Cal | Pro (g) | CHO (g) | Fibre (g) | T.fat (g) | S.fat (g) | Chol (mg) | Na (mg) |
|---|---|---|---|---|---|---|---|---|
| 1242 | 300 | 18 | 10 | 3 | 20 | 3.5 | 194 | 275 |

MAIN MEALS: MEAT ALTERNATIVES

*Salmon Bagels*

## CHEESY PUMPKIN RICOTTA BAKE

*Butternut pumpkin peeled and chopped (400g)*
*4 spring onions chopped (50g)*
*2 eggs or low cholesterol egg mix (100g)*
*1 cup non fat milk (250ml)*
*1 cup ricotta or cottage cheese (250g)*
*2 tabsp grated parmesan cheese (18g)*
*¼ cup dried breadcrumbs (30g)*
*Paprika for sprinkling*

- Steam or microwave pumpkin until tender.
- Place in ovenproof dish with onion.
- Whisk together eggs, milk and ricotta cheese and pour over pumpkin.
- Sprinkle with parmesan, breadcrumbs and paprika.
- Bake at 200°C for 30 minutes until golden brown and set.
- Serve cut into wedges.

**Serves 4**

NUTRIENTS PER SERVE

| KJ | Cal | Pro (g) | CHO (g) | Fibre (g) | T.fat (g) | S.fat (g) | Chol (mg) | Na (mg) |
|---|---|---|---|---|---|---|---|---|
| 958 | 231 | 17 | 17 | 2 | 10 | 6 | 126 | 299 |

## QUICHE

*4 eggs or low cholesterol egg mix (200g)*
*1½ cups non fat milk (375ml)*
*Pepper to taste*
*1 cup grated less than 10% fat cheese (120g)*
*1 finely chopped onion (100g)*
*3 slices diced lean ham or turkey ham (60g)*
*½ cup self raising wholemeal flour (70g)*

- Beat eggs, milk and pepper together.
- In a separate bowl mix together cheese, onion, ham and flour.
- Add egg and milk mixture to flour mixture, folding until well blended.
- Pour into a lightly greased pie dish and bake in a 200°C oven for 40 minutes or microwave on **Medium** for 12 minutes.

**Serves 4**

*Note*
Cholesterol will be reduced to 27mg if low cholesterol egg mix is used.

NUTRIENTS PER SERVE

| KJ | Cal | Pro (g) | CHO (g) | Fibre (g) | T.fat (g) | S.fat (g) | Chol (mg) | Na (mg) |
|---|---|---|---|---|---|---|---|---|
| 973 | 234 | 25 | 15 | 2 | 8 | 2 | 209 | 614 |

MAIN MEALS: MEAT ALTERNATIVES

## HAM AND BOCCONCINI CHEESE BAGEL

*4 x 80g bagels (320g)*
*1/3 cup cottage cheese (100g)*
*Shaved ham (150g)*
*Lettuce leaves (150g)*
*Bocconcini cheese (120g)*
*Capers (25g)*

❑ Slice the bagels, cover liberally with cottage cheese then with shaved ham, lettuce and sliced bocconcini cheese.
❑ Sprinkle with capers.
**Serves 4**

*Variation*
**Salmon Bagels** Substitute ricotta cheese, smoked salmon, rocket lettuce and dill pickle for the listed ingredients. Carbohydrate will be the same but kilojoules will be a little less.

*Note*
Bocconcini cheese is a fresh mozzarella. It is sold as round balls floating in natural whey. The fat content is about 20%. Use in sandwiches, pizzas and bagels.

NUTRIENTS PER SERVE

| KJ | Cal | Pro (g) | CHO (g) | Fibre (g) | T.fat (g) | S.fat (g) | Chol (mg) | Na (mg) |
|---|---|---|---|---|---|---|---|---|
| 1482 | 357 | 28 | 39 | 3 | 9 | 4.5 | 45 | 1216 |

## ZUCCHINI SLICE

*2 medium zucchini (350g)*
*1 medium chopped onion (100g)*
*5 eggs or low cholesterol egg mix (250g)*
*3 slices finely chopped lean ham or middle eye rasher bacon (100g)*
*1 cup grated less than 10% fat cheese (120g)*
*1/4 cup of mono/polyunsaturated oil (60ml)*
*1 1/4 cups of self raising wholemeal flour (175g)*

❑ Finely chop the zucchini.
❑ Sieve and dry with kitchen paper to remove as much moisture as possible.
❑ Mix together zucchini and onion.
❑ Beat eggs.
❑ Add ham, cheese, oil and prepared onion and zucchini to eggs.
❑ Fold in self raising flour.
❑ Place zucchini mixture in a 30cm x 20cm tin which has been sprayed with oil.
❑ Bake in 180°C oven for 40 minutes.
**Serves 6**

*Note*
This may be made vegetarian by substituting 150g cooked pumpkin for lean ham.

NUTRIENTS PER SERVE

| KJ | Cal | Pro (g) | CHO (g) | Fibre (g) | T.fat (g) | S.fat (g) | Chol (mg) | Na (mg) |
|---|---|---|---|---|---|---|---|---|
| 1247 | 301 | 19 | 17 | 4 | 17 | 3 | 172 | 614 |

# PASTA AND GRAIN DISHES

## VEGETABLE PASTA

*2 cups dry macaroni or vegeroni (250g)*
*1 large can peeled tomatoes (800g)*
*1 medium finely chopped onion (100g)*
*2 crushed cloves garlic (6g)*
*2 tsp dry mustard*
*1 tabsp Worcestershire sauce (20ml)*
*1/2 tsp paprika*
*Chilli powder to taste*
*1/2 tsp oregano*
*8 medium sliced mushrooms (125g)*
*2 finely sliced zucchini (500g)*
*440g can Four Bean mix drained (300g)*
*2 tabsp lemon juice or vinegar*
*1 tabsp sugar (18g) or equivalent substitute*
*1 cup grated less than 10% fat cheese (120g)*
*Parsley chopped*

❑ Cook macaroni until tender and drain.
❑ Roughly chop the canned tomatoes with liquid and place into a saucepan.
❑ Add sliced onion, garlic, mustard, Worcestershire sauce, paprika, chilli powder and oregano and stir well.
❑ Bring to the boil and simmer gently for 5 - 10 minutes.
❑ Add mushrooms, sliced zucchini and bean mix and cook for a further 5 minutes.
❑ Add lemon juice or vinegar with sugar.
❑ Fold in the cooked macaroni.
❑ Place in large casserole dish and sprinkle with cheese.
❑ Bake in 180°C oven for 20 minutes.
❑ Sprinkle with parsley and serve with green salad and crusty bread.
**Serves 6**

NUTRIENTS PER SERVE

| KJ | Cal | Pro (g) | CHO (g) | Fibre (g) | T.fat (g) | S.fat (g) | Chol (mg) | Na (mg) |
|---|---|---|---|---|---|---|---|---|
| 1209 | 290 | 18 | 47 | 9 | 3 | 0.45 | 8 | 389 |

MAIN MEALS: MEAT ALTERNATIVES

## CHICK PEAS WITH TOMATO AND MACARONI

*1 cup dry macaroni (125g)*
*1 tsp mono/polyunsaturated oil (5ml)*
*1 tabsp water (20ml)*
*1 crushed clove garlic (3g)*
*1 medium finely chopped onion (100g)*
*2 medium peeled and chopped tomatoes (200g)*
*1 tabsp tomato paste (25g)*
*½ tsp dried oregano*
*2 tsp fresh chopped basil or ½ tsp dried*
*2 tsp sugar (optional)*
*1 cup cooked or canned chick peas (185g)*
*Additional water as required*

- Cook macaroni until al dente.
- Heat oil and water in a saucepan and stir-fry garlic and onion for 3 to 5 minutes or until golden.
- Add tomato, tomato paste, oregano and basil.
- Simmer for 10 minutes.
- Add cooked drained chick peas and cooked drained macaroni.
- Stir until well combined.
- Simmer for 5 minutes. (Add a little water if required.)
- Serve with crusty bread and green salad.

**Serves 4**

*Variation*
Substitute an equal quantity of canned tomatoes for fresh.

*Nutritional Tip*
If your energy requirements are high a larger serve would be acceptable as it is a low glycaemic index recipe.

NUTRIENTS PER SERVE

| KJ | Cal | Pro (g) | CHO (g) | Fibre (g) | T.fat (g) | S.fat (g) | Chol (mg) | Na (mg) |
|---|---|---|---|---|---|---|---|---|
| 840 | 202 | 8 | 35 | 5 | 3 | 0.4 | 0 | 155 |

## MACARONI CHEESE

*1 cup dry macaroni (125g)*
*2 tabsp mono/polyunsaturated margarine (40g)*
*3 tabsp plain flour (30g)*
*2 cups non fat milk (500ml)*
*¼ tsp dry mustard*
*⅛ tsp paprika*
*Freshly ground black pepper*
*1½ cups grated less than 10% fat cheese (180g)*
*¼ cup dried breadcrumbs (25g)*

- Cook dry macaroni in boiling water until al dente, drain and set aside.
- Melt margarine in a saucepan, add flour and stir until smooth. Slowly add milk while stirring to form a smooth thick sauce.
- Add mustard, paprika, pepper and grated cheese.
- Stir and cook over a low heat until cheese is melted. Blend in cooked macaroni and pour into a well-greased casserole dish.
- Sprinkle with breadcrumbs and bake in a 180°C oven 15 - 20 minutes.
- Serve as a luncheon or vegetarian meal.

**Serves 6 x ⅔ cup**

NUTRIENTS PER SERVE

| KJ | Cal | Pro (g) | CHO (g) | Fibre (g) | T.fat (g) | S.fat (g) | Chol (mg) | Na (mg) |
|---|---|---|---|---|---|---|---|---|
| 992 | 239 | 16 | 25 | 1.4 | 8.2 | 1.5 | 15 | 224 |

## PASTA WITH LOW FAT PESTO SAUCE

*1 bunch fresh basil, stalks removed (50g)*
*6 crushed cloves garlic (18g)*
*2 tabsp finely chopped pinenuts (28g)*
*1¼ cups fresh ricotta cheese (300g)*
*Freshly ground black pepper*
*1 tabsp lemon juice (20g)*
*2 tabsp parmesan cheese (18g)*
*Dry pasta (300g)*
*Salt to taste*
*1 tabsp parmesan cheese (extra) (9g)*

- Mash basil, garlic, pinenuts, ricotta, black pepper, lemon juice and parmesan in a mortar and pestle or blend together to make sauce.
- Cook pasta in a large saucepan of boiling water until just cooked.
- Mix sauce through freshly cooked pasta and adjust seasoning for salt.
- Sprinkle top with extra tablespoon of parmesan cheese.

**Serves 6**

NUTRIENTS PER SERVE

| KJ | Cal | Pro (g) | CHO (g) | Fibre (g) | T.fat (g) | S.fat (g) | Chol (mg) | Na (mg) |
|---|---|---|---|---|---|---|---|---|
| 1217 | 294 | 13 | 37 | 3 | 10 | 4 | 25 | 161 |

*Paella*

## PAELLA

1 tabsp olive oil (20ml)
2 coarsely chopped chicken breasts (300g)
20 peeled raw prawns (200g)
2 finely sliced squid sleeves (100g)
1 large sliced onion (150g)
2 crushed cloves garlic (6g)
2 finely sliced stalks celery (150g)
1 medium finely chopped red capsicum (100g)
2 cups Arborio rice (400g)
2 tsp low sodium chicken stock powder (5g)
1/4 tsp saffron or 1 tsp turmeric
Black pepper
1 tsp thyme
1 tsp oregano
2 cups water (500ml)
5 Roman tomatoes quartered (400g)
1 cup cooked frozen peas (70g)
1/2 cup stuffed olives (30g)
18 cleaned fresh shelled mussels (300g)

- Heat olive oil in a large electric fry pan or heavy stove top saucepan.
- Stir-fry chicken, prawns and squid; remove.
- Add garlic, celery, capsicum to saucepan and stir-fry 2 - 3 minutes.
- Add rice, stock powder, saffron, black pepper, thyme, oregano and stir-fry for 5 minutes.
- Place in a stove top casserole or microwave dish and add water.
- Cover and simmer on stove, on low for 20 minutes or in a covered microwave dish on **High** for 10 minutes, stirring once until all rice is absorbed.
- Stir in chicken, seafood, tomato, peas, olives.
- Place mussels on top, cover and simmer for a further 20 minutes or microwave on **High** for 10 minutes.
- When the mussels have opened the dish should be ready for serving.
- Discard any unopened mussels.

**Serves 6**

*Note*
Arborio rice is fat-grained with a starch-rich surface. It can absorb large quantities of liquid and flavour without breaking up during cooking. Do not wash the rice.

*Variation*
Any combination of seafood, chicken or meat may be used in this recipe but try to use the same amount e.g. 600g of total protein. Vegetables may also be varied according to what is on hand.

NUTRIENTS PER SERVE

| KJ | Cal | Pro (g) | CHO (g) | Fibre (g) | T.fat (g) | S.fat (g) | Chol (mg) | Na (mg) |
|---|---|---|---|---|---|---|---|---|
| 1732 | 418 | 24 | 44 | 3.5 | 4.5 | 1 | 126 | 349 |

MAIN MEALS: MEAT ALTERNATIVES

## GNOCCHI

¾ cup ricotta cheese (200g)
2 tabsp finely chopped chives (20g)
1 egg (50g)
¼ cup parmesan cheese (27g)
Freshly ground black pepper
1 cup plain flour (130g)

**White Sauce**
1 cup non fat milk (250ml)
2 tsp cornflour (5g)
2 tabsp parmesan cheese (18g)
Freshly ground black pepper

- Drain ricotta in cheese cloth or a strainer until quite firm or buy moulded firm ricotta.
- Mix together ricotta, chives, beaten egg, parmesan cheese, pepper and flour to form a smooth soft dough.
- Work in extra flour with the hands until the dough is quite firm. Chill.
- Roll on floured board to form 4 long sausages.
- Cut each sausage into 1cm lengths and press in middle to give a bow look.
- Heat large saucepan of boiling water or stock.
- Place about 10 gnocchi in water at a time and simmer or lightly boil for 1 to 1½ minutes or until they come to the surface. Do not overcook as they will fall apart.
- Drain and place in a greased serving dish to keep warm.
- Prepare white sauce by mixing together milk, cornflour, parmesan cheese and pepper.
- Cook slowly on top of the stove or in the microwave until thickened and smooth.
- Serve gnocchi tossed in white sauce.

**Serves 4**

*Variation*
This low fat easy vegetarian meal may be varied by using a commercial pasta tomato sauce instead of White Sauce.

*Note*
This makes 4 small serves or 2 large serves for a main course. Analysis is done for 4 serves. Gnocchi is not difficult to make if the right consistency of dough is reached.

*Helpful Hint*
The sauce is easily prepared in a large glass jug in the microwave.

NUTRIENTS PER SERVE

| KJ | Cal | Pro (g) | CHO (g) | Fibre (g) | T.fat (g) | S.fat (g) | Chol (mg) | Na (mg) |
|---|---|---|---|---|---|---|---|---|
| 1207 | 291 | 17.5 | 29 | 1.3 | 11.5 | 7 | 85 | 325 |

## PASTA VERDE PRIMAVERA

6 medium prepared brussel sprouts (100g)
6 halved baby squashes (250g)
6 small sliced zucchini (150g)
½ bunch bite size broccoli florets (150g)
1 medium thinly sliced red capsicum (150g)
Dry spinach fettuccine (200g)
2 crushed cloves garlic (6g)
2 tsp fresh or ½ teaspoon dried sweet basil
2 tabsp finely chopped parsley
Freshly ground black pepper
1 tsp mono/polyunsaturated oil (5g)
1 tabsp water (20ml)
½ cup plain non fat yoghurt (100g)

- Place prepared brussel sprouts (refer **Brussel Sprouts** p85), halved baby squashes, prepared zucchini, bite size pieces of broccoli and capsicum in a steamer or microwave and cook until just tender crisp, then rinse in cold water.
- Cook fettuccine in a large saucepan of boiling water until al dente or soft but firm.
- Drain and rinse in cold water.
- Stir-fry garlic, sweet basil, parsley and black pepper with oil and water.
- Add steamed and microwaved vegetables to herbs and stir-fry for 1 to 2 minutes.
- Just before serving gently stir yoghurt into fettuccine and heat through.
- Add hot vegetables and serve.

**Serves 6**

NUTRIENTS PER SERVE

| KJ | Cal | Pro (g) | CHO (g) | Fibre (g) | T.fat (g) | S.fat (g) | Chol (mg) | Na (mg) |
|---|---|---|---|---|---|---|---|---|
| 697 | 168 | 9 | 29 | 5 | 1.5 | 0.2 | 0.8 | 36 |

## POLENTA PIE

4 cups cooked **Rich Coarse Polenta** p92
2 tsp mono/polyunsaturated margarine (10g)
1 tabsp plain flour (10g)
½ cup non fat milk (125ml)
1 tabsp parmesan cheese (9g)
Shaved ham (100g)
1 large red **Peeled Capsicum** p86 (300g)
Finely sliced artichokes (150g)
1 small bunch fresh washed spinach (100g)
2 tabsp parmesan cheese (18g)

- Prepare **Rich Coarse Polenta** as directed.
- Prepare white sauce by melting margarine, stirring in flour, slowly adding milk and cooking and stirring until thick and smooth.

## MAIN MEALS: MEAT ALTERNATIVES

**Polenta Pie**

- Flavour with parmesan cheese.
- Place ¹/₃ of **Polenta** in the bottom of a greased springform pan.
- Cover with ¹/₂ white sauce, shaved ham and **Peeled Capsicum**.
- Place ¹/₃ more of **Polenta** firmly on top.
- Cover with remaining white sauce.
- Top with artichokes and wilted spinach leaves previously steamed or microwaved in a bag for 1 minute and then drained.
- Cover with remaining **Polenta**.
- Sprinkle with additional parmesan cheese.
- Bake in 180°C oven for 30 minutes.
- Serve with variety of salad as main or course or as a luncheon dish.

**Serves 8 main course**

NUTRIENTS PER SERVE

| KJ | Cal | Pro (g) | CHO (g) | Fibre (g) | T.fat (g) | S.fat (g) | Chol (mg) | Na (mg) |
|---|---|---|---|---|---|---|---|---|
| 845 | 204 | 12 | 25 | 2 | 6 | 2.5 | 17 | 410 |

## VEGETABLE LASAGNE

**Sauce**
1 tabsp mono/polyunsaturated margarine (20g)
2 tabsp of plain flour (20g)
2 cups non fat milk (500ml)
¹/₂ cup grated less than 10% fat cheese (60g)

**Lasagne**
Fresh lasagne (250g)
¹/₂ medium steamed and mashed butternut pumpkin (200g)
1 medium steamed and mashed sweet potato (200g)
1 cup ricotta cheese (250g)
200g packet frozen drained spinach or 1 bunch of fresh cooked spinach (165g)
1 medium julienne capsicum (150g)
1 cup sliced mushrooms (70g)
1 medium thinly sliced Spanish onion (100g)
1 can of tomatoes (400g)
1 tabsp tomato paste (25g)
Nutmeg, pepper and herbs as desired
¹/₂ cup grated less than 10% fat cheese (60g)

- Prepare the sauce with margarine, flour, milk and cheese, stirring until thick and smooth.
- Pour ¹/₃ of sauce in the bottom of a lasagne dish and cover with fresh lasagne pasta.
- Spread the mashed butternut pumpkin and sweet potato over the pasta.
- Sprinkle with ¹/₂ of the ricotta and then with spinach.
- Cover with another layer of lasagne and another ¹/₃ of sauce.
- Finish with the rest of the ricotta and sprinkle with capsicum, mushrooms and onion slices.
- Pour over the canned tomatoes that have been puréed with tomato paste.
- Cover with remaining ¹/₃ of sauce and sprinkle liberally with nutmeg and pepper and grated cheese.
- Bake 180°C for 40 minutes.

**Serves 8**

NUTRIENTS PER SERVE

| KJ | Cal | Pro (g) | CHO (g) | Fibre (g) | T.fat (g) | S.fat (g) | Chol (mg) | Na (mg) |
|---|---|---|---|---|---|---|---|---|
| 1126 | 271 | 18 | 36 | 4 | 6 | 2 | 26 | 238 |

MAIN MEALS: MEAT ALTERNATIVES

# MAIN VEGETABLE DISHES

## BAKED RATATOUILLE

*1 crushed clove garlic (3g)*
*1 medium thinly sliced rings of capsicum (150g)*
*1 medium sliced unpeeled eggplant (300g)*
*1 medium sliced unpeeled zucchini (175g)*
*1 medium thinly sliced onion (100g)*
*1 tsp mono/polyunsaturated oil (5g)*
*1 tabsp water (20ml)*
*1 tsp oregano*
*1 medium chopped tomato (100g)*
*1 cup grated less than 10% fat cheese (120g)*

❏ Stir-fry prepared garlic, capsicum, eggplant, zucchini and onion in a non-stick pan with oil and water.
❏ Add oregano and tomato.
❏ Continue cooking uncovered for 5 - 10 minutes.
❏ Place in a casserole dish, sprinkle with cheese.
❏ Bake in 180°C oven for about 20 minutes or until cheese melts.

**Serves 4**

NUTRIENTS PER SERVE

| KJ | Cal | Pro (g) | CHO (g) | Fibre (g) | T.fat (g) | S.fat (g) | Chol (mg) | Na (mg) |
|---|---|---|---|---|---|---|---|---|
| 438 | 104 | 12 | 5 | 3.5 | 4 | 0.6 | 11 | 160 |

## VEGETABLE SAVOURY

*1 cup broccoli florets (200g)*
*7 medium mushrooms (100g)*
*3 sticks celery (225g)*
*1 onion (100g)*
*1 tsp mono/polyunsaturated oil (5ml)*
*1 tabsp water (20ml)*
*¼ cup low fat evaporated milk (65ml)*
*½ cup water (125ml)*
*2 lightly beaten eggs or low cholesterol egg mix (100g)*
*Pepper*
*2 tabsp roughly chopped, roasted almonds (25g)*
*½ cup grated less than 10% fat cheese (60g)*
*¼ cup dried bread crumbs (30g)*
*1 tabsp chopped chives*

❏ Prepare vegetables by cutting broccoli into florets, mushrooms into quarters, celery into 1cm slices and onion into wedges.
❏ Stir-fry broccoli, mushrooms, celery and onion for 4 - 5 minutes in a non-stick pan with oil and water.
❏ Spoon into a 3-litre greased casserole dish.
❏ Combine milk, water, eggs and pepper.
❏ Pour over vegetables.
❏ Mix together almonds, cheese, bread crumbs and chives.
❏ Sprinkle on top of the dish.
❏ Bake at 190°C for 25 - 30 minutes or until egg mixture is set.
❏ Serve hot with crusty wholemeal bread.

**Serves 4**

*Nutritional Tip*
Broccoli is one of the best sources of vitamin C. One large floret will give you your daily requirement. If you include the stalks, peel and cook but allow a little more cooking time.

NUTRIENTS PER SERVE

| KJ | Cal | Pro (g) | CHO (g) | Fibre (g) | T.fat (g) | S.fat (g) | Chol (mg) | Na (mg) |
|---|---|---|---|---|---|---|---|---|
| 769 | 185 | 15 | 10 | 5 | 9 | 1.6 | 101 | 239 |

## VEGETABLE PARCELS

*1 medium thinly sliced spanish onion (100g)*
*1 cup of canned, drained and washed kidney beans or chick peas (200g)*
*1 cup finely chopped red cabbage (100g)*
*1 small peeled and chopped apple (70g)*
*1 cup coarsely grated pumpkin (100g)*
*⅓ cup sultanas (50g)*
*1 cup bean sprouts (100g)*
*8 sheets of filo pastry (110g)*
*2 tsp sesame seeds (6g)*

❏ Mix together onion, beans, cabbage, apple, pumpkin, sultanas and bean sprouts. Soften for 3 - 5 minutes on **High** in microwave or steamer.
❏ Fold a sheet of filo pastry in half, place about ¾ cup of mixture in one corner, fold in edges, fold up to form a parcel. Repeat this with all 8 sheets.
❏ Place on a greased baking tray.
❏ Sprinkle with sesame seeds.
❏ Bake in 180°C oven for 40 minutes.

**Serves 4 (Total 8 parcels)**

NUTRIENTS PER SERVE

| KJ | Cal | Pro (g) | CHO (g) | Fibre (g) | T.fat (g) | S.fat (g) | Chol (mg) | Na (mg) |
|---|---|---|---|---|---|---|---|---|
| 850 | 203 | 9 | 37 | 7 | 2 | 0.33 | 0 | 371 |

MAIN MEALS: MEAT ALTERNATIVES

## MEDITERRANEAN PIE

1 large **Grilled Eggplant** p88 (400g)
1 large red **Peeled Capsicum** p86 (300g)
4 medium peeled and sliced potatoes (400g)
1 medium sliced Spanish onion (100g)
250g pkt frozen drained spinach (165g)
Low fat fetta cheese (300g)
375g jar drained artichoke hearts in brine (300g)
1 cup **Fresh Tomato Basil Salsa** p106
5 sheets filo pastry (70g)
1 tabsp parmesan cheese (9g)
Mono-unsaturated oil spray

- Prepare eggplant as per recipe **Grilled Eggplant**.
- Peel red capsicum as per recipe **Peeled Capsicum**.
- Cook prepared potato and onion in microwave or steam for about 5 minutes or until just beginning to soften.
- Thaw spinach and drain well to remove all liquid.
- Slice fetta into 1/2 cm slices.
- Drain artichokes and blot with kitchen paper.
- Prepare **Fresh Tomato Basil Salsa**.

**Assembly**
- Place 3 sheets of filo pastry in a large, deep 25cm greased pie plate.
- Trim off edges, leaving an overlap of 2cm.
- Cover bottom with cooked potato and onion, followed with **Grilled Eggplant** and then spread with **Fresh Tomato Basil Salsa**.
- Top this with spinach, artichokes, fetta and red **Peeled Capsicum**.

*Vegetable Parcels*

- Fold bottom pastry over filling.
- Cover with two sheets of filo pastry, trimmed and tucked in around sides.
- Spray with oil and sprinkle with parmesan cheese.
- Bake in 180°C oven for 45 minutes.
- Serve warm.

**Serves 6**

*Note*
Sodium is high due to the fetta and artichokes. Omit artichokes and use fresh mushrooms if this is of concern.

NUTRIENTS PER SERVE

| KJ | Cal | Pro (g) | CHO (g) | Fibre (g) | T.fat (g) | S.fat (g) | Chol (mg) | Na (mg) |
|---|---|---|---|---|---|---|---|---|
| 1123 | 270 | 20 | 23 | 7 | 10 | 5 | 32 | 853 |

## VEGETABLE CURRY

1/2 cup yellow split peas (110g)
1 tabsp mono/polyunsaturated oil (20ml)
2 medium chopped onions (200g)
1 crushed clove garlic (3g)
4 whole cloves
2 tabsp curry powder
1 tsp turmeric
2 medium chopped tomatoes (200g)
2 medium chopped carrots (200g)
2 chopped sticks celery (150g)
2 medium diced potatoes (200g)
2 cups water (500ml)
Finely ground black pepper
Salt to taste

- Bring split peas to the boil in a large quantity of water, leave for 1 hour and drain.
- Heat oil in a heavy saucepan; stir-fry onion, garlic and cloves for 3 - 4 minutes.
- Add curry powder and turmeric; stir-fry a further 1 - 2 minutes.
- Add tomato, carrot, celery, potato, drained split peas, water, pepper and salt to taste.
- Simmer slowly for about 1 hour or until the split peas are soft.
- Serve as a main meal with boiled rice.

**Serves 6**

NUTRIENTS PER SERVE

| KJ | Cal | Pro (g) | CHO (g) | Fibre (g) | T.fat (g) | S.fat (g) | Chol (mg) | Na (mg) |
|---|---|---|---|---|---|---|---|---|
| 363 | 87 | 3.3 | 10 | 4 | 3.6 | 0.4 | 0 | 45 |

## Chicken

Chicken breasts without skin should be used as often as possible. Thighs are more moist and are acceptable if all fat and skin is removed, but they do have a higher fat content. Skinless chicken is a high protein, low fat product which contributes to iron, zinc and essential B vitamins. Use it in stir fries, casseroles, kebabs, roasts, grills and cold in salads. Don't overcook as this will toughen and dry the flesh.

*Apricot Chicken Breast in Filo 64*
*Chicken and Asparagus in Filo 64*
*Chicken Dhal Curry 65*
*Chicken Ginger Kebabs 65*
*Grilled Tandoori Chicken 66*
*Chicken with Barbecue Sauce 63*
*Hungarian Chicken 62*
*Satay Chicken Kebabs 63*
*Sherried Mushroom Chicken 63*
*Turkey Breasts in Marinade Sauce 66*

### *Chicken Casseroles*
In casserole-style dishes all skin and fat should be removed before cooking to minimise the fat content. Try **Chicken Dahl Curry** p65 and **Sherried Mushroom Chicken** p63 when entertaining.

### *Roast Chicken*
When roasting a chicken, it is acceptable to leave the fat on to cook but don't add any additional fat and cook vegetables in a separate roasting pan. It works well to partially boil or microwave the vegetables then brush or spray with oil and roast for 45 minutes or until nicely browned and crisp.

### *Barbecue Chicken*
Barbecuing is ideal in summer weather. Try some of the following marinades and seasonings or prepare **Chicken Ginger Kebabs** p65, **Satay Chicken Kebab**s p63 or **Grilled Tandoori Chicken** p66.

### *Spicy Barbecue Chicken*
Brush chicken breasts with mono/polyunsaturated oil and sprinkle with spices such as tandoori, paprika, chilli, curry, Cajun, Indian, Mexican or crushed garlic. Cook on the barbecue hotplate.

### *Lemon Rosemary Chicken*
Place chicken fillets on aluminium foil and sprinkle with lemon juice, parsley and rosemary. Wrap in aluminium foil and barbecue till tender.

### *Chicken Burger and Sausages*
Use lean chicken mince to make chicken burgers or purchase chicken sausages and cook on barbecue. Shop around for low fat chicken mince and sausages. Some shops that specialise in chicken will have them. Check the fat content if possible. Some sausages and mince will be less than 10% fat but it depends on which parts of the chicken that are used.

## HUNGARIAN CHICKEN

*4 skinned boned chicken thighs (400g)*
*1 large finely chopped onion (150g)*
*2 medium finely chopped tomatoes (200g)*
*½ large capsicum (150g)*
*1 sliced stalk of celery (75g)*
*1 medium sliced carrot (100g)*
*10 medium sliced mushrooms (100g)*
*2 tabsp tomato paste (50g)*
*1 tabsp vinegar (20ml)*
*1 tabsp brown sugar (13g)*
*½ cup non fat yoghurt (125ml)*

- Place chicken thighs in a casserole dish.
- Mix onion, tomato, capsicum, celery, carrot, mushrooms, tomato paste, vinegar and brown sugar together.
- Cover chicken thighs with vegetable mixture, then cover with plastic wrap or a lid and microwave for thirty minutes at **Medium High** or bake for 40 minutes at 180°C.
- Remove from microwave or oven and stir in natural non fat yoghurt.
- Serve with rice or noodles, allowing about one chicken thigh of 100g each per serve.

**Serves 4**

### *Note*
You may substitute part or all of yoghurt with sour cream if desired but fat will be higher.

### *Handy Hint*
If you chop all the vegetables in the food processor, preparation time will only be about 10 minutes.

NUTRIENTS PER SERVE

| KJ | Cal | Pro (g) | CHO (g) | Fibre (g) | T.fat (g) | S.fat (g) | Chol (mg) | Na (mg) |
|---|---|---|---|---|---|---|---|---|
| 1005 | 240 | 33 | 12 | 4 | 6 | 3 | 104 | 236 |

## CHICKEN WITH BARBECUE SAUCE

*1 small finely chopped onion (75g)*
*1 crushed clove garlic (3g)*
*½ cup low sodium tomato sauce (125ml)*
*2 tsp Worcestershire sauce (10ml)*
*2 tabsp vinegar (40ml)*
*2 tabsp sugar (36g) or equivalent substitute*
*½ tsp dry mustard*
*½ tsp paprika*
*1 tsp low sodium chicken stock powder (2.5g)*
*Skinned, boned chicken thighs (600g)*

❏ Mix onion, garlic, tomato sauce, Worcestershire sauce, vinegar, sugar, mustard, paprika and chicken stock powder together.
❏ Remove any fat from chicken thighs.
❏ Place in a large casserole dish with marinade and refrigerate for 1 to 2 hours.
❏ Cover with a lid and bake in a 180°C oven for 30 minutes.
❏ Remove lid and bake a further ½ hour.
❏ Serve with rice, buttered ribbon noodles or **Cous Cous** p90.

**Serves 4**

*Note*
Small quantities of sugar are insignificant. The total carbohydrate is more important.

NUTRIENTS PER SERVE

| KJ | Cal | Pro (g) | CHO (g) | Fibre (g) | T.fat (g) | S.fat (g) | Chol (mg) | Na (mg) |
|---|---|---|---|---|---|---|---|---|
| 1422 | 341 | 44 | 21 | 1 | 10 | 5 | 154 | 236 |

## SHERRIED MUSHROOM CHICKEN

*1 kg skinned chicken breasts*
*1 cup chicken stock (250ml)*
*20 large fresh sliced mushrooms (400g)*
*1 package of cream of mushroom soup (yield 4 serves)*
*1½ tsp curry powder*
*1 can low fat evaporated milk (375ml)*
*1 tabsp medium dry sherry (20ml)*
*½ small carton non fat natural yoghurt (100g)*
*¼ cup parsley*

❏ Place chicken breasts and stock in a large casserole and microwave or bake until just done.
❏ Let cool and then drain stock and reserve.
❏ Chop chicken into bite size pieces.
❏ Heat mushrooms with chicken stock, mushroom soup and curry powder.
❏ Add chicken, milk and sherry.
❏ Place in a large casserole dish and heat in 160°C oven for 40 minutes.
❏ Stir in yoghurt and reheat.
❏ Sprinkle parsley on top and serve with **Sunflower Rice** p94.

**Serves 10**

NUTRIENTS PER SERVE

| KJ | Cal | Pro (g) | CHO (g) | Fibre (g) | T.fat (g) | S.fat (g) | Chol (mg) | Na (mg) |
|---|---|---|---|---|---|---|---|---|
| 1246 | 297 | 32 | 18 | 2 | 8 | 4 | 60 | 863 |

## SATAY CHICKEN KEBABS

*Skinned boned chicken breasts (500g)*

**Marinade**
*½ cup water*
*1 tsp low sodium chicken stock powder (2.5g)*
*1 small finely chopped onion (75g)*
*1 crushed clove garlic (3g)*
*1 tsp grated green ginger (5g)*
*¼ cup smooth peanut butter (75g)*
*1 tabsp sherry (20ml)*
*1 tabsp honey (20ml)*
*1 tabsp low sodium soy sauce (20ml)*
*2 tsp curry powder (10g)*
*1 tsp cumin*
*½ tsp ground coriander*

❏ Remove any remaining fat from chicken breasts and cut into 2cm cubes.
❏ Prepare marinade by mixing water, stock powder, onion, garlic, ginger, peanut butter, sherry, honey, soy sauce, curry powder, cumin and coriander together. Use a blender or food processor if available.
❏ Add to chicken and refrigerate for 6 hours or overnight.
❏ Soak 18 wood skewers in hot water for 1 hour.
❏ Thread chicken on skewers, allowing 3 per person.
❏ Grill on a barbecue or oven grill, basting with marinade.
❏ Cook remaining marinade on stove or in microwave for 2 to 3 minutes to reduce liquid and serve with cooked kebabs.

**Serves 6**

NUTRIENTS PER SERVE

| KJ | Cal | Pro (g) | CHO (g) | Fibre (g) | T.fat (g) | S.fat (g) | Chol (mg) | Na (mg) |
|---|---|---|---|---|---|---|---|---|
| 1643 | 397 | 20 | 6 | 2 | 8 | 1.5 | 86 | 274 |

CHICKEN RECIPES

*Apricot Chicken Breast in Filo*

## APRICOT CHICKEN BREAST IN FILO

*4 chicken breasts/butterfly (400g)*
*1 can light apricot halves (420g)*
*1/3 pkt French onion soup mix (12g)*
*2 tsp sesame seeds (7g)*
*Mono-unsaturated cooking spray*
*8 sheets filo pastry (110g)*
*Paprika*
*Pepper*

- Cut open and butterfly chicken breasts.
- Place 2 apricot halves inside each butterfly.
- Sprinkle each with 2 tsp of French onion soup mix.
- Fold chicken over to enclose fillings.
- Take 2 sheets of filo for each breast and fold in half.
- Place each chicken breast at one corner.
- Fold in sides and then roll up to form a parcel, putting the seam on the bottom.
- Place on a lightly greased baking tray.
- Brush or spray chicken with a little bit of oil.
- Sprinkle with sesame seeds, paprika and black pepper.
- Bake in a 180°C oven for 40 minutes.
- Purée remaining apricots with a little juice to give a smooth sauce or coulis.
- Serve chicken breast on warmed fruit coulis.

**Serves 4**

### Variation

**Chicken and Asparagus in Filo** Butterfly chicken breast, place 2 or 3 fresh spears of asparagus on each. Fold chicken over and wrap in filo. Place on a greased oven tray, spray with oil and sprinkle with sesame seeds. Bake in 180°C oven for 40 minutes.

NUTRIENTS PER SERVE

| KJ | Cal | Pro (g) | CHO (g) | Fibre (g) | T.fat (g) | S.fat (g) | Chol (mg) | Na (mg) |
|---|---|---|---|---|---|---|---|---|
| 1953 | 472 | 23 | 22 | 2.4 | 3 | 0.6 | 103 | 453 |

**Chicken and Asparagus in Filo**

# CHICKEN DHAL CURRY

**Curry**

2 large finely chopped onions (300g)
8 to 10 crushed garlic cloves (25 - 30g)
2cm piece of crushed ginger
2 tsp mono/polyunsaturated oil (10ml)
2 tabsp water (40ml)
2½ tabsp curry powder (25g)
1 tsp turmeric
Boned skinned chicken breast (1kg)
3 medium finely chopped tomatoes (300g)
2 tsp low sodium stock powder (5g)
1 cup water (250ml)
1 cup low fat evaporated milk (250ml)
Coconut essence to taste

**Dhal**

1 cup split dried peas (250g)
Boiling water to cover
2 cups boiling water

**Onions**

2 tsp oil (10ml)
2 tabsp water (40ml)
3 large finely sliced onions (450g)

**Preparation of chicken curry** (best done a day before to allow full flavour to develop)
- Place onion, garlic and ginger in a food processor and chop coarsely.
- Heat oil and water in a non-stick frying pan and add onion, garlic and ginger.
- Stir-fry until liquid evaporates and onion is golden.
- Add curry powder and turmeric and stir-fry 1 minute more.
- Add bite size pieces of chicken to curry mixture and stir-fry for 5 to 7 minutes or until a little brown.
- Add stock powder, water and tomato to chicken curry.
- Cover and cook slowly for 15 minutes, stirring occasionally.
- Refrigerate overnight if time allows.

**Preparation of dhal**
- Add boiling water to cover split peas, leave for 1 hour and then drain.
- Add 2 cups of boiling water to split peas in a microwave dish and cook on **Medium** for about 30 minutes or on stove top until water evaporates and peas are soft.
- Purée.

**Combining and serving of curry**
- Cook onions slowly in oil and water in a non-stick frying pan until golden.
- Drain on kitchen paper and dry in a low oven. Use as garnish.
- Reheat curry, stirring in puréed dhal.
- When hot, stir in milk and coconut essence. Reheat gently, do not boil as it will separate.
- Serve curry over rice or **Cous Cous** p90 with dried onions as a garnish.

**Serves 8**

NUTRIENTS PER SERVE

| KJ | Cal | Pro (g) | CHO (g) | Fibre (g) | T.fat (g) | S.fat (g) | Chol (mg) | Na (mg) |
|---|---|---|---|---|---|---|---|---|
| 1366 | 326 | 41 | 24 | 7 | 7.3 | 2 | 64 | 149 |

# CHICKEN GINGER KEBABS

Boned skinned chicken breast (500g)
2 tsp finely chopped green ginger
2 tabsp salt reduced soy sauce (40ml)
2 tabsp lemon juice (40ml)
3 tsp Worcestershire sauce (15ml)
1 tabsp brown sugar (13g)
1 tsp dry mustard (2g)

- Remove all fat from chicken breast and cut into 2cm pieces.
- Place in a bowl.
- Combine green ginger, soy sauce, lemon juice, Worcestershire sauce, sugar and mustard and pour over chicken.
- Leave to marinate for 4 to 6 hours in the refrigerator, stirring occasionally.
- Place 12 wooden skewers in a pan and pour over boiling water.
- Leave to steep and absorb moisture while chicken is marinating (this will prevent the skewers from burning while being grilled).
- Thread chicken on wooden skewers, allowing 3 per person.
- Grill on barbecue or oven griller, turning frequently and basting with remaining marinade.
- Serve on a bed of saffron rice or **Sunflower Rice** p94.

**Serves 4**

NUTRIENTS PER SERVE

| KJ | Cal | Pro (g) | CHO (g) | Fibre (g) | T.fat (g) | S.fat (g) | Chol (mg) | Na (mg) |
|---|---|---|---|---|---|---|---|---|
| 690 | 164 | 29 | 5 | 0.10 | 3 | 0.8 | 63 | 470 |

CHICKEN RECIPES

*Grilled Tandoori Chicken p66 and Fruity Cous Cous p91*

## GRILLED TANDOORI CHICKEN

*Skinned, boned chicken breast (1kg)*

**Marinade**
2 tsp grained mustard (10g)
1 tabsp mono/polyunsaturated oil (20ml)
1/3 cup non fat natural yoghurt (85ml)
1 1/2 cm piece fresh ginger (10g)
1/2 tsp cumin
1/2 tsp coriander
1/2 tsp ground turmeric
2 tabsp lemon juice (40ml)
3 - 4 mild fresh or bottled finely chopped sweet capsicum or peppers (150g)

- Remove any extra fat from skinned chicken and cut into large bite size pieces.
- Place into a bowl.
- Mix mustard, oil, yoghurt, ginger, cumin, coriander, turmeric, lemon juice and sweet capsicum or peppers together.
- Mix marinade into chicken and refrigerate overnight or for 4 - 6 hours.
- Cook on grill or barbecue until just done.
- Serve with rice and salad.

**Serves 8**

*Note*
Mix marinade together in a food processor or blender to save time.

NUTRIENTS PER SERVE

| KJ | Cal | Pro (g) | CHO (g) | Fibre (g) | T.fat (g) | S.fat (g) | Chol (mg) | Na (mg) |
|---|---|---|---|---|---|---|---|---|
| 728 | 173 | 29 | 1.4 | 0.3 | 5.5 | 1 | 63 | 95 |

## TURKEY BREASTS IN A MARINADE SAUCE

*4 turkey breasts (600g)*

**Marinade**
1 tabsp olive oil (20ml)
1/3 cup red or white wine (85ml)
1 tabsp mixed fresh or 1 tsp dried herbs - parsley, thyme, oregano
2 tsp low sodium soy sauce (10ml)
1 small finely chopped onion (75g)
1 crushed clove garlic (3g)
2 tsp cornflour (5g)

- Mix oil, wine, herbs, soy sauce, onion and garlic together. Add to turkey breasts in a dish and leave 6 - 8 hours to marinade.
- Lightly barbecue or fry turkey in a non-stick frying pan until cooked.
- Set aside in a warm oven.
- Strain the marinade juices.
- Mix a little juice with cornflour.
- Heat remaining juice and stir in cornflour paste.
- Cook until thickened.
- Pour over the turkey breasts and serve immediately.

**Serves 4**

NUTRIENTS PER SERVE

| KJ | Cal | Pro (g) | CHO (g) | Fibre (g) | T.fat (g) | S.fat (g) | Chol (mg) | Na (mg) |
|---|---|---|---|---|---|---|---|---|
| 291 | 71 | 0.5 | 2 | 0.4 | 5 | 0.7 | 0 | 9 |

# BEEF/LAMB/PORK RECIPES

## Meat

Meat includes beef, lamb and pork - all important sources of protein. Pork is a particularly good source of thiamin, and beef, pork and lamb of riboflavin and niacin. It is recommended that meat be included at least twice a week to ensure a well-balanced diet. Meat may be used in a wide variety of casseroles, mince dishes, roasts, for barbecues, kebabs or cold in salad. If good quality lean products are bought, wastage is kept to a minimum.

*Beef*
Beef Curry 68
Beef Stroganoff 68
Chilli Con carne 71
Cabbage Rolls 69
Cornish Pasties 70
Lasagne 68
Meat Balls with Sauce 72
Moussaka 71
Savoury Mince 70
   Shepherds Pie 70
Spaghetti Bolognaise 70
Steak Diane 72
Steak with Green Capsicum 72

*Lamb*
Lamb Kebabs 73
Lamb and Mushroom Curry 74
Lamb Shank & Dumpling
   Ragout 74
Lamb Shank Pie 74
Tropical Crown Lamb Roast 73

*Pork*
Barbecue Spare Ribs 76
Port Tenderloin Teriyaki 75
Spicy Pork Medallions 75
Sweet and Sour Pork 76

## *Casseroles and Mince Dishes*

Casseroles are ideal for cheaper cuts of meat such as lamb shanks for **Lamb Shank and Dumpling Ragout** p74 or blade steak for **Beef Curry** p68.

Mince should be as low fat as possible. There will be less shrinkage in cooking. Try **Cabbage Rolls** p69 and **Savoury Mince** p70.

## *Roasts*

Use well-trimmed cuts such as topside roast for beef, or pork or lamb fillet. Cook vegetables separately and make fat free gravy. Either set the stock in the refrigerator or freezer, or add ice cubes to congeal fat for easy removal. For a special occasion try **Pork Tenderloin Teriyaki** p75 or **Tropical Crown Lxoast** p73.

## *Barbecue Ideas*

On your next barbecue, instead of fatty chops and sausages, use lean beef, trim lamb steaks, or pork steaks. Allow approx 500g meat for four serves. Don't overcook and only turn once. For tougher cuts of meat marinading is recommended and it helps to reduce the risk of cancer.

Beef should be cooked thus, depending on the desired result —

   **Rare** - Seal for 2 to 3 minutes, turn and cook 2 to 3 minutes more.

   **Medium** - Seal for 2 to 3 minutes and then allow 2 to 3 more minutes for each side.

   **Well done** - Seal for 2 to 3 minutes and then allow 4 to 6 minutes for each side.

It is acceptable to serve pork and lamb medium rare. It will be more tender and moist.

Try some of the marinades or choose your own combination. We recommend **Spicy Pork Medallions** p75.

**Garlic Wine Marinade**
   2 tsp mono/polyunsaturated oil (10ml)
   1 tabsp lemon juice (20ml)
   ¼ cup dry wine (65ml)
   1 crushed clove garlic (3g)
   Pepper
   Herbs e.g. bay leaves, marjoram etc.

**Soy Honey Marinade**
   2 tabsp salt reduced soy sauce (40ml)
   1 tabsp vinegar (20ml)
   1 tabsp honey (20ml)
   1 tsp fresh ginger, chopped
   2 tabsp water (40ml)

**Wine Soy Marinade**
   ¼ cup dry wine (65ml)
   ¼ cup salt reduced soy sauce (65ml)
   ½ tabsp mono/polyunsaturated oil (10ml)
   1 crushed clove garlic (3g)

## *Meat Kebabs - photograph p73*

- Use lean meat and cut into cubes. Thread on skewers. (Wooden skewers need to be soaked in water for 1 to 2 hours.)
- Place kebabs in your choice of marinade for 2 to 3 hours or overnight. Meat may be marinaded before or after threading on skewers.
- Alternate cubes of meat with vegetables such as carrots, celery, mushrooms, cherry tomatoes, onions, zucchini, capsicum.

## *Burgers*

- Use lean mince (beef, lamb, pork) for meat patties, burgers, rissoles etc., and cook on barbecue. Frozen burgers with the Heart Tick (✓) may be used when time is short.

## *Sausages*

- Shop around for low fat sausages. Some butchers and supermarkets sell them.
- Fat content is approx 18% fat as compared to 25% fat for regular sausages.
- This is still high so consume sparingly.

# BEEF DISHES

## LASAGNE

1 cup ricotta cheese (250g)
1½ packets of instant lasagne pasta (375g)
4 cups **Spaghetti Sauce** p104
250g packet of frozen drained spinach (165g)
1 tabsp mono/polyunsaturated margarine (20g)
2 tabsp plain flour (20g)
¼ tsp nutmeg
Freshly ground black pepper
3 cups non fat milk (750ml)
1 cup grated less than 10% fat cheese (120g)
2 tabsp parmesan cheese (18g)

❑ Use a knife to spread ricotta evenly over lasagne pasta.
❑ Have **Spaghetti Sauce** prepared and spinach thawed.
❑ Prepare white sauce by melting margarine in a heavy based saucepan or microwave dish.
❑ Stir in flour, nutmeg and black pepper to form a smooth paste.
❑ Slowly add milk while cooking over low heat or stirring occasionally in the microwave.
❑ Cook and stir occasionally until thick and smooth.
❑ Pour a little white sauce into the bottom of a greased large oblong dish.
❑ Arrange ⅓ of the pasta that is spread with ricotta on the bottom, top with ⅓ of **Spaghetti Sauce** and ⅓ of cheese.
❑ Cover with a little white sauce.
❑ Place another layer of pasta and the next ⅓ of **Spaghetti Sauce** on top.
❑ Spread with spinach and ⅓ cheese.
❑ Cover with sauce.
❑ Top with remaining pasta, **Spaghetti Sauce** and white sauce.
❑ Push down any areas which are not covered with sauce.
❑ Sprinkle with remaining ⅓ cheese and parmesan cheese.
❑ Place in a 180°C oven and bake for 50 to 60 minutes or until tender and liquid is absorbed.

**Serves 12**

NUTRIENTS PER SERVE

| KJ | Cal | Pro (g) | CHO (g) | Fibre (g) | T.fat (g) | S.fat (g) | Chol (mg) | Na (mg) |
|---|---|---|---|---|---|---|---|---|
| 1089 | 284 | 22 | 30 | 3 | 8 | 3 | 42 | 218 |

## BEEF STROGANOFF

Topside steak, lean (500g)
1 tabsp plain flour (10g)
Freshly ground black pepper
1 tabsp mono/polyunsaturated oil (20ml)
1 medium finely chopped onion (100g)
1 crushed clove garlic (3g)
20 medium sliced mushrooms with stalks (200g)
1 tabsp flour (10g)
1 tabsp tomato paste (25g)
1 tsp low sodium beef stock powder (2.5g)
½ tsp nutmeg
1 cup water (250ml)
½ cup natural non fat yoghurt (125ml)

❑ Cut steak into thin strips.
❑ Toss in flour combined with pepper.
❑ Stir-fry meat in oil in a non-stick pan with onions, garlic and mushrooms until onion is soft and meat is brown.
❑ Remove meat and vegetables with a slotted serving spoon to a casserole dish.
❑ Mix remaining flour and tomato paste into juices to form a smooth sauce.
❑ Blend in stock powder, nutmeg and water.
❑ Cook and stir until thick and smooth.
❑ Add sauce to steak.
❑ Blend in yoghurt and reheat in a 180°C oven for 10 minutes.

**Serves 4**

NUTRIENTS PER SERVE

| KJ | Cal | Pro (g) | CHO (g) | Fibre (g) | T.fat (g) | S.fat (g) | Chol (mg) | Na (mg) |
|---|---|---|---|---|---|---|---|---|
| 1236 | 296 | 38 | 8.4 | 2.1 | 12 | 3.4 | 84 | 160 |

## BEEF CURRY

1 medium finely chopped onion (100g)
3 crushed cloves garlic (9g)
2cm piece of green ginger (10g)
1 tsp ground cumin
2 tabsp beef curry powder (20g)
½ tsp chilli powder (optional)
1 tsp turmeric
1 tabsp mono/polyunsaturated oil (20ml)
Lean cubed blade or round steak (500g)
1 tsp Lite salt (5g)
1 medium chopped tomato (100g)
1 large cubed potato (200g)

❑ Sauté onion, garlic, ginger, cumin, curry powder, chilli powder and turmeric with oil in pan.

# BEEF/LAMB/PORK RECIPES

- Cook and stir for 3 to 4 minutes until a curry paste has formed.
- Add cubed steak and salt. Cover and cook on low for 10 minutes.
- Add tomato and potato and continue to cook for about 10 minutes until soft and tender.

**Serves 4**

*Note*
Salt does draw out moisture. You may use regular salt as an alternative which will increase the sodium to 589mg.

NUTRIENTS PER SERVE

| KJ | Cal | Pro (g) | CHO (g) | Fibre (g) | T.fat (g) | S.fat (g) | Chol (mg) | Na (mg) |
|---|---|---|---|---|---|---|---|---|
| 1115 | 266 | 29 | 10 | 3 | 12 | 3 | 65 | 339 |

## CABBAGE ROLLS

¾ cup long grain raw rice (170g)
4 cups water (1 litre)
1 large finely chopped onion (150g)
2 crushed cloves garlic (6g)
2 tsp low sodium vegetable powder (5g)
Lean fine mince (500g)
10 large cabbage leaves (350g)
1 can tomatoes (400g)
½ cup low salt tomato sauce (125g)
1 cup water (250ml)

- Bring rice and water to the boil, cover and reduce heat, simmer on low for 20 minutes. This will yield 2¼ cups of cooked rice.
- Mix rice, onion, garlic, vegetable powder and mince together.
- Cut the core from the cabbage, pull apart and remove leaves and cut the very thick stalk from the end. Steam or boil in water until just softened, then drain.
- Place 100g (a bare ½ cup) of mince mixture on each cabbage leaf and fold to form a parcel.
- Place in a flat large (22cm square) dish.
- Mix tinned tomatoes that have been roughly chopped with tomato sauce and water.
- Pour over cabbage leaves.
- Bake uncovered in a 180°C oven for 1 hour.

**Serves 5 (2 cabbage rolls each)**

*Handy Hint*
Use scissors to cut the tomatoes while still in the can.

NUTRIENTS PER SERVE

| KJ | Cal | Pro (g) | CHO (g) | Fibre (g) | T.fat (g) | S.fat (g) | Chol (mg) | Na (mg) |
|---|---|---|---|---|---|---|---|---|
| 1128 | 324 | 25 | 40 | 5.4 | 7 | 3 | 63 | 212 |

## CORNISH PASTIES

*1½ cups* **Low Fat Fibre Pastry** *p131*

**Filling**
*2 medium finely cubed potatoes (200g)
2 small finely chopped turnips (250)
1 medium finely chopped onion (100g)
1 medium coarsely grated carrot (100g)
Lean mince (250g)
1 tsp oregano
½ tsp nutmeg
Freshly ground black pepper
¼ cup finely chopped parsley*

- Prepare **Low Fat Fibre Pastry**.
- Divide in half. Using half the pastry, line the base of a 27cm x 18cm lamington tin.
- Chill remainder.
- Combine potato, turnip, onion, carrot and lean mince.
- Season with oregano, nutmeg, black pepper and parsley.
- Mix well then fill pastry lined tin, pressing down firmly.
- Roll out remaining pastry, place on top and cut even with edge.
- Bake in 180°C oven for 30 minutes then reduce heat to 160°C for 35 - 40 minutes.
- Cut into serving pieces.

**Serves 6**

*Variation*
Use filo pastry instead of the **Low Fat Fibre Pastry**. Fat content will be even lower.

NUTRIENTS PER SERVE

| KJ | Cal | Pro (g) | CHO (g) | Fibre (g) | T.fat (g) | S.fat (g) | Chol (mg) | Na (mg) |
|---|---|---|---|---|---|---|---|---|
| 1066 | 257 | 15 | 25 | 6 | 10.4 | 3.3 | 31 | 82 |

## SAVOURY MINCE

*1 medium finely chopped onion (100g)
2 crushed cloves garlic (6g)
1 finely chopped stick celery (75g)
1 peeled and finely sliced carrot (100g)
1 tsp mono/polyunsaturated oil (5ml)
1 tabsp water (20ml)
Finely ground lean mince (400g)
1 tsp Worcestershire sauce (5ml)
1 tabsp low sodium soy sauce (20ml)
2 tabsp tomato paste (50g)
2 tabsp plain flour (20g)
¼ cup water (65ml)*

- Stir-fry onion, garlic, celery, carrot in oil and water in a non-stick fry pan 3 to 4 minutes.
- Add mince and stir-fry for 5 minutes more.
- Season with Worcestershire sauce, soy sauce and tomato paste.
- Make a paste of flour and water and stir to thicken.
- Adjust water until desired thickness is gained.
- Cook and occasionally stir over low heat for 5 to 10 minutes more.
- Serve with mashed potatoes and vegetables or over toast or as a delicious filling for baked potato.

**Serves 4**

*Variation*
**Shepherds Pie** Place in a deep pie dish and top with mashed potato and low fat grated cheese. Brown for 30 minutes in 180°C oven.

NUTRIENTS PER SERVE

| KJ | Cal | Pro (g) | CHO (g) | Fibre (g) | T.fat (g) | S.fat (g) | Chol (mg) | Na (mg) |
|---|---|---|---|---|---|---|---|---|
| 564 | 188 | 22 | 8.3 | 2.5 | 7.5 | 2.9 | 63 | 321 |

## SPAGHETTI BOLOGNAISE

*4 cups* **Spaghetti Sauce** *p104*
*Raw pasta (500g)
2 tabsp parmesan cheese (18g)*

- Have 4 cups of **Spaghetti Sauce** on hand.
- Cook pasta in boiling water until al dente.
- Serve pasta topped with **Spaghetti Sauce**.
- Allow 1 cup pasta, ½ cup sauce and 1 tsp parmesan cheese per serve.

**Serves 8**

# BEEF/LAMB/PORK RECIPES

*Note*
Pasta is a low glycaemic index food. When combined with a moderate quantity of low fat sauce it makes an excellent meal.

NUTRIENTS PER SERVE

| KJ | Cal | Pro (g) | CHO (g) | Fibre (g) | T.fat (g) | S.fat (g) | Chol (mg) | Na (mg) |
|---|---|---|---|---|---|---|---|---|
| 1302 | 347 | 22 | 49 | 5 | 6.7 | 2.5 | 42 | 133 |

## MOUSSAKA

2 medium **Grilled Eggplant** p88 (600g)
Lean topside mince (300g)
2 medium finely chopped onions (200g)
2 crushed cloves garlic (6g)
1 tsp low sodium beef stock powder (2.5g)
1 bay leaf
3 medium finely chopped tomatoes (300g)
Mono-unsaturated oil spray
1½ cups **Bechamel Sauce** p106
3 tabsp parmesan cheese (27g)

- Prepare **Grilled Eggplant**.
- Brown mince, onion and garlic in a dish in microwave or in a non-stick pan for about 5 minutes.
- Add beef stock powder, bay leaf and tomato. Cook for a further 5 minutes.
- Reduce heat in microwave and cook for 30 minutes or cover and simmer on stove for 30 minutes.
- Spray a large 25cm oven or microwave dish with oil.
- Place a ½ of eggplant in a layer on the bottom. Top with ½ of the mince.
- Finish with rest of eggplant and mince.
- Prepare **Bechamel Sauce** adding 2 tabsp parmesan cheese.
- Top mixture with **Bechamel Sauce** and sprinkle with remaining 1 tabsp of parmesan cheese.
- Bake in a 200°C oven for 20 to 25 minutes or until slightly brown and bubbly.

**Serves 8**

*Note*
Potato could be substituted for eggplant.

NUTRIENTS PER SERVE

| KJ | Cal | Pro (g) | CHO (g) | Fibre (g) | T.fat (g) | S.fat (g) | Chol (mg) | Na (mg) |
|---|---|---|---|---|---|---|---|---|
| 820 | 197 | 13 | 10 | 3 | 12 | 3.5 | 51 | 149 |

*Moussaka*

## CHILLI CON CARNE

2 cloves garlic (6g)
1 medium finely chopped onion (100g)
Low fat mince (500g)
400g can no added salt drained kidney beans (300g)
1 cup finely chopped celery (150g)
1 can tomatoes (400g)
¼ cup no added salt tomato paste (65ml)
¼ cup water (65ml)
2 tsp chilli powder or to taste (5g)
1 tsp sugar (5g)
Black pepper to taste

- Finely chop garlic and onion and mix with the mince.
- Cook in a non-stick fry pan or microwave on **High** until brown, breaking up with a fork occasionally.
- Add beans, celery, tomato, tomato paste, water, chilli powder, sugar and black pepper.
- Continue to microwave, covered at **Medium High** for 1 hour or alternatively cook 3 - 4 hours on **High** in a slow cooker or on stove.

**Serves 6**

*Note*
Using no added salt kidney beans in the recipe matches the sodium content of fresh beans.

NUTRIENTS PER SERVE

| KJ | Cal | Pro (g) | CHO (g) | Fibre (g) | T.fat (g) | S.fat (g) | Chol (mg) | Na (mg) |
|---|---|---|---|---|---|---|---|---|
| 874 | 275 | 32 | 18 | 8 | 8.3 | 3.5 | 79 | 222 |

## STEAK DIANE

*Steak (400g)*
*2 tablespoons of wholegrain mustard (40g)*
*4 crushed cloves garlic (12g)*
*1 tabsp Worcestershire sauce (20ml)*
*2 tabsp tomato sauce (40ml)*
*²/₃ cup low fat evaporated milk (165g)*
*Black pepper to taste*

- Take four pieces of lean steak weighing about 100g each and cut shallow slits on the surface.
- Mix together mustard and garlic and spread on both sides.
- Grill steak until just medium rare.
- Place in oven to keep warm.
- Mix Worcestershire sauce, tomato sauce, milk and pepper together to form a smooth paste.
- Cook slowly over low heat to thicken.
- Place steak on the plate and pour over sauce.

**Serves 4**

### Variations
Add stir-fried mushrooms or finely chopped spring onions.

### Note
This is low in fat using the low fat evaporated milk instead of cream but is still delicious.

NUTRIENTS PER SERVE

| KJ | Cal | Pro (g) | CHO (g) | Fibre (g) | T.fat (g) | S.fat (g) | Chol (mg) | Na (mg) |
|---|---|---|---|---|---|---|---|---|
| 766 | 182 | 28 | 10 | 1 | 4 | 2 | 70 | 433 |

## STEAK WITH GREEN CAPSICUM

*Blade steak (500g)*
*¼ cup cornflour (30g)*
*1 medium finely sliced onion (100g)*
*3 medium finely sliced tomatoes (300g)*
*2 medium finely sliced green capsicum (300g)*
*2 tabsp mono/polyunsaturated oil (40ml)*
*1½ cups water (375ml)*
*1 tsp low sodium beef stock powder (2.5g)*
*2 tabsp low sodium soy sauce (40ml)*

- Cut blade steak in very thin slices across the grain. Dip in cornflour.
- Prepare onion, tomatoes and capsicum.
- Heat 2 tabsp oil in a wok or heavy frypan.
- Sauté onions until golden. Add steak and sauté until brown.
- Add sliced capsicum and stir-fry for 5 minutes.
- Stir in water, stock powder, soy sauce and lastly sliced tomatoes.
- Cook for another 5 minutes and serve.

**Serves 4**

NUTRIENTS PER SERVE

| KJ | Cal | Pro (g) | CHO (g) | Fibre (g) | T.fat (g) | S.fat (g) | Chol (mg) | Na (mg) |
|---|---|---|---|---|---|---|---|---|
| 1338 | 320 | 30 | 12 | 2 | 16.6 | 4 | 65 | 480 |

## MEATBALLS WITH SAUCE

*Lean mince (500g)*
*4 slices crumbed grained bread (100g)*
*1 medium finely chopped onion (100g)*
*¼ cup finely chopped parsley*
*2 crushed cloves garlic (6g)*
*¼ cup non fat milk (65ml)*
*Black pepper*
**Italian Pasta Sauce** *p104*

- Place mince, bread, onion, parsley, garlic, milk and black pepper in the kitchen whiz or mix by hand.
- Blend until smooth.
- Make into 30 small balls (about the size of ping pong balls).
- Stir fry balls in non-stick pan until lightly brown.
- Place balls in **Italian Pasta Sauce** and simmer on the stove for 10 minutes or reheat in the microwave.
- Serve with pasta or **Rich Coarse Polenta** p92

**Serves 6 (Allow 5 balls per person)**

NUTRIENTS PER SERVE

| KJ | Cal | Pro (g) | CHO (g) | Fibre (g) | T.fat (g) | S.fat (g) | Chol (mg) | Na (mg) |
|---|---|---|---|---|---|---|---|---|
| 862 | 206 | 22 | 15 | 4 | 7 | 2.5 | 53 | 211 |

BEEF/LAMB/PORK RECIPES

*Lamb Kebabs*

# LAMB DISHES

## LAMB KEBABS

*Minced lean lamb (700g)*
*1 medium finely chopped onion (100g)*
*4 crushed cloves garlic (12g)*
*2 tsp ground cumin*
*1 tsp cinnamon*
*½ tsp paprika*
*2 tabsp chopped fresh coriander or 2 tsp dry*
*3 tabsp fresh chopped parsley*
*3 tabsp fresh chopped mint*
*½ cup* **Yoghurt Sauce** *p108*

- Re-mince lamb in a food processor with onion, garlic, cumin, cinnamon, paprika, coriander, parsley and mint.
- Soak 24 wooden skewers for 1 hour.
- Firmly mound lamb around 24 soaked skewers and refrigerate for 2 hours.
- Grill on a barbecue or oven grill, turning to brown evenly.
- Serve with **Yoghurt Sauce** as a dip plus rice.

**Serves 6**

NUTRIENTS PER SERVE

| KJ | Cal | Pro (g) | CHO (g) | Fibre (g) | T.fat (g) | S.fat (g) | Chol (mg) | Na (mg) |
|---|---|---|---|---|---|---|---|---|
| 622 | 147 | 28 | 2 | 0.7 | 3 | 1.2 | 78 | 92 |

## TROPICAL CROWN LAMB ROAST

*2 racks of lamb well trimmed of all fat (1kg)*
*1 cup commercial stuffing mix (100g)*
*¼ cup pinenuts (40g)*
*⅓ cup dried finely chopped apricots (50g)*
*6 - 7 finely chopped prunes (50g)*
*½ cup water (125ml)*

- Fold trimmed rack so outer skin is to inside and tie ends together with string to form a crown (you may ask your butcher to do this).
- Make the stuffing by mixing together stuffing mix, pinenuts, apricots, prunes and water.
- Place crown in a baking dish lined with foil or baking paper. Place stuffing in middle.
- Bake at 180°C for 1 hour.
- Serve 2 chops per person with **Plum Sauce** p106.

**Serves 6**

*Note*
Make sure that lamb is well trimmed of fat. A tunnel boned leg of lamb could be used with this stuffing mixture to give lower fat.

NUTRIENTS PER SERVE

| KJ | Cal | Pro (g) | CHO (g) | Fibre (g) | T.fat (g) | S.fat (g) | Chol (mg) | Na (mg) |
|---|---|---|---|---|---|---|---|---|
| 1381 | 331 | 37.5 | 8 | 2 | 16.5 | 5.5 | 112 | 206 |

## LAMB SHANK AND DUMPLING RAGOUT

*500g lamb shank meat (about 3 to 4 lamb shanks)*
*Mono-unsaturated oil spray*
*1 small finely chopped onion (75g)*
*1 crushed clove garlic (3g)*
*1 tsp mono/polyunsaturated oil (5ml)*
*2 tsp water (10ml)*
*1 small finely grated carrot (75g)*
*1 tsp Worcestershire sauce (5ml)*
*1 tabsp tomato paste (25g)*
*1 bay leaf*
*½ cup chicken stock or ½ tsp low sodium stock powder plus water (1.25g)*
**Dumplings** p128

- Bone or have the butcher bone the lamb shanks, removing all fat and cutting into large chunks.
- Stir-fry meat in a non stick pan or heavy based frying pan sprayed with oil. Transfer to a deep 2-litre casserole dish.
- Stir-fry onion and garlic in oil and water in frying pan until golden brown.
- Add carrot, Worcestershire sauce, tomato paste, bay leaf and stock.
- Stir to form a smooth sauce and then pour over meat.
- Press meat firmly into sauce to cover as much as possible.
- Cover with foil or baking paper to prevent the top from drying out.
- Bake in 180°C oven for about 2 hours or in a pressure cooker for 30 minutes.
- Drop **Dumplings** onto meat and cook uncovered at 200°C for 20 minutes, or in pressure cooker for 10 minutes uncovered and 10 minutes covered.

**Serves 4**

### Variation
**Lamb Shank Pie** - the lamb mixture may be put into a pie dish and topped with mashed potato and sprinkled with cheese, or line dish with filo pastry to make a pie. Cool filling first. Spray a little mono-unsaturated oil on top.

### Note
A flavoursome and inexpensive ragout which definitely lends itself to company fare. Combine it with tossed salad and vegetables in season.

NUTRIENTS PER SERVE

| KJ | Cal | Pro (g) | CHO (g) | Fibre (g) | T.fat (g) | S.fat (g) | Chol (mg) | Na (mg) |
|---|---|---|---|---|---|---|---|---|
| 1405 | 337 | 36 | 26 | 4 | 9 | 2 | 84 | 314 |

## LAMB AND MUSHROOM CURRY

*1 tabsp mono/polyunsaturated oil (20ml)*
*2 tabsp water (40ml)*
*2 medium coarsely chopped onions (200g)*
*2 large crushed cloves garlic (6g)*
*2 tsp freshly grated ginger (10g)*
*2 tsp brown sugar (6g)*
*1 tsp sweet chilli sauce (6ml)*
*1 bay leaf*
*3 tsp curry powder (10g)*
*1 tsp turmeric*
*½ tsp ground coriander*
*½ tsp ground cumin*
*Lean cubed lamb (prefer leg lamb) (600g)*
*20 medium sliced fresh mushrooms (200g)*
*2 medium coarsely chopped tomatoes (200g)*
*Zest of 1 lemon*
*Juice of 1 lemon (60ml)*
*½ cup low fat evaporated milk (125ml)*
*Coconut essence to taste*

- Heat oil and water in a heavy based saucepan or non-stick frying pan and stir-fry onion, garlic and ginger.
- Blend in brown sugar, chilli sauce, bay leaf, curry powder, turmeric, coriander and cumin.
- Add lamb and stir-frying for 5 minutes.
- Add mushrooms, tomatoes, lemon zest and lemon juice.
- Cover and cook slowly for 30 - 40 minutes or until tender.
- Just before serving stir in milk and coconut essence.

**Serves 6**

### Note
Serve with **Sunflower Rice** p94 or **Cous Cous** p90, curry condiments such as chopped onion and tomato, mango chutney or chopped cucumber and non fat natural yoghurt.

NUTRIENTS PER SERVE

| KJ | Cal | Pro (g) | CHO (g) | Fibre (g) | T.fat (g) | S.fat (g) | Chol (mg) | Na (mg) |
|---|---|---|---|---|---|---|---|---|
| 801 | 191 | 27 | 7 | 2.5 | 6 | 1.5 | 67 | 108 |

### Note
Low fat evaporated milk plus coconut essence is an excellent substitute for coconut cream and is low in saturated fat.

*Pork Tenderloin Teriyaki*

# PORK DISHES

## PORK TENDERLOIN TERIYAKI

*3 finely chopped spring onions (40g)*
*3cm piece crushed ginger (10g)*
*2 tsp sugar (10g) or equivalent substitute*
*1 tabsp white wine (20ml)*
*2 tabsp sherry (40ml)*
*3 tabsp low sodium soy sauce (60ml)*
*3 crushed cloves garlic (9g)*
*Freshly ground black pepper*
*2 x 300g pork tenderloins (600g)*

- Mix together onion, ginger, sugar, white wine, sherry, soy sauce, garlic and black pepper.
- Marinate pork tenderloins in the mixture for 4 - 6 hours or overnight.
- Place in a baking pan and bake at 180°C for 15 - 20 minutes. Stop and baste while cooking.
- Slice and serve

**Serves 6**

*Note*
Pork may be served rare and it is more juicy and tender. Pork tenderloins are very lean with no wastage. They may be thickly sliced and barbecued.

### NUTRIENTS PER SERVE

| KJ | Cal | Pro (g) | CHO (g) | Fibre (g) | T.fat (g) | S.fat (g) | Chol (mg) | Na (mg) |
|---|---|---|---|---|---|---|---|---|
| 555 | 132 | 25 | 3 | 0.4 | 1 | 0.3 | 54 | 415 |

## SPICY PORK MEDALLIONS

*4 well trimmed pork medallions (500g)*
*2 tsp mono/polyunsaturated oil (10ml)*
*1 tabsp lemon juice (20ml)*
*1/4 cup dry white wine (65ml)*
*1 crushed clove garlic (3g)*
*Freshly ground black pepper*
*2 tabsp fresh herbs or 2 tsp dry*
*Chutney (optional)*

- Trim pork medallions of all fat.
- Mix marinade of oil, lemon juice, wine, garlic, black pepper and herbs.
- Marinate pork for 3 to 4 hours in the refrigerator.
- Grill quickly allowing 3 to 4 minutes per side.
- Brush with marinade while cooking.
- Serve with a little chutney if desired.

**Serves 4**

### NUTRIENTS PER SERVE

| KJ | Cal | Pro (g) | CHO (g) | Fibre (g) | T.fat (g) | S.fat (g) | Chol (mg) | Na (mg) |
|---|---|---|---|---|---|---|---|---|
| 712 | 169 | 31 | 0.3 | 0.1 | 4 | 0.7 | 68 | 69 |

BEEF/LAMB/PORK RECIPES

*Barbecue Spare Ribs*

## BARBECUE SPARE RIBS

*Lean trimmed pork spare ribs (2kg)*
*Sauce*
*1 large finely chopped onion (150g)*
*2 crushed cloves garlic (6g)*
*¾ cup of low sodium tomato sauce (190ml)*
*3 tsp Worcestershire sauce (15ml)*
*3 tabsp vinegar (60ml)*
*2 tabsp sugar (36g) or equivalent substitute*
*½ tsp dry mustard (2.5g)*
*½ tsp paprika*
*1 tsp low sodium chicken stock powder (2.5g)*

- Trim and cut spare ribs into individual ribs, removing any remaining fat.
- Blend onion, garlic, tomato sauce, Worcestershire sauce, vinegar, sugar, dry mustard, paprika and chicken stock powder together.
- Place spare ribs in a large pan, pour sauce over, marinade for 4 - 6 hours turning occasionally.
- Bake in an oven for 2 hours at 180°C.
- Turn and brush occasionally with sauce while cooking.
- Serve with steamed **Sunflower Rice** p94, with finger bowls on the side.

**Serves 6**

*Note*
This can be cooked very successfully on the barbecue.

NUTRIENTS PER SERVE

| KJ | Cal | Pro (g) | CHO (g) | Fibre (g) | T.fat (g) | S.fat (g) | Chol (mg) | Na (mg) |
|---|---|---|---|---|---|---|---|---|
| 1978 | 475 | 45 | 19 | 1.2 | 24 | 8.4 | 155 | 185 |

## SWEET AND SOUR PORK

*1 large diced onion (150g)*
*1 crushed clove garlic (3g)*
*1 tsp grated green ginger (optional)*
*1 tabsp water (20ml)*
*1 tsp mono/polyunsaturated oil (20ml)*
*Lean diced pork steak (500g)*
*2 medium sliced carrots (200g)*
*2 sticks sliced celery (150g)*
*1 small diced red capsicum (75g)*
*1 small julienne zucchini (100g)*
*2 tabsp tomato paste (50g)*
*1 tabsp vinegar (20ml)*
*1 can unsweetened pineapple pieces and juice (420g)*
*2 tsp cornflour (5g)*
*2 tabsp water (40ml)*
*Black pepper to taste*
*1 tabsp low sodium soy sauce (20ml)*

- Sauté onions, garlic and ginger in water and oil until onion is translucent.
- Add pork and continue to sauté until liquid has evaporated and pork is lightly browned.
- Add carrot, celery and saute for another 2 minutes more.
- Add capsicum and zucchini along with tomato paste, vinegar, pineapple pieces and juice.
- Thoroughly mix all ingredients and stir and steam lightly for 3 to 4 additional minutes until vegetables are tender crisp.
- Mix cornflour and water and add to mixture with black pepper and soy sauce. Stir until thick and smooth.
- Serve with rice and steamed cauliflower or broccoli.

**Serves 4**

*Note*
Julienne is to cut into thin strips. Substitute any vegetables that you have on hand.

NUTRIENTS PER SERVE

| KJ | Cal | Pro (g) | CHO (g) | Fibre (g) | T.fat (g) | S.fat (g) | Chol (mg) | Na (mg) |
|---|---|---|---|---|---|---|---|---|
| 1138 | 272 | 31 | 20 | 5.5 | 7 | 1 | 61 | 389 |

## Fish and Seafood

Fish is low in fat and high in protein. It takes very little grilling or baking time, so it is quick and easy.
**Curried Fish** p80, **Tuna Hotpot** p82 and **Chilli Mussels** p79 are for those who like that extra flavour and spice.
If you are tired of the everyday grilled or fried fish try **Lemon Fish Rolls** p80 or **Schnapper Fillets Julienne** p83.
Dress up baked fish with **Barramundi Almondine** p81 or **Fish Fillet Puff** p83. Seafood such as oysters, mussels and scallops can be included, even if you are watching cholesterol. **Stir Fry Scallops** p79 is quick and easy and other seafood could be substituted in the basic recipe. **Paella** p57, found under Pasta and Grains, combines seafood and chicken.
Refer to the extra suggestions for cooking fish below.

*Barramundi Almondine 81*
*Chilli Mussels 79*
*Curried Fish 80*
*Curried Prawns with Fish 80*
*Dhufish with Cucumber Sauce 82*
*Fish Fillet Puff 83*
*Lemon Fish Rolls 80*
*Pan-fried Fish with Salsa 78*
*Salmon Steaks 78*
*Schnapper Fillets Julienne 83*
*Stir Fry Scallops 79*
*Tuna Hotpot 82*

### Suggestions for Cooking Fish

**Microwave**
- Fish only takes a few minutes to cook in the microwave. Don't overcook, but allow it to stand for a few minutes to complete the cooking.
- Place fish (whole or fillet) on plate and sprinkle with lemon juice and herbs or add a little milk and pepper.
- Cover with plastic film and cook for a few minutes. Allow 10 to 12 minutes per kilo depending on size and thickness.
- Allow to stand another few minutes.

**Steamed Fish**
- Place fish fillets in steamer or on ovenproof plate which sits on top of saucepan with boiling water.
- Cover and allow to steam until fish flakes easily.
- Steamed or microwaved fish may also be served with **Sweet and Sour Sauce** p106.

**Mornay Sauce (for steamed or microwaved fish)**
1 cup non fat milk (250ml)
1 tabsp flour (10g)
1 tabsp parmesan cheese (9g)

- Mix flour with a little cold milk and add to remainder of milk which has been heated.
- Cook until sauce thickens.
- Mix half the parmesan cheese through the sauce.
- Pour sauce over fish and sprinkle with remaining parmesan cheese.

**Grilled Fish**
- Place fish fillet on foil, sprinkle with lemon juice and herbs such as parsley, dill and pepper. Wrap and grill or barbecue.
or
- Brush fish fillets with oil, sprinkle with herbs and spices such as paprika, chilli, cumin, Indian and Mexican and grill or barbecue.

**Baked Fish Fillets**
- Spray or brush baking dish with a little oil, add fish and top with chopped spring onions, sliced tomato, chopped celery, parsley and lemon juice.
- Bake in moderate oven till tender.
or
- Place fish fillets in baking dish, cover with tomato purée, sliced mushrooms, chopped capsicum, chopped spring onions, basil and oregano.
- Bake in 180°C oven until tender. (This goes well with boiled noodles and salad or vegetables.)
or
- Place fish fillets in baking dish, brush with tomato paste, sprinkle with fresh breadcrumbs and a little parmesan cheese.
- Bake at 180°C oven until tender.

**Baked Whole Fish**
- Brush fish with oil and sprinkle with lemon juice, pepper, parsley and spring onions.
- Wrap or cover with foil and bake in 180°C oven until tender.
or
- Make a stuffing with fresh breadcrumbs, chopped parsley, chopped celery, shallots, dill and pepper.
- Mix stuffing together with a beaten egg or a little dry white wine then insert stuffing into fish cavity and bake as above.

### Barbecue Fish Fillet
- Brush fish fillets with oil, sprinkle with spices such as Tandoori, paprika, chilli, curry, Cajun, Indian, Mexican or crushed garlic.
- Barbecue until tender using minimum mono/polyunsaturated oil.

or
- Place fish fillets on foil, sprinkle with lemon juice, pepper, dill and parsley.
- Wrap in foil and barbecue.

or
- Coat fish fillets with seasoned flour and barbecue in minimum mono/polyunsaturated oil.

or
- Use salmon, tuna or cooked fish to make fish cakes and cook on barbecue in minimum mono/polyunsaturated oil.

### Pan-Fried Fish
- Coat fish fillets with seasoned flour and shallow fry in minimal mono/polyunsaturated oil in a non-stick pan.

or
- Dip fish fillets in beaten egg and breadcrumbs and shallow fry in minimal mono/polyunsaturated oil in a non-stick pan.

### Fish In Filo
- Sprinkle fish with lemon juice and herbs and wrap in filo pastry.
- Brush pastry with skim milk and bake in 180°C oven.

### Fish Pie
- Steam or microwave fish, cut into small pieces and mix with **Mornay Sauce** p77. (A little curry powder may be added to taste and some chopped steamed vegetables such as celery, carrot, cauliflower, broccoli may also be added.)
- Place in casserole dish, top with mashed potato and sprinkle with grated low fat cheese.
- Bake in 180°C oven until heated through and cheese melts.

### Fish Cakes
- Combine salmon, tuna or cooked fish fillets with mashed potato, lemon juice, chopped onion, parsley and pepper.
- Shape into patties, coat with seasoned flour.
- Grill, barbecue or cook in non-stick pan with minimal oil.

## PAN-FRIED FISH WITH FRESH TOMATO SALSA

*3 tabsp flour (30g)*
*Pepper*
*1 tsp low sodium stock powder (2.5g)*
*500g barramundi or any white flesh fillets*
*2 tsp mono/polyunsaturated oil (10ml)*
*1 cup* **Fresh Tomato Basil Salsa** *p106*

- Dip fish in mixture of flour, pepper and stock powder and lightly fry in oil in a non-stick pan.
- Prepare and heat **Fresh Tomato Basil Salsa**
- Place fish on a plate and pour over sauce.

**Serves 4**

*Note*
If time is short a commercial salsa could be substituted. Add a little chopped fresh tomato to the salsa

*Variation*
Cook fish, add **Fresh Tomato Basil Salsa** and a little grated cheese. Grill or bake until cheese has melted.

NUTRIENTS PER SERVE

| KJ | Cal | Pro (g) | CHO (g) | Fibre (g) | T.fat (g) | S.fat (g) | Chol (mg) | Na (mg) |
|---|---|---|---|---|---|---|---|---|
| 794 | 190 | 27 | 8.5 | 1 | 5 | 1 | 76 | 138 |

## SALMON STEAKS

*2 tsp mono/polyunsaturated margarine (10g)*
*2 tsp grated orange zest*
*1 tabsp orange juice (20ml)*
*1 tsp lemon juice (5ml)*
*4 salmon steaks (600 grams)*

- Melt margarine in non-stick fry pan and add orange zest, orange juice, lemon juice and blend with a wooden spoon.
- Add salmon steaks and toss in marinade to coat thoroughly.
- Lightly poach, turning after 5 minutes on one side until lightly brown and liquid has evaporated.
- Serve with fresh green salad and brown rolls.

**Serves 4**

NUTRIENTS PER SERVE

| KJ | Cal | Pro (g) | CHO (g) | Fibre (g) | T.fat (g) | S.fat (g) | Chol (mg) | Na (mg) |
|---|---|---|---|---|---|---|---|---|
| 1229 | 295 | 27 | 0.6 | 0 | 20 | 1.7 | 105 | 150 |

FISH AND SEAFOOD

## CHILLI MUSSELS

*1kg fresh farm mussels*
*1 small finely chopped green capsicum (100g)*
*½ small finely chopped red capsicum (50g)*
*1 large finely chopped onion (150g)*
*3 crushed cloves garlic (9g)*
*1 stick finely chopped celery (75g)*
*1 medium finely chopped carrot (100g)*
*1 tsp low sodium chicken stock powder (2.5g)*
*1 can tomatoes (400g)*
*2 tabsp chopped chives (10g)*
*1 - 2 hot red chillies or ½ to 1 tsp of chilli sauce or dry chilli powder*
*1 cup white wine (250ml)*

*Chilli Mussels*

- Place fresh mussels in water until ready to use. Use a scrubbing brush to clean mussels and remove hairy bit by pulling to one end.
- Make a tomato mixture by bringing red and green capsicum, onion, garlic, celery, carrot, stock powder, tomatoes, chives, chillies and wine to the boil and simmer for 10 minutes.
- Add mussels, cover, return to the boil, reduce heat and simmer for 10 or 15 minutes or until most mussels are open.
- Serve mussels with fresh bread, with sauce as a soup.
- Any mussels that don't open should be discarded as they may not be fresh.

**Serves 4**

*Note*
This will serve 6 as an entrée.

NUTRIENTS PER SERVE

| KJ | Cal | Pro (g) | CHO (g) | Fibre (g) | T.fat (g) | S.fat (g) | Chol (mg) | Na (mg) |
|---|---|---|---|---|---|---|---|---|
| 1344 | 321 | 46 | 11 | 4 | 6 | 2.4 | 250 | 75 |

## SCALLOPS

*1 tabsp crushed ginger (10g)*
*1 large finely sliced onion (150g)*
*1 tabsp mono/polyunsaturated oil (20ml)*
*1 tsp sesame oil (5ml)*
*Scallops (500g)*
*1 small coarsely chopped bunch broccoli (200g)*
*2 medium julienne carrots (200g)*
*15 sliced fresh mushrooms (200g)*
*½ large finely sliced red capsicum (150g)*
*2 tabsp water (40ml)*
*1 tsp low sodium vegetable stock (2.5g)*
*2 tabsp sherry (40ml)*
*1 tabsp low sodium soy sauce (20ml)*
*3 - 4 bunches coarsely chopped bok choy (350g)*

- Stir-fry ginger and onion in oils for 3 to 4 minutes or until onion is soft.
- Add scallops and stir-fry for 5 minutes or until scallops are opaque. Do not overcook.
- Remove scallops to keep warm.
- Add broccoli, carrot, mushrooms, capsicum, water, stock powder, sherry and soy sauce.
- Stir-fry for 4 minutes.
- Add bok choy and stir-fry for a further 2 minutes.
- Add scallops, reheat and serve immediately.

**Serves 4**

*Note*
Substitute prawns or firm fish such as barramundi for scallops or use a combination. Other vegetables in season may be added or omitted as desired. Make sure to wash bok choy thoroughly to remove all sand.

NUTRIENTS PER SERVE

| KJ | Cal | Pro (g) | CHO (g) | Fibre (g) | T.fat (g) | S.fat (g) | Chol (mg) | Na (mg) |
|---|---|---|---|---|---|---|---|---|
| 898 | 215 | 23.4 | 9.3 | 8.4 | 8 | 1 | 41.5 | 468 |

***Stir Fry Scallops***

*Curried Prawns with Fish*

## CURRIED FISH

*Fresh fish fillet (500g)*
*1 tabsp mono/polyunsaturated oil (20ml)*
*1 medium chopped onion (100g)*
*2 crushed cloves garlic (6g)*
*2 bay leaves*
*4 cloves*
*¼ cup water (65ml)*
*1 tabsp curry powder (10g)*
*1 tsp ground coriander*
*1 tsp turmeric*
*1 tsp cumin*
*½ tsp chilli powder*
*1 tsp low sodium chicken stock powder (2.5g)*
*1 cup low fat evaporated milk (250ml)*
*Coconut essence*

- ❑ Cut fish fillet into 1cm cubes.
- ❑ Heat oil in a non-stick frypan.
- ❑ Gently sauté onion, garlic, bay leaves and cloves with water until soft.
- ❑ Add curry powder, coriander, turmeric, cumin, chilli powder, chicken stock powder and stir-fry to form a smooth paste.
- ❑ Add fish to mixture and stir-fry gently for 1 - 2 minutes. Add milk, cover and simmer for 5 minutes.
- ❑ Add coconut essence to taste.
- ❑ Serve immediately with plain boiled rice and other curry condiments.

**Serves 4**

*Variation*
**Curried Prawns with Fish** Prepare as in **Curried Fish**, adding a dozen cleaned prawns with tails. Serve on a bed of rice.

NUTRIENTS PER SERVE

| KJ | Cal | Pro (g) | CHO (g) | Fibre (g) | T.fat (g) | S.fat (g) | Chol (mg) | Na (mg) |
|---|---|---|---|---|---|---|---|---|
| 1041 | 249 | 32 | 9 | 1.3 | 10 | 2.5 | 91 | 203 |

## LEMON FISH ROLLS

*4 white fish fillets (400g)*

**Stuffing**
*2 slices crumbed wholemeal bread (50g)*
*2 tabsp chopped spring onion (20g)*
*1 tsp grated lemon zest*
*2 tsp lemon juice (10ml)*
*4 medium sliced mushrooms with stalks (50g)*
*1 egg (50g)*
*2 tabsp water (40ml)*
*2 tabsp dried breadcrumbs (15g)*
*1 tabsp mono/polyunsaturated oil (20ml)*

- ❑ Slit and butterfly fish fillets (e.g. king clip, schnapper) to form a large flat area.
- ❑ Mix breadcrumbs, spring onion, lemon zest, lemon juice, mushrooms and egg yolk together. **Note:** Keep egg white for crumbing.

# FISH AND SEAFOOD

**Lemon Fish Rolls**

- Place ¼ of stuffing on one end of each fillet.
- Beat egg white mix with water.
- Roll up fillets, dip in beaten egg white then coat with breadcrumbs.
- Heat oil in a heavy based fry pan and fry fish until flaky, about 5 minutes each side.

**Serves 4**

NUTRIENTS PER SERVE

| KJ | Cal | Pro (g) | CHO (g) | Fibre (g) | T.fat (g) | S.fat (g) | Chol (mg) | Na (mg) |
|---|---|---|---|---|---|---|---|---|
| 910 | 217 | 25 | 8 | 1.4 | 10 | 2 | 117 | 190 |

- Pour over fish.
- Bake in a 180°C oven for 20 minutes or until fish is opaque and flakes easily.
- Serve with ½ cup boiled new mint potatoes, silverbeet and carrot coins.

**Serves 4**

NUTRIENTS PER SERVE

| KJ | Cal | Pro (g) | CHO (g) | Fibre (g) | T.fat (g) | S.fat (g) | Chol (mg) | Na (mg) |
|---|---|---|---|---|---|---|---|---|
| 914 | 218 | 28 | 3 | 1 | 10 | 2.2 | 88 | 111 |

## BARRAMUNDI ALMONDINE

*500g filleted barramundi or other white fleshed fish*
*2 tabsp wholemeal flour (20g)*
*Salt to taste*
*¼ tsp freshly ground black pepper*
*2 tabsp chopped spring onions (10g)*
*2 tabsp slivered almonds (20g)*
*2 tabsp mono/polyunsaturated margarine (40g)*
*2 tsp lemon zest*
*2 tabsp lemon juice (40ml)*
*Lemon wedges as garnish*

- Dust barramundi with flour mixed with salt and pepper and place in well-greased baking dish.
- Sprinkle spring onions and slivered almonds over the top.
- Melt margarine. Add lemon zest and lemon juice.

**Barramundi Almondine**

*Dhufish with Cucumber Sauce*

## DHUFISH WITH CUCUMBER SAUCE

*1 tabsp chopped fresh dill or 1 tsp dried*
*1 tabsp lime or lemon juice (20ml)*
*Freshly ground black pepper*
*2 crushed cloves garlic (6g)*
*2 tsp mono/polyunsaturated oil (10ml)*
*500g dhufish or white flesh fish*
*½ cup chopped cucumber (85g)*
*½ cup non fat yoghurt (125ml)*
*2 tabsp finely chopped chives (20g)*
*Freshly ground black pepper*

- Make a paste of dill, lime juice, black pepper, garlic and oil.
- Rub into fillets of fish and leave for a ½ hour or more.
- Pan fry fillets in a non-stick pan or grill until a fork easily pierces the flesh.
- Mix cucumber, yoghurt, chives and black pepper together to form a sauce.
- Heat sauce in a microwave for 1 to 2 minutes or until warmed through.
- Place fish on plate and pour over sauce.
- Serve with a squeeze of fresh lime juice and a sprig of dill.

**Serves 4**

### Nutritional Tip
Fish is low in fat (especially saturated fat) and rich in Omega 3 fatty acids. This is recommended for heart disease and cancer prevention.

NUTRIENTS PER SERVE

| KJ | Cal | Pro (g) | CHO (g) | Fibre (g) | T.fat (g) | S.fat (g) | Chol (mg) | Na (mg) |
|---|---|---|---|---|---|---|---|---|
| 781 | 186 | 28 | 3 | 0.5 | 7 | 2 | 91 | 135 |

## TUNA HOTPOT

*4 medium size tomatoes (400g)*
*455g canned water packed tuna (drained 312g)*
*5 medium cooked potatoes (500g)*
*2 cups **Cheese Sauce** p108*
*¼ cup grated less than 10% fat cheese (30g)*

- Slice tomatoes; place half in the bottom of a 1-litre greased casserole dish.
- Drain and flake tuna and place on top of tomatoes.
- Add remaining tomatoes and then potatoes which have been cooked and sliced.
- Prepare **Cheese Sauce** and pour over potato tuna mixture.
- Sprinkle extra cheese on top.
- Bake in 180°C oven for 20 minutes.

**Serves 4**

NUTRIENTS PER SERVE

| KJ | Cal | Pro (g) | CHO (g) | Fibre (g) | T.fat (g) | S.fat (g) | Chol (mg) | Na (mg) |
|---|---|---|---|---|---|---|---|---|
| 1362 | 327 | 35 | 27 | 3.8 | 8 | 1.9 | 54 | 528 |

*Schnapper Fillets Julienne*

## SCHNAPPER FILLETS JULIENNE

*500g schnapper or any white flesh fillets*
*1 tsp lemon juice (5ml)*
*Black pepper*
*²/₃ cup dry cider or dry white wine (165ml)*
*1 medium julienne carrot (100g)*
*½ small julienne zucchini (50g)*
*2 sticks julienne celery (150g)*
*½ medium julienne capsicum (75g)*
*2 tsp mono/polyunsaturated margarine (10g)*
*1 tabsp plain flour (10g)*
*½ cup low fat evaporated milk (125ml)*
*1 tsp chopped parsley (5g)*

- Wash and dry the fish and cut into 4 portions.
- Sprinkle fish with the lemon juice and black pepper.
- Place fish in a lightly greased flat casserole dish and add 100ml dry cider or wine. (Reserve remainder.)
- Cover and microwave on **High** for 10 minutes or baked for 15 minutes at 180°C.
- Cook carrot, zucchini, celery and capsicum with the remaining dry cider or wine, covered in microwave or stir-fried until tender crisp.
- Drain juices from fish and vegetables and reserve.
- Place fish onto a serving plate.
- Melt margarine, mix in flour and blend in reserved juices from fish and vegetables and milk.
- Cook in microwave or on stove, stirring occasionally until smooth and thick.
- Add chopped parsley and pour around fish fillets. Arrange julienne vegetables on the top of each serve.
- Reheat before serving.

**Serves 4**

NUTRIENTS PER SERVE

| KJ | Cal | Pro (g) | CHO (g) | Fibre (g) | T.fat (g) | S.fat (g) | Chol (mg) | Na (mg) |
|---|---|---|---|---|---|---|---|---|
| 928 | 221 | 30 | 8 | 2 | 5 | 2 | 89 | 195 |

## FISH FILLET PUFF

*500g of white flesh fish such as schnapper*
*1 egg white (30g)*
*2 tsp mono/polyunsaturated margarine (10g)*
*2 tabsp of slivered almonds (20g)*

- Place the fish in a lightly greased casserole dish.
- Beat egg white and fold in melted margarine.
- Cover the fish with egg white mixture and sprinkle with slivered almonds.
- Bake in 180°C oven for 15 minutes until brown on top and fish is opaque.
- Simple but good for entertaining.

**Serves 4**

NUTRIENTS PER SERVE

| KJ | Cal | Pro (g) | CHO (g) | Fibre (g) | T.fat (g) | S.fat (g) | Chol (mg) | Na (mg) |
|---|---|---|---|---|---|---|---|---|
| 784 | 187 | 28 | 0.3 | 0.6 | 8.4 | 1.9 | 88 | 121 |

## Vegetables and Grains

Vegetables and grains are important sources of energy, carbohydrate, vitamins and minerals. Apart from the many recipes included, this section offers valuable tips on buying, storing, preparing and serving both vegetables and grains.

### Low Joule Low Carbohydrate Vegetables

Low joule vegetables such as asparagus, broccoli, tomatoes, pumpkin and carrot will add variety, fibre and nutrients. Always try to include colour with each meal such as choosing a green, yellow and red. It will look good and be good for you.

*Asparagus 84*
  *Asparagus with Cheese Sauce 84*
  *Asparagus with Lemon Sauce 84*
  *Asparagus Soufflé 84*
  *Marinated Asparagus Salad 84*
  *Savoury Cases with Asparagus 84*
  *Cocktail Puffs with Asparagus 85*
  *Asparagus Rolls 85*
*Beans 85*
  *Green Beans and Cherry Tomatoes 85*
  *Green Bean Bundles 85*
*Broccoli 85*
  *Cheesy Broccoli 85*
  *Lemon Broccoli 85*
*Brussel Sprouts 85*
  *Brussel Sprouts with Baby Corn 85*
  *Lemon Brussel Sprouts 85*
  *Seasoned Brussel Sprout Salad 85*
*Cabbage 86*
  *Sweet and Sour red Cabbage 86*
  *Cabbage and Bacon 86*
*Capsicum 86*
*Peeled Capsicum 86*
*Cauliflower 86*
  *Cauliflower Cheese 86*
  *Baked Cauliflower Cheese 86*
  *Mustard Tarragon Cauliflower 87*
*Eggplant 87*
  *Stuffed Eggplant 87*
*Grilled Eggplant 88*
*Globe Artichokes 87*
*Stuffed Artichokes 87*
*Pumpkin 88*
*Spinach 88*
  *Spinach Triangles 88*
*Savoury Spinach 88*
*Tomatoes 89*
*Sun Dried Tomatoes 89*
*Zucchini 90*
  *Savoury Tomato Zucchini 90*

## ASPARAGUS

Fresh asparagus is available in spring. Prepare by discarding the woody bottom 1/3 of the asparagus (use this in a sauce or a soup). Tie the remaining asparagus spears with string so that they can stand upright unsupported. Place in a tall saucepan of boiling water so that the ends are immersed but the tips are just steamed. Cover and cook for 8 to 10 minutes. Serve with pepper or crushed garlic and margarine. Include fresh chilled, canned or pickled asparagus in salad platters, sandwiches or salads.

**Asparagus with Cheese Sauce**
Prepare fresh asparagus as directed, arrange attractively on a plate and pour over prepared **Cheese Sauce** p108. Sprinkle with paprika.

**Asparagus with Lemon Sauce**
Prepare fresh asparagus as directed.
Prepare **Low Fat White Sauce** p108. Flavour with a little lemon juice and black pepper. Pour over asparagus and serve.

**Asparagus Soufflé**
Substitute canned asparagus for broccoli in **Broccoli Souffle** p52.

**Marinated Asparagus Salad**
Pour 'No Oil Italian Dressing' or **Balsamic French Dressing** p95 over freshly cooked and drained asparagus. Chill and serve cold as part of a salad.

**Savoury Cases with Asparagus Sauce**
Prepare **Savoury Cases** p130. Prepare **Low Fat White Sauce** p108 substituting some of the milk with the juice of canned asparagus.
Stir in drained asparagus. Heat and serve with 1

tabsp of mixture per case.

**Cocktail Puffs with Asparagus**
Prepare **Choux Pastry** p131 making small Choux Puffs.
Prepare **Asparagus Sauce** as directed in **Savoury Cases with Asparagus Sauce** p84. Make a slit in the side of Choux Puffs and remove any excess. Fill, reheat and serve.

**Asparagus Rolls**
Cut crust off fresh multigrain bread, spread with **Hommos** p39 or **Yoghurt Cheese** p39. Cut cooked or canned asparagus spears to fit, roll up and pin with tooth pick and chill before serving.

## BEANS

There are several varieties of beans, the smaller green or french beans or the larger coarser runner beans or snake, wax or yellow beans. Green beans should be firm, crisp, of bright colour and non wrinkled without damaged ends or discoloured patches. They are better young.

*Preparation and Cooking*
Remove strings if present and cut and tail ends; wash well. They may be steamed or microwaved for 4 to 5 minutes until they are tender but maintain their colour.
Serve with black pepper and a spot of olive oil. The addition of a few toasted almonds will dress up beans. Green beans may be left whole if very small, sliced on the angle or straight across.

**Green Beans and Cherry Tomatoes**
Prepare and cook green beans until just tender. Add cherry tomatoes and heat for 1 minute only so they don't split.
Sprinkle toasted pinenuts on top and serve.

**Green Bean Bundles**
Tie raw beans in servable bundles with spring onion or bacon. Steam or microwave and serve.

## BROCCOLI

Broccoli is a very nutritious and versatile vegetable which is available fresh all year around. A valuable source of vitamin C, it may be used cooked or raw in salads.
Care and storage is very important as broccoli will deteriorate rapidly after picking if not refrigerated. The head should be dark green and tightly packed. Old or poorly stored broccoli will start to go yellow and flower. It should be discarded.

*Preparation and Cooking*
To prepare broccoli for cooking, remove thick stalks and cut broccoli into bite size florets. It may be boiled in minimum water for 4 to 5 minutes or steamed for an equal length of time. Microwave a small head for 4 to 5 minutes on **High** in a covered dish with only the water after washing adhering to it. Broccoli should be served immediately as holding after cooking will allow it to become strong flavoured and soft. The stalks may be used, but peel first and allow a little longer cooking.
Broccoli may be used in **Broccoli Soup** (refer to **Cauliflower Soup** p43) and in **Broccoli Soufflé** p52 or **Baked Frittata** p52.

**Cheesy Broccoli**
Cook broccoli until just tender. Prepare **Cheese Sauce** p108. Pour over broccoli, reheat for 1 minute and serve. Sprinkle with chopped pinenuts if desired.

**Lemon Broccoli**
Cook broccoli until just tender. Prepare **Low Fat White Sauce** p108. Flavour with lemon zest and black pepper. Pour over broccoli, reheat for 1 minute and serve.

## BRUSSEL SPROUTS

Use small tightly packed brussel sprouts. Remove any outer yellowing leaves. Cut off excess stem. Cut a cross in the base of each to assist in cooking. Wash well. Cook or steam for 6 to 8 minutes or until fork pierces the brussel sprout easily but the green colour is maintained. They go well with **Baked Ratatouille** p60.

**Brussel Sprouts with Baby Corn**
Stir-fry brussel sprouts with lean bacon, chopped hazelnuts and baby corn in a little oil and water.

**Lemon Brussel Sprouts**
Season with a little nutmeg, lemon or black pepper.

**Seasoned Brussel Sprout Salad**
Pour 'No Oil Dressing' over cooked and drained brussel sprouts and chill.
To serve sprinkle with chopped nuts and peeled red capsicum strips. See **Peeled Capsicum** p86.

## CABBAGE

Cabbage is a low kilojoule vegetable which is available in different varieties such as English, Chinese, Savoy and Red. All contain high fibre and moderate quantities of vitamin C and carotene. Cabbage will store well in the refrigerator if covered with plastic wrap and not cut. As soon as the vegetable is cut it should be used to avoid any vitamin loss.

Just before cooking cabbage, remove all tough centre stalks; wash and shred finely. It should be boiled quickly in as little water as possible until just crisp. Do not overcook or nutrient value will be lost.

Serve cabbage as a plain vegetable with pepper or with the addition of a little cinnamon and margarine.

Prepare **Red Cabbage Salad** p101 or use in **Vegetable Parcels** p60.

### Sweet and Sour Red Cabbage
Cook red cabbage with the addition of a little vinegar, apple and brown sugar.

### Cabbage and Bacon
Use Savoy or English cabbage, steamed with the addition of a little lean bacon, turkey bacon or lean ham.

## CAPSICUM

There are yellow, green and red capsicum, of which the latter is the sweetest. They should be bright of colour and firm with no blemishes. The skin is tough and indigestible and often causes wind and bloating in people with sensitive stomachs. If this is the case, refer to **Peeled Capsicum** p86.

It is an excellent source of vitamin C and rich in carotene which is made into vitamin A by the body. It is one of the most nutritious vegetables.

Use them in salads such as **Chinese Mixed Vegetable Salad** p102, in soups such as '**CCC**' p43, as a dip e.g. **Red Capsicum Dip** p38, in sauces such as **Italian Pasta Sauce** p104, and in vegetable dishes such as **Mediterranean Pie** p61. The list is endless. Buy in bulk, make **Peeled Capsicum** p86.

## PEELED CAPSICUM

*Capsicum (red, green or yellow) (200g)*

- Cut capsicum in quarters, remove seeds and flatten.
- Place flesh side down under a hot grill.
- Grill for about 10 minutes or until skin is black and charred then place in a plastic bag and leave to sweat for 10 minutes.
- Remove capsicum and peel off skin with fingers. It usually comes away quite easily.
- Use in salads or recipes as called for.
- May be kept by placing in olive oil, garlic and herbs in the refrigerator.

**Serves 4**

*Note*
Use oil from capsicum in salad dressings for additional flavour.

NUTRIENTS PER SERVE

| KJ | Cal | Pro (g) | CHO (g) | Fibre (g) | T.fat (g) | S.fat (g) | Chol (mg) | Na (mg) |
|---|---|---|---|---|---|---|---|---|
| 52 | 13 | 0.85 | 2 | 0.6 | 0.1 | 0 | 0 | 0.5 |

## CAULIFLOWER

Cauliflower should be crisp and white with no dark brown or green spots. It stores well in the refrigerator if sealed with plastic wrap. Cauliflower is a low kilojoule vegetable which is adaptable to many dishes. It is excellent in a soup or casserole to give body without kilojoules. It may be served raw as an accompaniment to dips or as part of a salad.

To prepare, wash well and section florets into bite size pieces. Boil, steam or microwave until just tender crisp.

Prepare **Cauliflower Soup** p42 or **Baked Frittata** p52.

### Cauliflower Cheese
Prepare ½ quantity of **Cheese Sauce** p108 and add ½ teaspoon of mustard. Prepare florets and steam or microwave until just soft. Place cauliflower in a dish, pour over sauce and serve. Substitute some of the milk with the cauliflower water if desired.

### Baked Cauliflower Cheese
Prepare **Cauliflower Cheese** as directed, but place in a baking dish and pour over sauce. Sprinkle with 2 tabsp of breadcrumbs mixed with 2 tabsp of finely grated less than 10% fat cheese. Bake 20 minutes at 180°C or until

brown and heated through.

**Mustard Tarragon Cauliflower**
Prepare cauliflower and **Low Fat White Sauce** p108, which has been flavoured with 1 tabsp fresh or 1/2 tsp dried tarragon and 1/2 tsp dried mustard. Pour sauce over cauliflower, sprinkle with a little parsley and serve.

## GLOBE ARTICHOKES

Choose plump, dull green or purple tinged artichokes with tightly packed leaves and a firm stem.

*Preparation and Cooking*
Wash and trim base to sit flat and remove a few outer leaves until you see the yellow green base of the leaves. Cut off the top third and trim the top of any prickly leaves. Rub all cut surfaces with lemon to prevent discolouration. Place each one on a plate, cover with plastic wrap and microwave on **High** for 3 - 4 minutes or until the centre is soft.
Serve with margarine and lemon or a vinaigrette dressing. Scrape out the choke from the middle and then eat the heart.
Prepare **Stuffed Artichokes** p87. Use artichoke hearts in **Mediterranean Pie** p61.

## STUFFED ARTICHOKES

4 artichokes (500g)
2 slices crumbed wholegrain bread (50g)
1 tabsp capers
1 tabsp chopped parsley
2 crushed cloves garlic (6g)
Black pepper
1/2 cup 17% low fat mozzarella cheese (60g)
2 tabsp water (40ml)
1 tabsp lemon juice (20ml)
Mono-unsaturated oil spray

- Cut 2cm from top of artichoke.
- Cut off its base to sit flat.
- Turn upright and cut off sharp points of artichoke leaves with scissors.
- Rinse and place in microwave dish, cover with plastic wrap and microwave on **High** for 8 to 10 minutes. It will be done when easily pierced with a fork.
- Turn upside down and when cool enough to handle remove the hairy choke and purple leaves in the centre.
- Turn upright and place on baking tray. Fan or open out leaves.
- Combine fresh breadcrumbs, capers, parsley, garlic, black pepper and 4 tabsp of mozzarella cheese. (Reserve 2 tabsp.)
- Divide filling between artichokes, dropping between leaves. Sprinkle with water, lemon juice and remaining 2 tabsp of cheese.
- Spray lightly with oil.
- Bake at 180°C for 10 to 15 minutes or until cheese topping is crisp.

**Serves 4**

*Note*
Serve as an entrée or luncheon dish. To eat, scrape flesh and crumbs from bottom of leaves using teeth. Heart may be cut up with a knife and fork. This is a finger meal so supply a finger bowl!

NUTRIENTS PER SERVE

| KJ | Cal | Pro (g) | CHO (g) | Fibre (g) | T.fat (g) | S.fat (g) | Chol (mg) | Na (mg) |
|---|---|---|---|---|---|---|---|---|
| 403 | 96 | 9 | 7 | 2 | 3 | 2 | 9 | 123 |

## EGGPLANT

Eggplant are often known as aubergine or eggfruit. The most common varieties are either a medium size globe or sausage shape. Colour often varies from purple through to white and green. They should be a bright colour with a smooth tight skin without wrinkles or blemishes. They are low in kilojoules and carbohydrate and so are ideal for adding to stews, casseroles, curries and soups. They make good dips and are excellent grilled and served hot or cold in sandwiches, rolls and Focaccia. Don't forget to serve them as a vegetable.
Extend sauces like **Italian Pasta Sauce** p104, **Sweet and Sour Sauce** p106 or **Spaghetti Sauce** p104 with extra chopped and peeled eggplant.
Try **Eggplant Soup** p43, **Baked Ratatouille** p60 or **Mediterranean Pie** p61. Make **Grilled Eggplant** p88 and have on hand.

**Stuffed Eggplant**
Cut an eggplant in half lengthwise, hollow out, leaving a 1cm rim. Roughly chop eggplant and stir-fry with onion and garlic. Add canned sweetcorn, tomato and leftover chopped roast meat. Vary ingredients according to what is available. Bake at 180°C for 40minutes.

## VEGETABLES AND GRAINS

## GRILLED EGGPLANT

*1 medium eggplant (300g)*
*2 tsp Worcestershire sauce (10g)*
*2 tsp olive oil (10g)*
*2 tsp lemon juice (10ml)*

- Peel and slice eggplant in 1cm slices.
- Place in salted water for 1 hour to extract juices. Dry on kitchen paper.
- Mix Worcestershire sauce, olive oil and lemon juice together for marinade.
- Brush marinade on one side of eggplant.
- Place under griller and grill for about 4 to 5 minutes or until beginning to brown.
- Turn, brush with remaining marinade and grill for a further 3 - 5 minutes.
- Serve with **Fresh Tomato Basil Salsa** p106.

**Serves 4**

NUTRIENTS PER SERVE

| KJ | Cal | Pro (g) | CHO (g) | Fibre (g) | T.fat (g) | S.fat (g) | Chol (mg) | Na (mg) |
|---|---|---|---|---|---|---|---|---|
| 158 | 38 | 0.85 | 2 | 2 | 3 | 0.35 | 0.05 | 30 |

## PUMPKIN

Choose a firm dark Queensland blue, Japanese or butternut pumpkin. The flesh should be hard, firm and a dark yellow colour.
Peel and remove and discard the seeds. Place in a covered dish and microwave until soft.
If you need pumpkin purée, then wrap unpeeled pumpkin with plastic wrap, make a couple of holes and microwave until soft. Leave to cool and then the flesh may be scooped out. Pumpkin may be baked with the skin on for extra fibre.
Use in **Vegetable Lasagne** p59, **Cheesy Pumpkin Ricotta Bake** p54, **Baked Frittata** p52, **Zucchini Slice** p55 and in **Pumpkin and Ginger Soup** p44.
Pumpkin is a high fibre, low glycaemic index vegetable which is high in carotene. Add it to dishes as often as possible and it can even be used as a pasta sauce or a spread on rolls or Lavash bread.

## SPINACH

Spinach is a general term that may refer to English spinach or silverbeet. In this book, spinach is the English variety but fresh young silverbeet may be used instead.

Spinach is high in iron although not readily absorbed by the body due to the presence of oxalic acid. Silverbeet is high in iron as well but has much higher sodium levels.
Frozen chopped English spinach is handy to have on hand and is fine in dishes such as **Spinach Dip** p37.
To prepare spinach or silverbeet, wash well 2 to 3 times to remove all sand. With English spinach cut off stems with scissors before washing then cook and chop. Silverbeet should have the white stems removed and each leaf individually washed. Finely slice before cooking.
Use raw spinach in **Lasagne** p68 or in quiches or spinach slices. Serve cooked, on its own with freshly ground black pepper and lemon juice. Prepare **Savoury Spinach** p88.

**Spinach Triangles**
Mix spinach with ricotta or fetta, garlic and an egg and place on strips of filo and fold to make a parcel. Spray with oil and bake in a 180°C oven for 15 minutes or until crisp and brown. Serve hot.

## SAVOURY SPINACH

*2 bunches spinach ready for cooking (400g)*
*1 small chopped onion (75g)*
*2 slices lean chopped ham or turkey bacon (50g)*
*1 tsp mono/polyunsaturated oil (5g)*

- Steam or microwave spinach for 2 to 3 minutes or until soft.
- Drain and chop.
- Stir-fry onion and ham or turkey bacon in oil.
- Add spinach, stir-fry for 1 minute and serve.

**Serves 6**

*Variation*
**Savoury Pinenut Spinach** Omit ham and stir-fry 2 tabsp of pinenuts with onion and oil.

NUTRIENTS PER SERVE

| KJ | Cal | Pro (g) | CHO (g) | Fibre (g) | T.fat (g) | S.fat (g) | Chol (mg) | Na (mg) |
|---|---|---|---|---|---|---|---|---|
| 138 | 33 | 3.4 | 1.3 | 2 | 1.5 | 0.3 | 5 | 83 |

*Savoury Spinach*

## TOMATOES

Tomatoes are really a fruit rather than a vegetable, but they are used more as a vegetable and hence included in this section.

They are one of the most versatile fruit or vegetables. Use them to add flavour in many basic dishes.

Three main types are popular in Australia; the normal tomato, the Roman or pear shaped tomato and the small or cherry tomato.

Tomatoes are rich in vitamin C and carotene which forms vitamin A.

Best when ripened on the vine, they should be a bright red colour, firm and sweet. Store in the refrigerator. You can grow extra and make sauce in bulk or prepare **Sundried Tomatoes** p89.

Often a simple meal will be complete with a slice or half of a tomato. Dress it up with chopped chives or parsley or grill with grated low fat cheese until just heated through. Cut into wedges, slices or seed and cut into julienne strips. Add to salads or stews and casseroles. For convenience, use canned tomatoes which come whole, peeled or chopped for casseroles and sauces.

Fresh tomatoes form the basis of dishes such as **Bruschetta** p40 or **Fresh Tomato Basil Salsa** p106. They are the basis of **Spaghetti Bolognaise** p70 or **Chicken with Barbecue Sauce** p63.

## SUNDRIED TOMATOES

*12 Roman or pear shaped tomatoes (1200g)*
*Fresh mixed herbs*
*Salt to taste*
*Freshly ground black pepper*
*4 crushed cloves garlic (12g)*
*Olive oil to cover*

- Cut tomatoes into 6ths and scoop out seeds.
- Place on a rack and sprinkle liberally with salt and then fresh mixed herbs (oregano, thyme, basil). Use dried if fresh not available.
- Add freshly ground black pepper and garlic.
- Cover with a light net and place in the sun to dry for 2 to 3 days or until they are leathery. They may be dried in the oven on a tray for 6 to 8 hours at very low heat.
- Place in a jar and cover with olive oil and leave to soften and mature for at least 2 to 3 weeks.

**Serves 36 x 2 pieces**

*To Use*
Remove from oil, pat dry with kitchen paper and cut in strips. They are quite tart and add a unique flavour to many salads. Use leftover oil in cooking or salad dressings. Analysis is done allowing 1 tsp oil per serve; some will adhere after blotting dry. No allowance is made for salt.

NUTRIENTS PER SERVE

| KJ | Cal | Pro (g) | CHO (g) | Fibre (g) | T.fat (g) | S.fat (g) | Chol (mg) | Na (mg) |
|---|---|---|---|---|---|---|---|---|
| 109 | 26 | 0.4 | 0.8 | 0.5 | 2.4 | 0.3 | 0 | 3 |

VEGETABLES AND GRAINS

*Savoury Tomato Zucchini*

## High Joule High Carbohydrate Vegetables and Grains

Always try to use a variety of starchy vegetables and grains for energy in each meal. Potatoes, sweet potatoes, corn, peas and then the grains such as rice, pasta, polenta and cous cous are the basis of the main energy foods.
High carbohydrate vegetables are equivalent to bread and must be considered as such when planning menus. Examples of low glycaemic index vegetables and grains are polenta or corn, pasta and sweet potato.

*Cous Cous 90*
   *Cous Cous 90*
   *Fruity Cous Cous 91*
*Noodles 91*
*Pasta 91*
*Peas 92*
*Polenta 92*
*Grilled Fine Polenta 92*
*Rich Coarse Polenta 92*
*Potato 93*
   *Baked Potato 93*
   *Stuffed Baked Potato 93*
*Armadillo Potatoes 93*
*Crunchy Cajun Chips 94*
*Scallop Potatoes 93*
*Rice 94*
*Sunflower Rice 94*
   *Steamed Rice 94*

## ZUCCHINI

Zucchini or courgettes are a low kilojoule inexpensive vegetable readily available all year. You should look for ones of medium size with firm flesh and shiny skins. Baby zucchini are simply miniature versions. They are attractive in some dishes, particularly salads.
To prepare zucchini wash well and remove ends. Peeling is not necessary. Either slice or cut into julienne strips. Steam or microwave in minimum water for 5 to 6 minutes and serve immediately. Do not overcook zucchini as it loses much of its appeal and becomes soft.
Make **Zucchini Soup**, a variation of **Cauliflower Soup** p43 or **Baked Ratatouille** p60. Serve zucchini with fresh herbs and garlic.

**Savoury Tomato Zucchini**
Place sliced zucchini in a greased baking dish. Pour **Cooked Tomato Savoury** p105 over zucchini and heat in a 180°C oven for 10 or 15 minutes. May add grated cheese and breadcrumbs before baking if desired.

## COUS COUS

Cous Cous is made from wheat and may be purchased as white or wholemeal. A higher fibre meal plan is always preferred. It is an easy grain to prepare as it requires the minimum of cooking and lends itself to the addition of spices and dried fruit. It is often used in combination with middle eastern dishes.

## COUS COUS

*1 small finely chopped onion (75g)*
*1 crushed clove garlic (3g)*
*1 tsp low sodium chicken stock powder (2.5g)*
*1 tsp mono/polyunsaturated oil (5g)*
*1 tabsp water (20ml)*
*1 cup wholemeal cous cous (170g)*
*2 cups boiling water (500ml)*
*Zest of 1 lemon*

# VEGETABLES AND GRAINS

*Fruity Cous Cous*

- ❏ Lightly stir-fry onion, garlic and stock powder in oil and 1 tabsp of water in a non-stick frying pan until soft and golden.
- ❏ Place cous cous in a bowl and pour over 2 cups of boiling water.
- ❏ Add onion mixture to cous cous with lemon zest.
- ❏ Leave to soften for 10 minutes.
- ❏ Cover with plastic wrap, poke a couple of holes to allow steam to escape and microwave for 5 minutes on **High**.
- ❏ Fluff with a fork and serve.

**Serves 6 x ½ cup (Total 3 cups)**

### Variation

For **Fruity Cous Cous** add 3 tabsp currants (35g), 3 tabsp slivered toasted almonds (30g), 2 tabsp chopped mint and 2 tabsp finely chopped coriander.

NUTRIENTS PER SERVE

| KJ | Cal | Pro (g) | CHO (g) | Fibre (g) | T.fat (g) | S.fat (g) | Chol (mg) | Na (mg) |
|---|---|---|---|---|---|---|---|---|
| 332 | 80 | 2 | 15 | 1 | 1 | 0.2 | 0 | 21 |

## NOODLES

Noodles are associated with Asian cooking and are based on wheat or rice. As rice gives a very fast absorption of carbohydrate, it must be consumed with care. Those based on wheat are better. Noodle dishes have been included such as **Laksa** p46 and **Lombok Fish Soup** p45. Use noodles in combination with stir fries, with kebabs and casseroles and stews.

## PASTA

Pasta, a staple of Italian cuisine, has become more popular in Australia, and its low glycaemic index makes it ideal in a diabetic diet.
It may be made with wholemeal or regular flour and flavoured with such vegetables as spinach, carrots or pumpkin.
It comes in many different shapes such as lasagne, fettuccine or spaghetti. You may buy it fresh or dried. One half cup cooked is equivalent in carbohydrate to 1 slice of bread. It is important to restrict other concentrated carbohydrate foods when pasta forms a significant part of the meal. Use pasta instead of potato or rice or as a main meal dish as in **Macaroni Cheese** p56 or **Gnocchi** p58. Refer to the **Main Meal** section under **Pasta and Grain Dishes** p55.

VEGETABLES AND GRAINS

## PEAS

Use frozen bright green peas which are not icy. Ice indicates they have been allowed to partially thaw and been refrozen.
Cover and cook in microwave on **High** or steam 4 to 5 minutes until just tender. Flavour with a little finely chopped white or Spanish onion or with chopped mint before cooking.
Peas have a low glycaemic index and may supplement or replace other starchy or grains such as potatoes, rice or pasta.

## POLENTA

Polenta may be instant, regular, fine or coarse. The type used will depend on the recipe and time available. Polenta is ground corn and has a low glycaemic index.
The long cooking regular variety will take some minutes of constant stirring on top of the stove or periodically stirring in the microwave. If time is short then the instant is an ideal solution. The fine is good as polenta slices — use like toast and season or sprinkle with various herbs.
Prepare **Grilled Fine Polenta** 92.
A substitute for potato is the coarse polenta in **Rich Coarse Polenta** p92. Use as an accompaniment for stews and casseroles. This is very popular in Italian cooking.

## GRILLED FINE POLENTA

*1 cup fine polenta (180g)*
*4 cups boiling water (1 litre)*

❑ Bring water to the boil, add polenta in a steady stream and stir until smooth.
❑ Continue to cook and stir periodically for 5 to 10 minutes or until a thick porridge type consistency is formed.
❑ Spread mixture in a lightly greased 24cm by 32cm Swiss roll tin and allow to cool.
❑ Slice into rectangles, place under grill and cook until golden brown.
❑ Serve to accompany **Lentil Sauce** p105, **Baked Ratatouille** p60 and stew-type mixtures.
❑ This freezes well so keep some available.
**Serves 8 x 1/2 cup (Total 4 cups )**

*Variation*
Spray 1 large or 8 individual moulds with oil. Fill with hot polenta and allow to cool and set. Unmould on to plate and reheat. This presents well.

NUTRIENTS PER SERVE

| KJ | Cal | Pro (g) | CHO (g) | Fibre (g) | T.fat (g) | S.fat (g) | Chol (mg) | Na (mg) |
|---|---|---|---|---|---|---|---|---|
| 311 | 75 | 2 | 16 | 0.6 | 0.4 | 0.06 | 0 | 0.2 |

## RICH COARSE POLENTA

*3 cups of water (750ml)*
*1 tsp low sodium chicken stock powder (2.5g)*
*1 can low fat evaporated milk (375ml)*
*1 cup coarse polenta (180g)*
*1/2 medium finely chopped onion (50g)*
*1 crushed clove garlic (3g)*
*1 tabsp finely chopped basil*
*1 tsp mono/polyunsaturated oil (5ml)*
*1 tabsp water (20ml)*
*2 tabsp parmesan cheese (18g)*
*Freshly ground black pepper*

❑ Bring 3 cups of water, stock powder and milk to the boil in a large microwave dish.
❑ Using a whisk, beat in polenta to form a smooth mixture.
❑ Microwave on **High** for 15 minutes, stopping to stir every 4 to 5 minutes.
❑ Remove from heat.
❑ Stir-fry onion, garlic and basil in oil and 1 tabsp of water.
❑ Stir into polenta with parmesan cheese.
❑ Add freshly ground black pepper to taste.
❑ Serve immediately or place in greased ring mould and microwave for a further 2 minutes on **High**.
❑ Allow to cool before removing from mould.
**Serves 8 x 1/2 cup (Total 4 cups)**

*Variation*
**Traditional Cooking** Prepare this in a saucepan on the stove. Cook and stir for about 10 to 20 minutes or until the polenta is thick, taking care it doesn't burn. Cooking time may vary depending on the type of polenta used. The instant is much faster than the traditional.

*Note*
Excellent with a **Fresh Tomato Basil Salsa** p106 or use in **Polenta Pie** p58. May substitute non fat milk for a lighter polenta.

NUTRIENTS PER SERVE

| KJ | Cal | Pro (g) | CHO (g) | Fibre (g) | T.fat (g) | S.fat (g) | Chol (mg) | Na (mg) |
|---|---|---|---|---|---|---|---|---|
| 580 | 141 | 7 | 21 | 0.8 | 3 | 1 | 7 | 97 |

## VEGETABLES AND GRAINS

## POTATO

Potato is a starchy vegetable that can be used instead of bread. Choose firm potatoes without blemishes or decay that are not sprouting. Store in a cool dry cupboard that is well ventilated. Make sure not to use any with a green tinge. Potatoes may be peeled or not and boiled or microwaved, mashed, baked, oven roasted or used in any number of the recipes that we have suggested. Try **Armadillo Potatoes** p93, **Crunchy Cajun Chips** p94 or **Scalloped Potatoes** p93 as a separate accompaniment to the main meal. Prepare **German Potato Salad** p100 for a barbecue or buffet meal.

*Rich Coarse Polenta p92*

### Baked Potato
Bake medium to large well-scrubbed, pricked potatoes about 1 hour at 180°C or 5 to 7 minutes on **High** in the microwave until soft. Time will depend on the number and size of the potatoes. Cut a cross on top and squeeze bottom to make potatoes open out. Top with any combination of chopped chives, pepper, lean ham, yoghurt, **Hommos** p39, low fat cheese, paprika or parsley.

### Stuffed Baked Potato
Prepare baked potatoes as indicated. Cut in half horizontally and scoop out potato and mash. Mix mashed potato with **Lentils Sauce** p105, **Savoury Baked Beans** p33, **Savoury Corn Spread** p32. Refill potato shells with chosen mixture, reheat for 10 minutes in 180°C oven or for 2 to 3 minutes in the microwave on **High.**

## ARMADILLO POTATOES

*4 medium potatoes (400g)*
*¼ cup non fat milk (65ml)*
*½ cup grated less than 10% fat cheese (60g)*
*1 tabsp chopped chives*

- Scrub potatoes well and pierce the skin with a fork.
- Cook in their jackets for 1 hour in a 180°C oven.
- Remove potatoes from oven and make ¼cm deep slices across each.
- Place in a baking dish, pour over milk and sprinkle cheese and chives on the top.
- Return to the oven and bake a further 10 - 15 minutes or until the potatoes are heated through.
- Serve immediately.

**Serves 8**

NUTRIENTS PER SERVE

| KJ | Cal | Pro (g) | CHO (g) | Fibre (g) | T.fat (g) | S.fat (g) | Chol (mg) | Na (mg) |
|---|---|---|---|---|---|---|---|---|
| 209 | 50 | 4 | 7 | 0.8 | 0.6 | 0.11 | 3 | 43 |

## SCALLOPED POTATOES

*3 medium peeled and sliced potatoes (300g)*
*1 medium sliced onion (100g)*
*1 tabsp parmesan cheese (9g)*
*½ tsp dried dill weed*
*Freshly ground black pepper*
*1 tabsp mono/polyunsaturated margarine (20g)*
*2 tabsp plain flour (20g)*
*1 cup non fat milk (250ml)*

- Layer potato and onion in a greased casserole.
- Sprinkle with parmesan cheese, dill and pepper.
- Prepare a white sauce by melting margarine in a heavy based saucepan or in microwave.
- Remove from microwave or stove and stir in flour to form a smooth paste. Slowly add milk while stirring.
- Return to microwave or stove to cook, stirring occasionally until the sauce is thick and smooth. If on stove top, stir continuously.
- Cover potato and onion with sauce and bake for 20 minutes in a 180°C oven.
- Remove lid and continue to bake for a further 40 minutes or until potatoes can be easily pierced with a fork.

**Serves 6**

NUTRIENTS PER SERVE

| KJ | Cal | Pro (g) | CHO (g) | Fibre (g) | T.fat (g) | S.fat (g) | Chol (mg) | Na (mg) |
|---|---|---|---|---|---|---|---|---|
| 400 | 97 | 4 | 12 | 1 | 3 | 78 | 3 | 45 |

## CRUNCHY CAJUN CHIPS

*4 medium potatoes (400g)*
*1 tsp chilli powder (2g)*
*1 tsp low sodium stock powder (2.5g)*
*Freshly ground black pepper*
*1 tsp mono/polyunsaturated oil (5ml)*
*Salt to taste*

- Peel and cut potatoes into wedges.
- Parboil for 3 to 4 minute and drain well.
- Place on greased baking tray.
- Brush with oil.
- Sprinkle with a mix of chilli powder, stock powder and black pepper.
- Bake in 220°C oven for 30 minutes or until crisp and golden brown.
- Turn a couple of times to brown evenly.
- Add salt to taste.

**Serves 4**

*Note*
These are low in fat, tasty and less expensive than frozen oven fries.

NUTRIENTS PER SERVE

| KJ | Cal | Pro (g) | CHO (g) | Fibre (g) | T.fat (g) | S.fat (g) | Chol (mg) | Na (mg) |
|---|---|---|---|---|---|---|---|---|
| 345 | 83 | 2.6 | 13.6 | 1.6 | 1.5 | 0.2 | 0.2 | 81 |

## RICE

Rice is a staple of many Asian countries and has become very popular as an alternative to potatoes and pasta in Australia.
Rice is a fast absorbing carbohydrate so quantities must be carefully controlled.
Brown or long grain rice is preferred to short grain or gluggy rice. It is better to boil rice in a large quantity of water and then to rinse to remove excess starch than to use the more traditional steaming method as in a rice cooker. Basmati rice has a low Glycaemic Index and is recommended.
Consider half a cup of cooked rice has the same carbohydrate as 1 slice of bread. It helps absorption if it is consumed with high fibre vegetables and protein.
Rice forms the basis of a number of main meal dishes such as **Cabbage Rolls** p69, **Paella** p57 and **Kidney Bean Rice Medley** p48.
Serve **Sunflower Rice** p94 as an accompaniment to a meal.

## SUNFLOWER RICE

*½ cup uncooked brown rice (100g)*
*½ cup uncooked white rice (100g)*
*Salt to taste*
*Water*
*½ cup sunflower seeds (75g)*
*2 tsp mono/polyunsaturated margarine (10g)*

- Boil brown rice in a large saucepan of salted water for 25 minutes.
- Add white rice to brown rice and continue to cook for 10 to 15 minutes more or until rice is soft.
- Strain and rinse.
- Toast sunflower seeds in a 200°C oven for 10 minutes or microwave for 2 to 3 minutes on **Medium High**.
- Toss white rice, brown rice and sunflower seeds together with margarine.
- Reheat and serve.

**Serves 6**

*Variation*
**Steamed Rice** Steam brown rice in water over low heat for 40 minutes. Steam white rice over low heat for 15 minutes. Make sure the lid is tightly closed and that it doesn't burn. Allow 2 cups of water to each cup of rice.

NUTRIENTS PER SERVE

| KJ | Cal | Pro (g) | CHO (g) | Fibre (g) | T.fat (g) | S.fat (g) | Chol (mg) | Na (mg) |
|---|---|---|---|---|---|---|---|---|
| 630 | 153 | 4 | 20 | 2 | 6 | 0.6 | 0 | 1.3 |

**Crunchy Cajun Chips**

# Salads and Dressings

Salads can be an addition to a meal as in **Chinese Mixed Vegetable Salad** p102 or **Red Cabbage Salad** p101 or a meal on its own such as **Asian Salad** p98 or **Thai Fish Salad** p100. There are many variations in salads. Be adventurous and add whatever is on hand. Refer to the **Salad Maker Chart** p103 for additional ideas and combination.
Try the different salad dressings with a range of lettuce and salad vegetables to come up with your own combinations. A good idea is to see what you have in the refrigerator and then go on from there. Produce a new main meal salad with leftover meat, chicken or canned fish.

*Rare Roast Beef Salad p98*

DRESSINGS
*Balsamic French Dressing* 95
*Cider Vinegar Dressing* 95
*Creamy Mustard Dressing* 96
*Honey Orange Dressing* 96
*Horseradish Dressing* 96
*Low Joule Caesar Salad Dressing* 97
*Mustard Herb Dressing* 97
*Spicy Cream Dressing* 96
*Thai Dressing* 97
*Tomato Yoghurt Dressing* 97

SALADS
<u>Main Meal Salads</u>
*Asian Salad (Hot or Cold)* 98
*Macaroni Bean Salad* 99
*Mango Chicken Salad* 99
*Rare Roast Beef Salad* 98
*Thai Fish Salad* 100
*Thai Chicken Salad* 100

<u>Side Salads</u>
*Salad Maker Chart* 103
*Chinese Mixed Vegetable Salad* 102
*German Potato Salad* 100
*Low Joule Caesar Salad* 101
*Red Cabbage Salad* 101
*Roast Vegetable Salad* 101
*Spinach Tomato Salad* 100
*Tropical Sicilian Salad* 102

# SALAD DRESSINGS

## BALSAMIC FRENCH DRESSING

¼ cup olive oil (65ml)
2 tabsp water (40ml)
¼ cup balsamic or other highly flavoured vinegar (65ml)
1 tsp sugar (5g) or equivalent substitute
1 crushed clove garlic (3g)

❏ Blend or shake oil, water, vinegar, sugar and garlic until smooth.
❏ Store in an airtight jar in the refrigerator.
❏ Use about ¼ to ½ cup on **Spinach Tomato Salad** p100 according to kilojoule requirements.

**Serves 8 x 1 tabsp (Total ¾ cup)**

NUTRIENTS PER SERVE

| KJ | Cal | Pro (g) | CHO (g) | Fibre (g) | T.fat (g) | S.fat (g) | Chol (mg) | Na (mg) |
|---|---|---|---|---|---|---|---|---|
| 317 | 77 | 0.03 | 0.7 | 0.06 | 8 | 0.7 | 0 | 0.4 |

## CIDER VINEGAR DRESSING

⅓ cup sugar (70g) or equivalent substitute
2 tabsp mono/polyunsaturated oil (40ml)
2 tabsp water (40ml)
⅓ cup cider vinegar (85ml)

❏ Mix sugar, oil, water and cider vinegar together.
❏ Let stand for 15 minutes to allow flavour to develop.
❏ Use in **Chinese Mixed Vegetable Salad** p102 or any light salad.

**Serves 10 (Total 1 cup)**

NUTRIENTS PER SERVE

| KJ | Cal | Pro (g) | CHO (g) | Fibre (g) | T.fat (g) | S.fat (g) | Chol (mg) | Na (mg) |
|---|---|---|---|---|---|---|---|---|
| 265 | 65 | 0 | 7 | 0 | 4 | 0.3 | 0 | .4 |

NS

| KJ | Cal | CHO (g) |
|---|---|---|
| 166 | 40 | 0.8 |

**Note** NS = No Added Sugar

## CREAMY MUSTARD DRESSING

*3/4 cup non fat natural yoghurt (175ml)*
*2 tabsp light (97% fat free) mayonnaise (40ml)*
*2 tabsp chopped spring onion (5g)*
*1 tsp curry powder (5g)*
*1 tsp grained mustard (5g)*
*1 tabsp fresh dill or 1 tsp dried*

- Prepare dressing by mixing yoghurt, mayonnaise, spring onion, curry powder, mustard and dill together.
- Pour dressing over hot potatoes and use in **German Potato Salad** p100 or use as a dressing for cubed cucumber.

**Serves 8 x 1½ tabsp (Total 1 cup).**

NUTRIENTS PER SERVE

| KJ | Cal | Pro (g) | CHO (g) | Fibre (g) | T.fat (g) | S.fat (g) | Chol (mg) | Na (mg) |
|---|---|---|---|---|---|---|---|---|
| 96 | 23 | 2 | 3 | 0.2 | 0.5 | 0.2 | 2.3 | 56 |

## HONEY ORANGE DRESSING

*1 tabsp orange juice (20ml)*
*1 tabsp honey (20ml)*
*1 tabsp balsamic vinegar (20ml)*
*1 tabsp mono/polyunsaturated oil (20ml)*
*1 tsp grain mustard (5g)*

- Mix orange juice, honey, vinegar, oil and mustard in a food processor or in a jar.
- Whiz or shake until smooth.
- Use in **Red Cabbage Salad** p101 or add to mixed green salad.

**Serves 4 x 1 tabsp (Total ⅓ cup)**

NUTRIENTS PER SERVE

| KJ | Cal | Pro (g) | CHO (g) | Fibre (g) | T.fat (g) | S.fat (g) | Chol (mg) | Na (mg) |
|---|---|---|---|---|---|---|---|---|
| 289 | 70 | 0.4 | 5 | 0 | 5.5 | 0.6 | 0 | 1 |

## HORSERADISH DRESSING

*1 tabsp lemon juice (20ml)*
*2 tabsp horseradish (40g)*
*½ cup non fat yoghurt (125g)*
*2 tabsp light (97% fat free) mayonnaise (40g)*
*Freshly ground black pepper*
*½ tsp paprika*
*1 tabsp chives*

- Mix lemon juice, horse radish, yoghurt, mayonnaise together and season lightly with black pepper.
- Place in a bowl and sprinkle with paprika and chopped chives.
- Serve with **Rare Roast Beef Salad** p98.

**Serves 6 x 2 tabsp (Total 1 cup)**

*Variation*
**Ginger Lime Sauce** Substitute ginger for horseradish and lime juice for lemon juice. Serve over grilled chicken breast or skinless thigh.

NUTRIENTS PER SERVE

| KJ | Cal | Pro (g) | CHO (g) | Fibre (g) | T.fat (g) | S.fat (g) | Chol (mg) | Na (mg) |
|---|---|---|---|---|---|---|---|---|
| 174 | 42 | 1.4 | 4 | 0.2 | 2 | 0.6 | 5 | 211 |

## SPICY CREAM DRESSING

*¼ cup light (97% fat free) mayonnaise (65ml)*
*¼ cup non fat yoghurt (65ml)*
*1 tabsp low sodium soy sauce (20ml)*
*1 crushed clove garlic (3g)*
*2 tabsp chopped spring onion (5g)*
*¼ tsp chilli sauce (1.25ml)*
*1 tabsp lemon juice (20ml)*
*2 tabsp fresh chopped basil or 2 tsp dry*
*1 tabsp fresh tarragon or 1 tsp dry*

- Place mayonnaise, yoghurt, soy sauce, garlic, spring onion, chilli sauce, lemon juice, basil and tarragon in blender or food processor and blend until smooth or use a mortar and pestle.
- Refrigerate for 4 hours or more to allow flavour to develop.
- Use in **Mango Chicken Salad** p99 or with fresh crab, or poached fish.

**Serves 6 x 2 tabsp (Total 1 cup)**

NUTRIENTS PER SERVE

| KJ | Cal | Pro (g) | CHO (g) | Fibre (g) | T.fat (g) | S.fat (g) | Chol (mg) | Na (mg) |
|---|---|---|---|---|---|---|---|---|
| 93 | 22 | 0.9 | 3.5 | 0.2 | 0.4 | 0.3 | 3 | 220 |

## LOW JOULE CAESAR SALAD DRESSING

1/2 cup light (97% fat free) mayonnaise (65ml)
2 tabsp lemon juice (40ml)
1 tsp Worcestershire sauce (5ml)
1 crushed clove garlic (3g)
1 - 2 well drained anchovies (10g)
1/2 tsp Dijon mustard (3g)
Black pepper
2 tabsp parmesan cheese (18g)

- Blend mayonnaise, lemon juice, Worcestershire sauce, garlic, anchovies, mustard, black pepper and parmesan cheese together in a kitchen whiz or blender.
- Serve with **Low Joule Caesar Salad** p101.

**Serves 6 x 1 tabsp (Total 1/2 cup)**

*Variation*
Vary the seasoning according to taste, increasing or decreasing the anchovies and the Dijon mustard.

*Note*
Anchovies are very high in sodium and therefore may need to be omitted.

NUTRIENTS PER SERVE

| KJ | Cal | Pro (g) | CHO (g) | Fibre (g) | T.fat (g) | S.fat (g) | Chol (mg) | Na (mg) |
|---|---|---|---|---|---|---|---|---|
| 220 | 53 | 2 | 3 | 0.2 | 3.5 | 0.9 | 7 | 230 |

## MUSTARD HERB DRESSING

1/2 cup low fat cottage cheese (125g)
1/2 cup non fat natural yoghurt (125g)
1/2 tsp grain mustard (2.5g)
1 tabsp chopped fresh oregano or 1 tsp dried
2 tabsp chopped fresh basil or 2 tsp dried

- Place cottage cheese, yoghurt, mustard, oregano and basil in food processor and blend until smooth or mash with a mortar and pestle.
- Use in coleslaw or pasta salads.

**Serves 6 x 2 tabsp (Total 1 cup)**

NUTRIENTS PER SERVE

| KJ | Cal | Pro (g) | CHO (g) | Fibre (g) | T.fat (g) | S.fat (g) | Chol (mg) | Na (mg) |
|---|---|---|---|---|---|---|---|---|
| 134 | 32 | 5 | 1.5 | 0 | 0.5 | 0.2 | 4 | 41 |

## THAI DRESSING

2 tabsp sugar (36g) or equivalent substitute
2 tabsp lemon or lime juice (40ml)
1/3 cup fish sauce (85ml)
2 small seeded and sliced chillies or chilli powder to taste

- Mix sugar, lemon or lime juice, fish sauce and chillies together.
- Place in container and refrigerate for 3 - 4 hours to allow flavour to develop.
- Serve with **Thai Fish Salad** p100.

**Serves 4 x 2 tabsp (Total 2/3 cup)**

*Note*
This is high in sodium. Substitute low sodium soy sauce for fish sauce if this is of concern.

NUTRIENTS PER SERVE

| KJ | Cal | Pro (g) | CHO (g) | Fibre (g) | T.fat (g) | S.fat (g) | Chol (mg) | Na (mg) |
|---|---|---|---|---|---|---|---|---|
| 198 | 49 | 1.5 | 10 | 0.3 | 0.1 | 0 | 0 | 1596 |

NS

| KJ | Cal | CHO (g) |
|---|---|---|
| 86 | 21 | 3 |

## TOMATO YOGHURT DRESSING

1 tabsp tomato paste (25g)
2 tabsp non fat natural yoghurt (40ml)
1 tabsp mono/polyunsaturated oil (20ml)
2 tsp sugar (8g) or equivalent substitute
1 tsp Worcestershire sauce (5ml)
2 tabsp vinegar (40ml)
1 crushed clove of garlic (3g)

- Place tomato paste, yoghurt, oil, sugar, Worcestershire sauce, vinegar and garlic in blender or mortar and pestle and mix together.
- Use in **Macaroni Bean Salad** p99.

**Serves 8 x 3 tsp (Total 1/2 cup)**

NUTRIENTS PER SERVE

| KJ | Cal | Pro (g) | CHO (g) | Fibre (g) | T.fat (g) | S.fat (g) | Chol (mg) | Na (mg) |
|---|---|---|---|---|---|---|---|---|
| 134 | 32 | 0.4 | 2 | 0.2 | 3 | 0.3 | 0.3 | 11 |

**Note** NS = No Added Sugar

# MAIN MEAL SALADS

## ASIAN SALAD (HOT OR COLD)

500g lean beef rump or pork fillet
2 tabsp low sodium soy sauce (40ml)
1 tsp mono/polyunsaturated oil (5ml)
2 tbsp lemon juice (40ml)
1 crushed clove garlic (3g)
1 tsp chopped ginger
3 cups mixed vegetables (400g)
1 tabsp pinenuts (15g)

- Grill thick meat until medium rare, let rest for a moment and then slice thinly.
- Blend soy sauce, oil, lemon juice, garlic, and ginger together, add to beef and leave.
- Prepare a range of vegetables, such as snow peas, capsicum, baby corn, broccoli or cauliflower, allowing about ¾ cup per serve.
- Microwave vegetables until just tender and crisp. If serving cold then rinse vegetables in cold water before chilling.
- Immediately toss with beef and sprinkle with pinenuts.
- Serve hot or cold.

**Serves 4**

NUTRIENTS PER SERVE

| KJ | Cal | Pro (g) | CHO (g) | Fibre (g) | T.fat (g) | S.fat (g) | Chol (mg) | Na (mg) |
|---|---|---|---|---|---|---|---|---|
| 877 | 209 | 32.5 | 3.3 | 2.9 | 7.2 | 1.6 | 83.8 | 557 |

## RARE ROAST BEEF SALAD

2 cups mixed leafy greens (150g)
Thinly sliced rare topside roast beef (400g)
1 cup finely shredded cabbage (100g)
1 small grated beetroot 100g)
1 large grated carrot (100g)
1 medium red (150g) **Peeled Capsicum** p86
½ cup alfalfa (25g)
1 cup **Horse Radish Dressing** p96

- Wash and chill a mixture of greens including coloured lettuce, rocket, and spinach.
- Place a piece of topside in a little water in a pan on a trivet and roast medium rare by allowing 15 minutes per 500g at 180°C.
- As soon as topside is cooked, wrap in foil, cool slightly and refrigerate.
- When required slice thinly.
- On a bed of leafy greens make mounds of shredded cabbage, beetroot and carrot.
- Place **Peeled Capsicum** attractively around.
- Roll roast beef and place on platter and sprinkle with alfalfa. (Refer to picture p95.)
- Place **Horseradish Sauce** in middle of the platter. Allow about 2 tablespoons per serve.

**Serves 6**

*Addition*
Vary the ingredients with artichokes, blanched snow peas or asparagus.

NUTRIENTS PER SERVE

| KJ | Cal | Pro (g) | CHO (g) | Fibre (g) | T.fat (g) | S.fat (g) | Chol (mg) | Na (mg) |
|---|---|---|---|---|---|---|---|---|
| 763 | 182 | 25 | 8 | 3 | 6 | 3 | 59 | 272 |

*Asian Salad (Hot or Cold)*

*Mango Chicken Salad*

## MANGO CHICKEN SALAD

*1 large peeled mango (150g)*
*1 medium red apple with skin (100g)*
*1 medium peeled avocado (150g)*
*1 tabsp lemon juice (20ml)*
*Smoked or grilled chicken breast (500g)*
*Leafy greens (500g)*
*Bean sprouts (250g)*
*6 slices proscuitto or lean ham, trimmed (120g)*
*1 cup* **Spicy Cream Dressing** *p96*
*1 tabsp toasted sesame seeds (10g)*

- Cut mango into strips.
- Core and cut apple into wedges and avocado into strips and dip in lemon juice.
- Cut chicken breast into strips.
- Arrange washed and chilled lettuces including spinach attractively on a large platter with bean sprouts.
- Place mango, apple and avocado around sides.
- Arrange chicken and ham in the middle and dribble over **Spicy Cream Dressing** and garnish with toasted sesame seeds.

**Serves 6**

*Variation*
Substitute according to what is available e.g. fish instead of chicken, or banana, capsicum, pineapple or artichokes.

NUTRIENTS PER SERVE

| KJ | Cal | Pro (g) | CHO (g) | Fibre (g) | T.fat (g) | S.fat (g) | Chol (mg) | Na (mg) |
|---|---|---|---|---|---|---|---|---|
| 1827 | 441 | 25 | 11 | 5 | 9 | 2 | 99 | 650 |

## MACARONI BEAN SALAD

*1 cup raw vegetable macaroni (100g)*
*1 can Four Bean mix (310g)*
*1 1/2 cups sliced French beans (200g)*
*1/2 medium zucchini (100g)*
*1/2 cup* **Tomato Yoghurt Dressing** *p97*
*Pepper to taste*

- Cook macaroni in boiling water until just tender.
- Drain, rinse under cold water and cool.
- Drain and rinse Four Bean Mix.
- Cook French beans until just tender, drain and cool.
- Coarsely grate unpeeled raw zucchini.
- Toss macaroni, Four Bean Mix, French beans and zucchini together with **Tomato Yoghurt Dressing.**
- Season to taste with freshly ground pepper.
- Chill well before serving.

**Serves 8 x 1/2 cup (Total 4 cups)**

NUTRIENTS PER SERVE

| KJ | Cal | Pro (g) | CHO (g) | Fibre (g) | T.fat (g) | S.fat (g) | Chol (mg) | Na (mg) |
|---|---|---|---|---|---|---|---|---|
| 481 | 116 | 5 | 17 | 4 | 3 | 0.4 | 0.3 | 133 |

## THAI FISH SALAD

*6 cups mixed lettuce (300g)*
*1 small peeled and shredded beetroot (100g)*
*1 medium grated carrot (100g)*
*White firm flesh fish (shark or schnapper) (500g)*
*¼ cup plain flour (30g)*
*1 tsp low sodium stock powder (2.5g)*
*¼ cup non fat milk (65ml)*
*½ cup breadcrumbs (60g)*
*Mono-unsaturated oil spray*
*2 medium red apples with skin (200g)*
*2 tsp lemon juice (10ml)*
*¼ cup toasted pinenuts (40g)*
*⅔ cup **Thai Dressing** p97*

- Wash and dry mixed lettuce.
- Divide lettuce between four plates.
- Sprinkle shredded beetroot and carrot on top.
- Cut fish into strips; dip into flour and stock powder, then milk and breadcrumbs.
- Place on a greased baking tray.
- Spray with oil.
- Bake at 180°C for 15 minutes.
- Prepare apple by slicing finely in wedges and dipping in lemon juice.
- Arrange attractively on salad, alternating hot fish and apple.
- Sprinkle with toasted pinenuts and serve with **Thai Dressing,** allowing 2 tabsp per serve.

**Serves 4**

*Variation*
**Thai Chicken Salad** Substitute strips of grilled chicken breast for fish or add some fresh cooked prawns. Use toasted peanuts rather than pinenuts.

*Note*
Analysis includes **Thai Dressing** with sweetener. The fish sauce is high in sodium. You may substitute low sodium soy sauce.

NUTRIENTS PER SERVE

| KJ | Cal | Pro (g) | CHO (g) | Fibre (g) | T.fat (g) | S.fat (g) | Chol (mg) | Na (mg) |
|---|---|---|---|---|---|---|---|---|
| 1500 | 361 | 33 | 31 | 5.8 | 11 | 2 | 88 | 1880 |

## SIDE SALADS

### GERMAN POTATO SALAD

*5 large clean skinned cooked potatoes or small potatoes to equal 1kg*
*1 medium Spanish onion (100g)*
*3 finely chopped spring onions (10g)*
*1 cup **Creamy Mustard Dressing** p96*

- Wash potatoes and if large, slice or if small, leave whole. Do not peel. Cook until tender.
- Finely slice Spanish onion and cook until just soft, about 2 - 3 minutes in microwave.
- Prepare **Creamy Mustard Dressing.**
- Toss through hot potato and garnish with Spanish onion and spring onion.
- Serve slightly chilled or warm.

**Serves 8**

NUTRIENTS PER SERVE

| KJ | Cal | Pro (g) | CHO (g) | Fibre (g) | T.fat (g) | S.fat (g) | Chol (mg) | Na (mg) |
|---|---|---|---|---|---|---|---|---|
| 452 | 109 | 5 | 20 | 2.5 | 0.7 | 0.2 | 2 | 61 |

### SPINACH TOMATO SALAD

*Fresh spinach or available greens (300g)*
*1 medium finely sliced Spanish or white onion (100g)*
*2 tabsp parmesan cheese (18g)*
*½ cup prepared **Low Joule Garlic Croutons** p130*
*20 cherry tomatoes or 3 regular tomatoes cut into 8ths (300g)*
*¾ cup **Balsamic French Dressing** p95*

- Use fresh spinach or other available greens such as different lettuces e.g. rocket.
- Wash well, towel and refrigerate to crisp and dry.
- Place in a bowl and toss with onion, parmesan cheese, **Low Joule Garlic Croutons** and tomato.
- Just before serving add **Balsamic French Dressing.**

**Serves 8**

NUTRIENTS PER SERVE

| KJ | Cal | Pro (g) | CHO (g) | Fibre (g) | T.fat (g) | S.fat (g) | Chol (mg) | Na (mg) |
|---|---|---|---|---|---|---|---|---|
| 515 | 125 | 3 | 5 | 2 | 10 | 1.5 | 2 | 79 |

## LOW JOULE CAESAR SALAD

*4 cups well washed greens - cos, iceberg or other lettuces (200g)*
*3 finely chopped anchovy fillets (10g)*
*½ cup **Low Joule Caesar Salad Dressing** p97*
*½ cup **Low Joule Garlic Croutons** p130*
*2 tabsp parmesan cheese (18g)*
*1 finely chopped middle eye rasher of bacon (50g) optional*

❏ Wash and toss crisp lettuces with chopped anchovies.
❏ Just before serving add **Low Joule Caesar Salad Dressing**, tossing well and sprinkle with **Low Joule Garlic Croutons**, parmesan cheese and bacon if desired.

**Serve 6**

*Note*
A regular Caesar salad dressing may be used but kilojoules and fat will be much higher.

NUTRIENTS PER SERVE

| KJ | Cal | Pro (g) | CHO (g) | Fibre (g) | T.fat (g) | S.fat (g) | Chol (mg) | Na (mg) |
|---|---|---|---|---|---|---|---|---|
| 358 | 86 | 5 | 7 | 1.5 | 4 | 2 | 11 | 415 |

## RED CABBAGE SALAD

*1 cup finely shredded white cabbage (100g)*
*1 cup finely shredded red cabbage (100g)*
*1 medium peeled and chopped apple (100g)*
*2 tabsp chopped pecan nuts (20g)*
*2 tsp lemon juice (10ml)*
*½ cup **Honey Orange Dressing** p96*

❏ Mix white and red cabbage together.
❏ Add lemon to chopped apple to prevent browning and then add with pecan nuts to cabbage and mix well.
❏ Pour **Honey Orange Dressing** over salad and serve.

**Serves 4**

NUTRIENTS PER SERVE

| KJ | Cal | Pro (g) | CHO (g) | Fibre (g) | T.fat (g) | S.fat (g) | Chol (mg) | Na (mg) |
|---|---|---|---|---|---|---|---|---|
| 531 | 128 | 2 | 9.5 | 3 | 9 | 0.8 | 0 | 9 |

## ROAST VEGETABLE SALAD

*1 medium red capsicum (150g)*
*2 large peeled cubed potatoes (400g)*
*1 cup peeled cubed butternut pumpkin (150g)*
*1 cup peeled cubed sweet potato (150g))*
*1 teaspoon mono/polyunsaturated oil (5ml)*
*1 medium red onion cut into 8ths (100g)*
*1 cob of fresh corn or ¾ cup frozen kernels (200g)*
*4 large Roman tomatoes cut lengthwise into 6ths (400g)*
*Mono-unsaturated oil spray*
*1 tsp salt (5g)*
*2 stems rosemary*
*2 tablespoon chopped pistachios (25g)*

❏ Cut capsicum into 8ths and remove seeds. Grill with skin side up until blackened. Place in a plastic bag to sweat and then peel off skin.
❏ Microwave prepared potato, pumpkin and sweet potato for 8 minutes or until soft.
❏ Toss in oil and barbecue until crisp or bake at 220°C for 30 minutes.
❏ Mix prepared onion and kernels from corn cob together and add to vegetables.
❏ Barbecue or cook for 10 minutes more.
❏ Spray tomatoes with oil and sprinkle with salt.
❏ Add tomatoes and previous peeled capsicum to barbecue or oven and place sprigs of rosemary on top.
❏ Cook for 5 minutes more.
❏ Roast chopped pistachio nuts in microwave or oven until crisp.
❏ Place cooked vegetables garnished with rosemary on a platter.
❏ Sprinkle with chopped pistachio nuts and serve warm.

**Serves 8**

NUTRIENTS PER SERVE

| KJ | Cal | Pro (g) | CHO (g) | Fibre (g) | T.fat (g) | S.fat (g) | Chol (mg) | Na (mg) |
|---|---|---|---|---|---|---|---|---|
| 387 | 93 | 3.6 | 13.5 | 3 | 2.5 | 0.3 | 0 | 262 |

*Tropical Sicilian Salad*

## CHINESE MIXED VEGETABLE SALAD

*1 cup sliced runner beans (130g)*
*1 cup broad beans (100gms)*
*1 cup sliced butter beans (100g)*
*300g can drained, washed kidney beans (200g)*
*1 medium finely sliced red capsicum (100g)*
*1 medium finely sliced white onion (100g)*
*1 cup* **Cider Vinegar Dressing** *p95*

❑ Cook fresh or frozen broad, runner and butter beans for 5 minutes or until just tender crisp in a saucepan with minimum water.
❑ Toss beans, capsicum and onion together in a bowl.
❑ Stir in 1 cup **Cider Vinegar Dressing.**
❑ Refrigerate for at least 2 hours (preferably overnight) to develop the flavours.

**Serves 10 x ½ cups**

*Note*
Will keep in the fridge for up to 1 week. This may be prepared in the microwave, cooking the runner, broad and butter beans on **High** for about 10 minutes until tender crisp.

NUTRIENTS PER SERVE

| KJ | Cal | Pro (g) | CHO (g) | Fibre (g) | T.fat (g) | S.fat (g) | Chol (mg) | Na (mg) |
|---|---|---|---|---|---|---|---|---|
| 512 | 124 | 4 | 11.4 | 3.6 | 7 | 0.8 | 0 | 4 |

NS

| KJ | Cal | CHO (g) |
|---|---|---|
| 413 | 99 | 5.3 |

## TROPICAL SICILIAN SALAD

*3 cups mixed lettuces (150g)*
*1 dozen Kalamata olives (75g)*
*Low fat fetta cheese (about 15% fat) (60g)*
*5 well drained* **Sundried Tomatoes** *p89*
*2 tabsp pinenuts (30g)*
*1 dozen cherry tomatoes or 4 small ones cut in 6ths (350g)*
*2 tabsp parmesan or grated Romano cheese (20g)*

❑ Wash greens.
❑ Wrap in a clean towel and chill before serving.
❑ Toss greens in a salad bowl.
❑ Garnish with olives, cubed fetta, **Sundried Tomatoes** cut in strips, lightly toasted pinenuts and cherry tomatoes.
❑ Pour your favourite low joule dressing over salad and sprinkle parmesan or Romano cheese on top.

**Serves 4**

*Note*
This is high in salt and not suitable when sodium is restricted.

NUTRIENTS PER SERVE

| KJ | Cal | Pro (g) | CHO (g) | Fibre (g) | T.fat (g) | S.fat (g) | Chol (mg) | Na (mg) |
|---|---|---|---|---|---|---|---|---|
| 553 | 133 | 9 | 4 | 4 | 9 | 3 | 14 | 757 |

**Note** NS = No Added Sugar

# SALAD MAKER CHART

| LIGHT VEGETABLES & GREENS | STARCHY SUBSTANTIAL | CONDIMENTS | MEATS, CHEESES & ALTERNATIVES | DRESSINGS |
|---|---|---|---|---|
| Artichokes<br>Asparagus- canned, fresh or pickled.<br>Beans, green<br>Broccoli<br>Cauliflower<br>Cabbage- chopped or shredded<br>Celery- strips or slices<br>Cucumber - regular, burpless or Lebanese.<br>Italian Greens<br>Lettuce - all types<br>Onion - Spanish or white<br>Rocket lettuce<br>Spinach<br>Silverbeet<br>Snow peas<br>Sprouts - all types<br>Spring onions or chives<br>Witlof<br><br>**GELATINE**<br>Tomato Aspic<br>Lemon Jelly & vegetables<br>Lemon Jelly, Vegetables & Fruit | Corn, kernels<br>Cous Cous<br>Pasta<br>Peas<br>Polenta<br>Potato<br>Sweet Potato<br><br>**OTHER VEGETABLES**<br>Pumpkin - cooked cubes.<br>Carrot - grated, julienne or sliced.<br>Tomato - sliced, wedges or julienne.<br>Corn, baby canned<br>Beetroot- canned slices or Baby Beetroot.<br>Fresh Beetroot, grated.<br>Capsicum- green, yellow, red, black- strips, cubes or circles.<br>Red Cabbage<br>Radish | Olives - Kalamata, green or black<br>**Sun Dried Tomatoes** p89 or capsicum.<br>Parmesan cheese, grated<br>Romano Cheese, shaved<br><br>**FRUIT**<br>Apple<br>Avocado<br>Banana<br>Dried Fruit - apricot, sultanas, currants, dates & prunes.<br>Grapes<br>Kiwi fruit<br>Mango<br>Peaches<br>Strawberries | Bean mix, canned<br>Blue Cheese<br>Cheese - cubed, julienne strips or grated.<br>Chick peas<br>Chicken Strips or cubes.<br>Cold meat- beef, lamb, pork.<br>Cottage Cheese<br>Eggs- hard cooked<br>Fetta Cheese<br>Kidney beans<br>Nuts- pecan, peanuts, walnuts, almonds.<br>Seed- sesame seeds, Sunflower seeds.<br>Salmon or tuna<br>Fresh fish- grilled & cooked.<br>Prawns<br>Schnapper or sardines<br>Smoked cheese | **Balsamic French Dressing** p95<br>Commercial Low Joule Dressings.<br>**Creamy Mustard Dressing** p96<br>**Honey Orange Dressing** p96<br>**Horseradish Dressing** p96<br>**Low Joule Caesar Salad Dressing.** p97<br>**Mustard Herb Dressing** p97<br>**Spicy Cream Dressing** p96<br>**Thai Dressing** p97<br>**Tomato Yoghurt Dressing** p97<br><br>**DRESSING INGREDIENTS**<br>Garlic<br>Ginger<br>Lemon Juice<br>Light Mayonnaise<br>Lime juice<br>Oil<br>Sugar<br>Tomato Sauce<br>Vinegar<br>Yoghurt |

## Sauces

*Bechamel Sauce 106*
*Cheese Sauce 108*
*Fresh Tomato Basil Salsa 106*
*Fresh Tomato Savoury Sauce 105*
    *Cooked Tomato Savoury 105*
*Italian Pasta Sauce 104*
    *Italian Seafood Sauce 104*
*Lentil Sauce 105*
*Low Fat Pesto Sauce 105*
*Low Fat White Sauce 108*
*Plum Sauce 106*
*Seafood Sauce 107*
*Spaghetti Sauce 104*
*Sweet and Sour Sauce 106*
*Yoghurt Sauce 108*

***Plum Sauce p106 with***
***Savoury Stuffed Crêpes p38***

---

Sauces dress up a meal and can be low fat but still flavoursome. The addition of basil, a little mustard, low fat cheese or parmesan cheese can dress up a white sauce. Sauces can be stirred through pasta or added to vegetables.
The **Fresh Tomato Savoury Sauce** p105 for pasta or **Italian Pasta Sauce** p104 are ideal for vegetarian pasta dishes.
**Lentil Sauce** p105 can be added to pasta, poured over rice or **Cous Cous** p90, used with bread as a dip or added to a scone roll or to a roulade.
A sauce over a mixture of steamed or stir-fried vegetables with added cheese can become a main meal.
**Spaghetti Sauce** can be used in **Lasagne** p68, as a pizza base, in a savoury scone roll, over pasta or to stuff cannelloni.

❑ Stir-fry garlic and onion with mushrooms and capsicum in a non-stick pan with oil and water until onion is soft.
❑ Add oregano, parsley, black pepper and stir.
❑ Place in a microwave dish or saucepan with tomatoes, tomato paste, sugar and water.
❑ Microwave on **High** for 10 minutes or simmer on stove for 30 minutes.
❑ Serve with **Meatballs with Sauce** p72

**Serves 6 x ¹/₂ cups (Total 3 cups)**

*Variation*
**Italian Seafood Sauce** Add ¹/₂ cup per serve mixed seafood.

NUTRIENTS PER SERVE

| KJ | Cal | Pro (g) | CHO (g) | Fibre (g) | T.fat (g) | S.fat (g) | Chol (mg) | Na (mg) |
|---|---|---|---|---|---|---|---|---|
| 196 | 47 | 3 | 6 | 3 | 1.2 | 0.1 | 0 | 48 |

## ITALIAN PASTA SAUCE

2 crushed cloves garlic (6g)
1 large peeled and chopped onion (150g)
10 medium sliced mushrooms with stems (150g)
1 medium finely chopped red capsicum (150g)
1 tsp olive oil (5ml)
1 tabsp water (20ml)
1 tabsp fresh oregano or 1 tsp dried
1 tabsp finely chopped parsley or 1 tsp dried
Freshly ground black pepper
1 can tomatoes chopped (400g)
2 tabsp tomato paste (50g)
1 tsp sugar (5g) or equivalent substitute
1 cup water (250ml)
1 small eggplant finely chopped (150g) (optional)

## SPAGHETTI SAUCE

2 crushed cloves garlic (6g)
1 medium finely chopped onion (100g)
2 tsp mono/polyunsaturated oil (10ml)
1 tabsp water (20ml)
Lean mince (500g)
1 can no added salt tomato paste (140g)
1 can tomatoes (400g)
¹/₂ cup water (125ml)
¹/₄ tsp ground nutmeg
Freshly ground black pepper
1 bay leaf
¹/₂ tsp ground oregano
1 tsp sugar (5g) or equivalent substitute

- ❏ Stir-fry garlic and onion in a non-stick pan with oil and 1 tabsp water until onion is golden and softened.
- ❏ Add mince and continue to stir-fry until brown.
- ❏ Place in a saucepan or in a microwave dish and add tomato paste, tomatoes, 1/2 cup water, nutmeg, black pepper, bay leaf, oregano and sugar.
- ❏ Stir to form a smooth paste, either microwave at **Moderate High** for 1 hour or simmer slowly on the stove for 1 1/2 hours, stirring occasionally.
- ❏ Use in **Spaghetti Bolognaise** p70 or **Lasagne** p68

**Serves 8 x 1/2 cup (Total 4 cups)**

NUTRIENTS PER SERVE

| KJ | Cal | Pro (g) | CHO (g) | Fibre (g) | T.fat (g) | S.fat (g) | Chol (mg) | Na (mg) |
|---|---|---|---|---|---|---|---|---|
| 1004 | 240 | 27 | 9 | 3 | 10.4 | 3.7 | 79 | 189 |

## FRESH TOMATO SAVOURY SAUCE

6 - 8 pear shaped or Roman tomatoes (500g)
2 tabsp finely chopped basil or 2 tsp dried
1/2 small finely chopped Spanish onion (30g)
2 crushed cloves garlic (6g)
1 tsp mono/polyunsaturated oil (5ml)
1 tabsp water (20ml)
1 tsp sugar (5g) or equivalent substitute

- ❏ Blanch tomatoes in boiling water for 30 seconds, place in cold water, peel, cut in half and seed.
- ❏ Finely chop basil and Spanish onion.
- ❏ Stir-fry onion and basil with garlic in oil and water until onion is soft.
- ❏ Add prepared tomatoes and sugar and stir-fry for 2 - 3 minutes more.
- ❏ Serve as a fresh tomato sauce with pasta.
- ❏ Allow 1 cup of pasta per person

**Serve 4 x 1/2 cups (Total 2 cups)**

*Variation*
To prepare **Cooked Tomato Savoury** thicken sauce with 1 tbsp of cornflour and 2 tsp of water, cook for a further 2 to 3 minutes, then serve on toast at breakfast or over zucchini with grated low fat cheese.

NUTRIENTS PER SERVE

| KJ | Cal | Pro (g) | CHO (g) | Fibre (g) | T.fat (g) | S.fat (g) | Chol (mg) | Na (mg) |
|---|---|---|---|---|---|---|---|---|
| 133 | 32 | 1 | 4 | 2 | 1.4 | 0.2 | 0 | 8 |

## LENTIL SAUCE

1 medium finely chopped onion (100g)
1 crushed clove garlic (3g)
1 tsp mono/polyunsaturated oil (5ml)
1 tabsp water (20ml)
1 cup dry brown lentils cooked until tender, drained (220g)
1/2 cup celery chopped (50g)
1 can peeled tomatoes (400g)
2 tabsp tomato paste (50g)
1/4 tsp ground black pepper

- ❏ Sauté onion and garlic until tender in oil and water mixture.
- ❏ Add cooked, drained lentils and celery to onion mixture with tomatoes, tomato paste and pepper.
- ❏ Simmer until tender. (Add more tomato paste and water for a thinner sauce.)
- ❏ Serve with wholemeal pasta, as a dip with crusty bread or toast or as a hot dish with rice.

**Serves 6 x 2/3 cups (Total 4 cups)**

*Addition*
May add carrot and zucchini with celery.

NUTRIENT PER SERVE

| KJ | Cal | Pro (g) | CHO (g) | Fibre (g) | T.fat (g) | S.fat (g) | Chol (mg) | Na (mg) |
|---|---|---|---|---|---|---|---|---|
| 233 | 56 | 4 | 7.4 | 3 | 1 | 0.13 | 0 | 98 |

## LOW FAT PESTO SAUCE

1 bunch fresh basil, stalks removed (50g)
4 crushed cloves garlic (12g)
2 tabsp pinenuts (28g)
1 1/4 cups fresh ricotta cheese (300g)
Freshly ground black pepper
1 tabsp lemon juice (20ml)
2 tabsp parmesan cheese (18g)
Salt to taste

- ❏ Place basil, garlic, pinenuts, ricotta, black pepper, lemon juice and parmesan cheese together in a food processor or blender.
- ❏ Blend until smooth.
- ❏ Serve with fresh pasta with a little more parmesan on top if desired.

**Serves 6 x 1/4 cups (Total 1 1/2 cups)**

NUTRIENTS PER SERVE

| KJ | Cal | Pro (g) | CHO (g) | Fibre (g) | T.fat (g) | S.fat (g) | Chol (mg) | Na (mg) |
|---|---|---|---|---|---|---|---|---|
| 474 | 115 | 7 | 2 | 1 | 8.6 | 3.6 | 24 | 137 |

## FRESH TOMATO BASIL SALSA

*2 medium finely chopped tomatoes (200g)*
*2 crushed cloves garlic (6g)*
*1 tsp sugar (5g) or equivalent substitute*
*¼ cup chopped basil*
*1 tabsp lemon juice (20ml)*

- Mix tomato, garlic, sugar, basil and lemon juice together.
- A fast and easy method is put everything in a kitchen blender and blend for 3 to 4 minutes.
- Use in recipes such as **Mediterranean Pie** p61 or as a dip with corn chips or vegetables or as a spread.

**Serve 4 x ¼ cups (Total 1 cup)**

*Additions*
2 tsp chilli sauce or ½ cup finely chopped chives.

NUTRIENT PER SERVE

| KJ | Cal | Pro (g) | CHO (g) | Fibre (g) | T.fat (g) | S.fat (g) | Chol (mg) | Na (mg) |
|---|---|---|---|---|---|---|---|---|
| 59 | 14 | 0.6 | 2.5 | 0.9 | 0.1 | 0 | 0 | 3 |

## BECHAMEL SAUCE

*1 tabsp mono/polyunsaturated margarine (20g)*
*1 tabsp mono/polyunsaturated oil (20ml)*
*4 tabsp plain flour (40g)*
*1 cup non fat milk (250ml)*
*¼ tsp nutmeg*
*Freshly ground black pepper*
*1 egg or low cholesterol egg mix (50g)*

- Melt margarine and stir in oil and flour to form a smooth paste. Slowly add milk, nutmeg and black pepper.
- Cook in microwave or on top of stove for 4 to 5 minutes, stopping to stir vigorously to prevent any lumps. When thick and smooth, beat in egg.
- Use in recipes such as **Moussaka** p71.

**Serves 6 x ¼ cups (Total 1½ cups)**

*Handy Hint*
If not using immediately cover with plastic wrap to prevent a skin forming.

NUTRIENT SERVES

| KJ | Cal | Pro (g) | CHO (g) | Fibre (g) | T.fat (g) | S.fat (g) | Chol (mg) | Na (mg) |
|---|---|---|---|---|---|---|---|---|
| 414 | 99 | 3 | 7 | 0.1 | 7 | 1 | 55 | 29 |

## PLUM SAUCE

*2 medium plums (160g)*
*2 tabsp sugar (36g) or equivalent substitute*
*1 tsp chilli sauce (5ml)*
*1 tabsp red wine vinegar (20ml)*

- Cut plums in half and remove stone.
- Place in bowl and cover with plastic wrap.
- Microwave on **High** for 3 minutes.
- Place plums in kitchen whiz with sugar, chilli sauce and red wine vinegar.
- Whiz until smooth or strain.
- Serve with **Savoury Stuffed Crêpes** p38.

**Serves 8 x 1 tabsp (Total ⅔ cup)**

*Note*
Particularly nice with cold items.

NUTRIENTS PER SERVE

| KJ | Cal | Pro (g) | CHO (g) | Fibre (g) | T.fat (g) | S.fat (g) | Chol (mg) | Na (mg) |
|---|---|---|---|---|---|---|---|---|
| 102 | 25 | 0.13 | 6 | 0.44 | 0.03 | 0 | 0 | 9 |

## SWEET AND SOUR SAUCE

*¼ cup unsweetened pineapple juice (65ml)*
*1 tabsp cornflour (10g)*
*1 tabsp sugar (18g) or equivalent substitute*
*2 tabsp cider vinegar (40ml)*
*¼ cup water (65ml)*
*2 sticks chopped celery (150g)*
*1 large chopped carrot (150g)*
*1 small chopped red capsicum (100g)*
*1 tsp mono/polyunsaturated oil (5ml)*
*2 tsp water (10ml)*
*½ cup chopped unsweetened pineapple (100g)*
*2 sliced pickled onions (70g)*

- Drain juice from the canned pineapple.
- Mix cornflour to a paste with unsweetened pineapple juice in a saucepan.
- Add sugar, vinegar and water.
- Heat over moderate heat, stirring occasionally until thick and clear.
- Place celery, carrot and red capsicum in a wok or heavy based saucepan with oil and 2 tsp of water.
- Stir-fry for 3 to 4 minutes or until vegetables are just tender crisp.
- Add vegetables to sauce with pineapple and pickled onion.
- Reheat and if desired, add a little red food colouring to improve eye appeal.
- This basic sauce may be used with fish, chicken or pork.

*Sweet and Sour Sauce*

**Serves 4 x ²/₃ (Total 2²/₃ cups)**

*Microwave Adaptation*
Mix cornflour to a paste with pineapple juice. Add sugar, vinegar and water. Place in a microwave dish and cook on **High** for 3 to 4 minutes. Stop and stir once while cooking. Cook vegetables with oil and 2tsp water in a covered dish on **High** for 5 minutes. Just before serving, combine sauce, vegetables, pineapple and pickled onions. Reheat on **High** for 3 to 4 minutes.

*Variation*
Greater variation may be obtained by using water chestnuts, mushrooms and green capsicum in addition to or instead of some of the other vegetables.

NUTRIENTS PER SERVE

| KJ | Cal | Pro (g) | CHO (g) | Fibre (g) | T.fat (g) | S.fat (g) | Chol (mg) | Na (mg) |
|---|---|---|---|---|---|---|---|---|
| 345 | 83 | 2 | 16 | 3 | 1.4 | 0.2 | 0 | 54 |

# SEAFOOD SAUCE

¹/₄ cup light (97% fat free) mayonnaise 65ml)
2 tabsp tomato sauce (40ml)
¹/₂ tsp Worcestershire sauce
1 tsp lemon juice (5ml)
¹/₂ tsp chilli sauce or to taste

❏ Combine mayonnaise, tomato sauce, Worcestershire sauce, lemon juice and chilli sauce.
❏ Serve with seafood such as prawns, or in **Seafood Avocado Dip** p41.

**Serves 6 x 1 tabsp (¹/₂ cup total)**

NUTRIENTS PER SERVE

| KJ | Cal | Pro (g) | CHO (g) | Fibre (g) | T.fat (g) | S.fat (g) | Chol (mg) | Na (mg) |
|---|---|---|---|---|---|---|---|---|
| 87 | 21 | 0.1 | 4 | 0.2 | 0.4 | 0.3 | 3 | 161 |

## LOW FAT WHITE SAUCE

*1 cup non fat milk (250ml)*
*2 tsp cornflour (5g)*
*2 tabsp parmesan cheese (18g)*
*Freshly ground black pepper*

- Prepare white sauce by mixing together milk, cornflour, parmesan cheese and black pepper in a saucepan.
- Cook slowly while stirring until thick and smooth.

This low fat white sauce is ideal with Fettuccine or with fish or chicken.
**Serves 4 x ¼ cups (Total 1 cup)**

### Variation
Add finely chopped spring onions or chives, or ½ tsp of dry mustard or extra grated cheese in order to achieve a more definite cheese-flavoured sauce.

### Note
This sauce can also be prepared as directed in a microwave proof dish; place in microwave and cook at **Medium High** for 3 to 4 minutes, stopping to stir at least once.

### Handy Hint
A standard white sauce starts with a roux of margarine and flour. This recipe omits it and therefore is very low in fat. You may substitute ¼ cup of skim milk powder and 1 cup of water instead of non fat milk for reduced cost but the same calcium.

NUTRIENTS PER SERVE

| KJ | Cal | Pro (g) | CHO (g) | Fibre (g) | T.fat (g) | S.fat (g) | Chol (mg) | Na (mg) |
|---|---|---|---|---|---|---|---|---|
| 203 | 49 | 4 | 4 | 0 | 1.7 | 1 | 7 | 100 |

## CHEESE SAUCE

*1½ cups non fat milk (375ml)*
*1 tsp low sodium chicken stock powder (2.5g)*
*1 tabsp mono/polyunsaturated margarine (20g)*
*2 tabsp plain white flour (20g)*
*½ cup grated less than 10% fat cheese (60g)*

- Stir stock powder into milk and heat in a saucepan until hot.
- Melt margarine in a heavy based saucepan and stir in flour to form a smooth paste.
- Slowly add milk while continuing to stir.
- Stir and cook until thick and smooth, about 3 to 5 minutes.
- Stir in cheese, cook for 30 seconds longer and remove.
- Use this Cheese Sauce in **Lasagne** p68, in **Cauliflower Cheese** p86, in **Tuna Hot Pot** p82, or over broccoli or mixed steamed or microwaved vegetables.

**Serve 8 x ¼ cups (Total 2 cups)**

### Microwave Variation
Heat milk and stock cube in a jug. Melt margarine in a microwave dish for 30 seconds. Remove and stir in flour to form a smooth paste. Slowly add hot milk and stir. Return to microwave for a further 1 minute. Stir in cheese.

### Handy Hint
Low fat cheese used to reduce fat content.

NUTRIENT PER SERVE

| KJ | Cal | Pro (g) | CHO (g) | Fibre (g) | T.fat (g) | S.fat (g) | Chol (mg) | Na (mg) |
|---|---|---|---|---|---|---|---|---|
| 253 | 61 | 4.5 | 4.4 | 0.1 | 3 | 0.6 | 4.3 | 92 |

## YOGHURT SAUCE

*½ cup non fat natural yoghurt (125ml)*
*2 tsp lemon juice (10ml)*
*1 crushed clove garlic (3g)*
*1 tabsp each of finely chopped mint, coriander and parsley or to taste*

- Blend yoghurt, lemon juice, garlic and herbs.
- Place in a bowl and serve as a dipping sauce with **Lamb Kebabs** p73 or Turkish bread.

**Serves 6 x 1tabsp (Total ½ cup)**

NUTRIENTS PER SERVE

| KJ | Cal | Pro (g) | CHO (g) | Fibre (g) | T.fat (g) | S.fat (g) | Chol (mg) | Na (mg) |
|---|---|---|---|---|---|---|---|---|
| 50 | 12 | 1.3 | 1.3 | 0.1 | .05 | .02 | 1 | 15 |

## DESSERTS RECIPES

## Desserts

*Cold Desserts*
*Fresh Fruit Ideas 109*
*Apple Orange Fool 110*
*Apricot Whip 110 & Variations*
*Blancmange Pudding 110 & Variations*
*Burgundy Pears 113*
*Chocolate Mousse 111 & Variation*
*Compôte of Fruit 112*
*Fresh Fruit Lemon Jelly 112 & Variation*
*Gingered Rockmelon 111*
*Lemon Sponge 111 & Variations*
*Ricotta Cream 114*
*Spanish Cream 116*
*Strawberry Pie 114*
*Strawberry Whirl 113 & Variations*
*Summer Pudding 116*
*Tulip Fruits 115*
*Hot Desserts*
*Apple Cottage Pudding 117 & Variations*
*Bread Pudding 119*
*Custard Sauce 119*
*Lemon Delicious 119*
*Lemon Meringue Pie 118*

Desserts should be light and small to finish off a meal. Heavier substantial desserts are only suitable for people with a large energy requirement or if the dessert is delayed and becomes supper.

Desserts have been divided into Cold and Hot for convenience with a range of carbohydrate throughout.

**Apple Orange Fool** p110, **Fresh Fruit Lemon Jelly** p112, **Lemon Sponge** p111, or **Burgundy Pears** p113 make light desserts to follow a heavier meal. Base them on fresh fruit whenever possible.

Cholesterol and heart disease are of concern, and hence recipes have been tested using a low cholesterol egg mix. This contains egg white with a mixture of unsaturated oil plus colouring and flavouring to give an equivalent flavour of a whole egg. It substitutes well in dessert recipes. Where just one egg is used, the amount of cholesterol per person may not be significant. Analysis have all been done using eggs. One egg yolk or whole egg contains 220mg of cholesterol.

*All recipes have been analysed with no added sugar where possible — shown on the nutritional bar analysis as NS.*

## COLD DESSERTS

### FRESH FRUIT IDEAS

❏ Rockmelon with fresh passionfruit.

❏ Cubed watermelon with chopped mint.

❏ Rockmelon, passionfruit, banana salad with fresh kiwi fruit (see photograph this page).

❏ Strawberries with sliced banana.

❏ **Strawberry Pie** p114 made with fresh strawberries.

❏ Peeled and sliced oranges with chopped fresh mint.

❏ Fresh peaches spiked with cloves and brushed with a mixture of brown sugar, mono/polyunsaturated margarine and grilled.

❏ Fresh raspberries with **Custard Sauce** p119.

## APRICOT WHIP

*1 can puréed unsweetened apricots (415g)*
*¼ cup sugar (55g) or equivalent substitute*
*2 tsp gelatine (6g)*
*2 tabsp hot water (40ml)*
*2 egg whites (65ml)*

- Blend or purée apricots, plus sugar.
- Dissolve gelatine in cold water, heat until clear in microwave or in saucepan.
- Add to apricot mixture and chill until beginning to set.
- Whip egg whites until stiff and fold through chilled purée.
- Place in six serving dishes or one bowl.
- Refrigerate until set.

**Serves 6**

### Variation
**Apple Whip** Substitute 4 medium stewed apples for apricots.
**Strawberry Whip** Substitute 200g strawberries for apricots.
**Raspberry Whip** Substitute 200g raspberries for apricots.
**Apple/Blueberry Whip** Substitute 2 apples/ 200g blueberries for apricots.

NUTRIENTS PER SERVE

| KJ | Cal | Pro (g) | CHO (g) | Fibre (g) | T.fat (g) | S.fat (g) | Chol (mg) | Na (mg) |
|----|-----|---------|---------|-----------|-----------|-----------|-----------|---------|
| 290 | 71 | 3 | 14 | 1 | 0.1 | 0 | 0 | 24 |

NS

| KJ | Cal | CHO (g) |
|----|-----|---------|
| 160 | 38 | 6 |

## BLANCMANGE PUDDING

*2½ cups non fat milk (625ml)*
*¼ cup cornflour (30g)*
*1 tsp vanilla (5ml)*
*¼ cup sugar (55g) or equivalent substitute*

- Measure 2½ cups milk and heat 2 cups in a microwave dish or heavy based saucepan, reserving ½ cup.
- Mix remaining milk with cornflour.
- Slowly add to scalded milk and stir.
- Continue to cook and stir until thick and smooth or microwave for 5 minutes, stopping every couple of minutes to whisk briskly.
- Remove, add sugar and vanilla, whisk again.

**Serves 8**

### Variations
**Apricot Blancmange Pudding** Add 200g of puréed unsweetened canned or stewed apricots.
**Banana Blancmange Pudding** Add 2 mashed bananas.
**Strawberry Blancmange Pudding** Add 35 medium coarsely chopped strawberries.
**Passionfruit Blancmange Pudding** Add the pulp of one large passionfruit.
**Chocolate Blancmange Pudding** Add 2 tablespoons of cocoa with the cornflour.

NUTRIENTS PER SERVE

| KJ | Cal | Pro (g) | CHO (g) | Fibre (g) | T.fat (g) | S.fat (g) | Chol (mg) | Na (mg) |
|----|-----|---------|---------|-----------|-----------|-----------|-----------|---------|
| 282 | 69 | 3 | 14 | 0 | 0.09 | 0.05 | 2 | 35 |

NS

| KJ | Cal | CHO (g) |
|----|-----|---------|
| 184 | 44 | 8 |

## APPLE ORANGE FOOL

*5 medium peeled, sliced cooking apples (500g)*
*2 tabsp water (40ml)*
*¼ cup sugar (55g) or equivalent substitute*
*⅓ cup fresh orange juice (85ml)*
*½ x 200g carton non fat natural yoghurt (100g)*
*Apple and mint garnish*

- Cook apples and water in a covered microwave dish or heavy saucepan until soft.
- Cool slightly, purée until smooth in blender then add sugar, orange juice and non fat natural yoghurt.
- Purée until smooth.
- Place in individual serving dishes and garnish with fresh red and green apple slices plus a sprig of mint.

**Serves 6**

NUTRIENTS PER SERVE

| KJ | Cal | Pro (g) | CHO (g) | Fibre (g) | T.fat (g) | S.fat (g) | Chol (mg) | Na (mg) |
|----|-----|---------|---------|-----------|-----------|-----------|-----------|---------|
| 376 | 91 | 1 | 22 | 2 | 0.1 | 0.02 | 0.8 | 13 |

NS

| KJ | Cal | CHO (g) |
|----|-----|---------|
| 246 | 58 | 13 |

## DESSERTS RECIPES

## GINGERED ROCKMELON

*1 medium rockmelon (700g)*
*¼ cup lemon juice (65ml)*
*½ tsp dry ginger*
*½ cup boiled water (125ml)*
*¼ cup sugar (55g) or equivalent substitute*

- Peel and seed rockmelon, cut into cubes and place into a dish.
- Mix lemon juice, dry ginger and water in a microwave dish or saucepan and bring to the boil. Remove.
- Add sugar and stir until dissolved.
- Pour over rockmelon and chill well before serving.

**Serves 6**

*Variation*
Add a little bit of liqueur after bringing lemon juice, dry ginger and water to the boil.

NUTRIENTS PER SERVE

| KJ | Cal | Pro (g) | CHO (g) | Fibre (g) | T.fat (g) | S.fat (g) | Chol (mg) | Na (mg) |
|---|---|---|---|---|---|---|---|---|
| 265 | 65 | 0.6 | 15 | 1 | 0.2 | 0 | 0 | 12 |

NS

| KJ | Cal | CHO (g) |
|---|---|---|
| 134 | 32 | 7 |

## LEMON SPONGE

*2 cups cold water (500ml)*
*2 tabsp gelatine (25g)*
*1 cup boiling water (250ml)*
*½ cup lemon juice (125ml)*
*Zest of ½ lemon*
*½ cup sugar (110g) or equivalent substitute*
*2 egg whites (65ml)*

- Measure 2 cups cold water, pour a little over gelatine and allow to soften. Reserve remainder.
- Boil a further 1 cup of water, add gelatine and stir until dissolved.
- Stir in remaining cold water with lemon juice and lemon zest with sugar.
- Allow to partially set and then beat until frothy.
- Fold in stiffly beaten egg whites.
- Place in 8 serving dishes or one large bowl and return to refrigerator to set.
- Serve plain or with **Custard Sauce** p119.

**Serves 8**

*Variations*
**Lemon Orange Sponge** Use ¼ cup orange juice and ¼ cup lemon juice.
**Lemon Passionfruit Sponge** Use 2 medium passionfruit pulp and ¼ cup lemon juice.

NUTRIENTS PER SERVE

| KJ | Cal | Pro (g) | CHO (g) | Fibre (g) | T.fat (g) | S.fat (g) | Chol (mg) | Na (mg) |
|---|---|---|---|---|---|---|---|---|
| 299 | 73 | 3.6 | 14 | 0.01 | 0.04 | 0 | 0 | 25 |

NS

| KJ | Cal | CHO (g) |
|---|---|---|
| 103 | 24 | 2 |

## CHOCOLATE MOUSSE

*3 tsp gelatine (9g)*
*1½ tabsp cocoa (15g)*
*½ cup water (125ml)*
*1 can Bear Brand™ reduced fat chilled evaporated milk (375ml)*
*½ cup sugar (110g) or equivalent substitute*
*1 tsp vanilla (5ml)*

- Stir gelatine and cocoa in water to form a smooth paste.
- Heat in microwave until gelatine melts.
- Place chilled evaporated milk in a chilled mixing bowl and beat until thick.
- Beat in sugar, vanilla and hot cocoa and gelatine mixture.
- Pour into 12 glass dishes, refrigerate until set.
- Serve with low fat ice cream and if desired finely chopped hazelnuts.

**Serves 12**

*Variation*
**Strawberry Mousse** Substitute 1 cup of finely chopped strawberries for cocoa.

*Note*
4% Bear Brand™ will whip if well chilled but lower fat content evaporated milks will not e.g. Carnation Light™.

NUTRIENTS PER SERVE

| KJ | Cal | Pro (g) | CHO (g) | Fibre (g) | T.fat (g) | S.fat (g) | Chol (mg) | Na (mg) |
|---|---|---|---|---|---|---|---|---|
| 337 | 82 | 3 | 14 | 0.05 | 1.5 | 0.9 | 3 | 35 |

NS

| KJ | Cal | CHO (g) |
|---|---|---|
| 207 | 49 | 5 |

## FRESH FRUIT LEMON JELLY

*2 tabsp gelatine (25g)*
*½ cup water (125ml)*
*½ cup lemon juice (125ml)*
*1½ cups water (375ml)*
*½ cup sugar (110g) or equivalent substitute*
*Yellow food colouring if desired*
*2 medium passionfruit (pulp only) (125ml)*
*1 tabsp sugar (18g) or equivalent substitute*

- Mix gelatine in cold water.
- Microwave or heat on stove until gelatine has dissolved.
- Add lemon juice, 1½ cups of water and sugar.
- If desired add food colouring to a pleasing appearance.
- Place in individual serving dishes or 1 large dish and set in fridge.
- Serve with passionfruit sweetened with a little sugar and a slice of orange.

**Serves 6**

### Variation

**Lemon Orange Jelly** Substitute ½ cup lemon juice with a mixture of ¼ cup lemon juice and ¼ cup of orange juice. Add a little bit of food colouring if desired.

NUTRIENTS PER SERVE

| KJ | Cal | Pro (g) | CHO (g) | Fibre (g) | T.fat (g) | S.fat (g) | Chol (mg) | Na (mg) |
|---|---|---|---|---|---|---|---|---|
| 465 | 113 | 4 | 23 | 3 | 0.1 | 0 | 0 | 19 |

NS

| KJ | Cal | CHO (g) |
|---|---|---|
| 161 | 38 | 4 |

## COMPOTE OF FRUIT

*4 peeled cored pears (700g)*
*1 cup water (250ml)*
*½ cup apple juice (125ml)*
*1 tabsp liqueur e.g. Grand Marnier (20ml)*
*15 medium apricots (100g)*
*15 medium pitted prunes (120g)*

- Quarter pears and add to saucepan with water and apple juice and simmer gently until just softening.
- Add liqueur and apricots that have been cut into strips.
- Bring to the boil and simmer for 2 minutes. Remove from heat, add prunes and chill.

*Fresh Fruit Lemon Orange Jelly*

**Serves 10**

### Variation

Add 1 tabsp toasted slivered almonds or substitute ½ punnet of frozen or fresh blueberries or raspberries for prunes. Must be added after fruit has been chilled to prevent staining. Use whatever fruit is in season in any combination that is pleasing. You may combine canned fruit in natural juice with fresh or dried fruit when time is short

NUTRIENTS PER SERVE

| KJ | Cal | Pro (g) | CHO (g) | Fibre (g) | T.fat (g) | S.fat (g) | Chol (mg) | Na (mg) |
|---|---|---|---|---|---|---|---|---|
| 312 | 74 | 0.6 | 17 | 3 | 0.1 | 0 | 0 | 4 |

## DESSERTS RECIPES

*Strawberry Whirl*

## STRAWBERRY WHIRL

1/2 cup ricotta cheese (125g)
15 medium fresh strawberries (150g)
1 small carton non fat natural yoghurt (200g)
2 tsp gelatine (6g)
2 tabsp water (40ml)
1/3 cup sugar (70g) or equivalent substitute.

- Blend or purée ricotta cheese, strawberries and yoghurt.
- Mix gelatine into cold water and then heat until clear in microwave.
- Blend gelatine and sugar into yoghurt mixture.
- Place in 4 individual serving dishes.
- Decorate with a whole strawberry and serve with low fat ice cream or **Ricotta Cream** p114.

**Serves 6**

*Variations*

**Banana Whirl** Substitute banana for strawberries.
**Passionfruit Whirl** Substitute passionfruit for strawberries.
**Raspberry Whirl** Substitute raspberries for strawberries.

NUTRIENTS PER SERVE

| KJ | Cal | Pro (g) | CHO (g) | Fibre (g) | T.fat (g) | S.fat (g) | Chol (mg) | Na (mg) |
|---|---|---|---|---|---|---|---|---|
| 406 | 98 | 5 | 15 | 0.5 | 2 | 1 | 10 | 67 |

NS

| KJ | Cal | CHO (g) |
|---|---|---|
| 241 | 58 | 4 |

## BURGUNDY PEARS

8 medium pears (800g)
1 cup burgundy or any red wine (250ml)
1 cup water (250ml)
Red food colouring if desired
1/4 cup sugar (55g) or equivalent substitute

- Peel pears leaving the stem intact.
- Place in a large saucepan with wine and water.
- Bring to the boil, cover and simmer until just soft, about 10 minutes.
- Remove pears to a serving dish.
- Reduce liquid to half by boiling, add a little red food colouring and sugar.
- Pour over the pears and refrigerate.
- Turn occasionally to allow colour to be absorbed evenly.
- Serve well chilled with low fat ice cream or **Custard Sauce** p119.

**Serves 8**

NUTRIENTS PER SERVE

| KJ | Cal | Pro (g) | CHO (g) | Fibre (g) | T.fat (g) | S.fat (g) | Chol (mg) | Na (mg) |
|---|---|---|---|---|---|---|---|---|
| 409 | 98 | 0.4 | 19 | 2 | 0.1 | 0 | 0 | 5 |

NS

| KJ | Cal | CHO (g) |
|---|---|---|
| 311 | 74 | 13 |

*Strawberry Pie*

## STRAWBERRY PIE

1 cup **Low Fat Fibre Pastry** *p131*
2 cups fresh washed and hulled strawberries (300g)
1 strawberry flavoured sugar free jelly
1 cup boiling water (250ml)
1 tabsp cornflour (10g)
1 cup cold water (250ml)

- Prepare **Low Fat Fibre Pastry** and line a 25cm pie dish. Prick well with a fork.
- Bake in 200°C oven for 12 to 15 minutes or until nicely golden. Remove and cool.
- Set aside about 1½ cups of the best strawberries and cut up the remainder.
- Mix jelly with boiling water in a saucepan and stir until dissolved.
- Mix cornflour with cold water.
- Stir into jelly mixture to form a smooth sauce.
- Add the cut up strawberries and cook and stir over moderate heat for 3 to 4 minutes or until mixture is clear.
- Remove and sieve.
- Refrigerate until cool (about 30 minutes).
- Arrange the remaining strawberries attractively in pie dish.
- Pour over cooled jelly mixture, refrigerate until set.

**Serves 6**

*Note*
May serve with **Ricotta Cream** p114.

NUTRIENTS PER SERVE

| KJ | Cal | Pro (g) | CHO (g) | Fibre (g) | T.fat (g) | S.fat (g) | Chol (mg) | Na (mg) |
|---|---|---|---|---|---|---|---|---|
| 573 | 139 | 6 | 13.5 | 3 | 6.6 | 1.3 | 3 | 23 |

## RICOTTA CREAM

2 tabsp non fat milk (40ml)
1 tsp gelatine (3g)
¼ cup ricotta cheese (65g)
2 tsp sugar (8g) or equivalent substitute
¼ tsp vanilla

- Blend milk and gelatine and heat over hot water or in microwave until dissolved.
- Beat milk, gelatine, ricotta cheese, sugar and vanilla together until smooth.
- Slightly chill and this may then be piped or scooped onto desserts.

**Serves 4**

*Note*
Sugar contributes an insignificant amount of carbohydrate in this recipe

NUTRIENTS PER SERVE

| KJ | Cal | Pro (g) | CHO (g) | Fibre (g) | T.fat (g) | S.fat (g) | Chol (mg) | Na (mg) |
|---|---|---|---|---|---|---|---|---|
| 165 | 40 | 3 | 3 | 0 | 2 | 1 | 8 | 39 |

## TULIP FRUITS

3 egg whites (1/3 cup) (85ml)
1/2 cup sugar (110g) or equivalent substitute
1/2 cup plain white flour (65g)
1/4 cup melted mono/polyunsaturated margarine (65g)
1 tabsp water (20ml)
1 tsp pure vanilla essence
3 cups mixed fruit e.g. blueberries, raspberries, peaches, grapes, rockmelon, strawberries (500g)
2 tabsp sugar (36g) or equivalent substitute

- Line 4 baking trays with baking paper, draw two circles on each using a saucer as a template. You may re-use the same trays if desired.
- Beat egg whites, sugar, flour, melted margarine, water and vanilla together until smooth.
- Spoon about two tablespoons of mixture into the centre of each circle using 1/4 cup dry measure, about 2/3 full.
- Using a metal spatula spread the mixture to fill the circles.
- Bake in 200°C oven for 6 to 8 minutes or until edges are crisp and starting to brown.
- Remove from oven, gently remove from tray with the aid of a metal spatula.
- Place on top of an inverted large glass, quickly press with fingers to create a fluted effect. If it has become too hard, put back in oven to soften and try again.

**Filling**
- Prepare fruit by peeling, chopping and mixing with sugar and leaving for 1 hour or more for flavour to develop.
- Serve with a 1/3 cup of fruit in each tulip. If desired a small scoop of low fat ice cream or **Ricotta Cream** p114 may be added

**Serves 8**

*Note*
**Tulip Fruits** are easy to remove from the tray when baking paper is used. Do not use greaseproof or wax paper. These will keep in an airtight container for a couple of days or longer in the freezer. If soft when thawed you may heat to crisp.

NUTRIENTS PER SERVE

| KJ | Cal | Pro (g) | CHO (g) | Fibre (g) | T.fat (g) | S.fat (g) | Chol (mg) | Na (mg) |
|---|---|---|---|---|---|---|---|---|
| 804 | 192 | 3 | 30 | 1 | 7 | 1 | 0 | 22 |

NS

| KJ | Cal | CHO (g) |
|---|---|---|
| 532 | 128 | 14 |

*Summer Pudding*

## SUMMER PUDDING

*3 cups mixed summer fruit (500g)*
*½ cup water (125ml)*
*¼ cup sugar (55g) or equivalent substitute*
*9 slices of white high fibre bread no crust (160g)*

- Prepare 3 cups of mixed fruit such as blueberries, raspberries, strawberries, kiwi fruit, grapes or any other in season. Some should be juicy.
- Blueberries and raspberries should be microwaved for 4 minutes on **High** with sugar and water until soft and juicy.
- Toss raspberries and blueberries in syrup with hulled and sliced strawberries, peeled and sliced kiwi fruit and seeded and halved grapes.
- Cut the crusts from the 9 slices of bread and discard crusts.
- Line the bottom and sides of a 1 litre bowl with bread. Pour in ½ the fruit mixture, cover with bread cut to fit. Add rest of fruit mixture and top with remaining bread cut to fit.
- Cover with plastic wrap; place a plate on top that is slightly smaller than the bowl.
- Weigh down with a couple of heavy cans.
- Refrigerate for 4 to 6 hours or overnight.
- Unmould and slice to serve. A good accompaniment is low fat ice cream or **Custard Sauce** p119.

**Serves 8**

NUTRIENTS PER SERVE

| KJ | Cal | Pro (g) | CHO (g) | Fibre (g) | T.fat (g) | S.fat (g) | Chol (mg) | Na (mg) |
|---|---|---|---|---|---|---|---|---|
| 423 | 102 | 3 | 21.5 | 2 | 0.6 | 0.1 | 0 | 90 |

NS

| KJ | Cal | CHO (g) |
|---|---|---|
| 312 | 75 | 14 |

## SPANISH CREAM

*2 cup non fat milk (500ml)*
*1 tabsp gelatine (12g)*
*2 egg yolks or ½ cup low cholesterol egg mix (100g)*
*1 tsp vanilla*
*¼ cup sugar (55g) or equivalent substitute*
*2 egg whites*

- Measure milk and reserve 1 cup.
- Stir gelatine into 1 cup of milk and cook or microwave until scalding.
- Beat egg with remaining milk and add to hot milk.
- Microwave for about 5 minutes, stopping to stir occasionally. Don't overcook or it will curdle. Alternatively this may be cooked in a heavy based saucepan on the stove. Stir continuously so that it doesn't burn.
- Remove from microwave or stove and add vanilla and sugar.
- Chill until slightly firm, about 1 hour.

*Spanish Cream with Raspberry Sauce*

- ❏ Beat egg whites until stiff but not dry.
- ❏ Fold into chilled gelatine mixture and place in a glass bowl.
- ❏ Refrigerate for 2 - 3 hours.
- ❏ As it sets it will separate to form a custard bottom and foamy top.

**Serves 8 x 1/2 cups**

*Note*
This is a light refreshing dessert on its own or beautiful with fresh fruit such as strawberries, raspberries or peaches which may be puréed if desired.
There will be 50g less of cholesterol by using low cholesterol egg mix

NUTRIENTS PER SERVE

| KJ | Cal | Pro (g) | CHO (g) | Fibre (g) | T.fat (g) | S.fat (g) | Chol (mg) | Na (mg) |
|---|---|---|---|---|---|---|---|---|
| 318 | 77 | 5 | 11 | 0 | 1 | 0.4 | 49 | 49 |

NS

| KJ | Cal | CHO (g) |
|---|---|---|
| 200 | 48 | 4 |

# HOT DESSERTS

## APPLE COTTAGE PUDDING

1/2 cup white self raising flour (65g)
1/2 cup wholemeal self raising flour (70g)
2 tabsp sugar (36g) or equivalent substitute
1 tabsp mono/polyunsaturated oil (20ml)
1/2 cup non fat milk (125ml)
1 egg or a low cholesterol egg mix (50g)
6 small apples, peeled, cored and sliced (600g)
2 tabsp water (40ml)

- ❏ Measure flours and sugar into a bowl.
- ❏ Mix together oil, milk and egg.
- ❏ Stir into dry ingredients until just moistened.
- ❏ Microwave or cook apples and water until soft e.g. about 5 minutes.
- ❏ Place apple in base of greased large casserole dish (20cm diameter).
- ❏ Cover with pudding mixture.
- ❏ Bake in a 180°C oven for 30 minutes.

**Serves 12**

*Variation*
**Apricot Cottage Pudding** Substitute fresh or pie apricots for apple.
**Peach Cottage Pudding** Substitute fresh or pie peaches for apple.
**Rhubarb Cottage Pudding** Substitute rhubarb for apple but precook with 1/4 cup sugar or equivalent substitute for 4 - 5 minutes in the microwave.
**Rhubarb Apple Cottage Pudding** Substitute rhubarb and apple for plain apple.

*Note*
Analysis is done using eggs but reduce cholesterol by 60mg per serve by using a low cholesterol egg mix.

NUTRIENTS PER SERVE

| KJ | Cal | Pro (g) | CHO (g) | Fibre (g) | T.fat (g) | S.fat (g) | Chol (mg) | Na (mg) |
|---|---|---|---|---|---|---|---|---|
| 390 | 94 | 2.5 | 16 | 2 | 2 | 0.4 | 16 | 88 |

NS

| KJ | Cal | CHO (g) |
|---|---|---|
| 347 | 84 | 13 |

DESSERTS RECIPES

*Lemon Meringue Pie*

## LEMON MERINGUE PIE

*1 cup* **Low Fat Fibre Pastry** *p131*

**Filling**
²/₃ cup lemon juice (170ml)
1¹/₂ cups water (375ml)
¹/₂ cup cornflour (65g)
Zest of 3 lemons
¹/₂ cup sugar (110grams) or equivalent substitute
4 egg yolks (68g)

**Meringue Topping**
4 egg whites (100g)
²/₃ cup castor sugar (140 grams) or sugar substitute e.g. Splenda™

❑ Line a 25cm pie dish with the **Low Fat Fibre Pastry**. Crimp edges. Prick with a fork.
❑ Cook pastry at 200°C for 12 minutes or until lightly brown.
❑ Heat lemon juice, 1 cup of water and lemon zest in a saucepan. (Reserve ¹/₂ cup water.)
❑ Mix cornflour to a paste with reserved ¹/₂ cup water and add to the lemon mixture cooking and stirring until thick and smooth.
❑ Lightly beat the sugar with the egg yolks. Slowly mix into lemon mixture and cook for 2 - 3 minutes more. Do not allow to boil.
❑ Pour into cooked pie shell.
❑ Beat egg whites until stiff but not dry then slowly beat in the castor sugar until thick and smooth.
❑ Spread meringue onto top of pie making sure to seal the edges with meringue completely.
❑ Bake in a 200°C oven for 10 minutes then 150°C for another 10 minutes.

**Serves 12**

*Note*
If time is short use filo rather than low fat fibre pastry.
Lemon zest is the finely grated outer rind of lemon. Be careful to avoid including the pith.
If using Splenda™ in meringue, beat egg whites till they just hold their peaks, then beat in Splenda™. Be careful not to overbeat. It will be light and fluffy.

NUTRIENTS PER SERVE

| KJ | Cal | Pro (g) | CHO (g) | Fibre (g) | T.fat (g) | S.fat (g) | Chol (mg) | Na (mg) |
|---|---|---|---|---|---|---|---|---|
| 809 | 197 | 5 | 34 | 1.7 | 4.5 | 1 | 61 | 133 |

NS

| KJ | Cal | CHO (g) |
|---|---|---|
| 512 | 124 | 16 |

**Note** NS = No Added Sugar

118

## BREAD PUDDING

*2 tsp mono/polyunsaturated margarine (10g)*
*4 slices wholemeal bread (100g)*
*2 eggs or low cholesterol egg mix (100g)*
*3 cups non fat milk (750ml)*
*¼ cup sugar (55g) or equivalent substitute*
*¼ cup sultanas (40g)*

- ❏ Spread margarine very thinly on bread and cut into cubes.
- ❏ Beat eggs, milk and sugar together.
- ❏ Place bread in a greased 1½-litre casserole dish.
- ❏ Sprinkle sultanas on top.
- ❏ Pour milk mixture over.
- ❏ Cover and bake in a 180°C oven for ½ hour.
- ❏ Remove lid and bake for further ½ hour or until a knife comes out clean.

**Serves 8**

*Note*
Analysis is done with eggs. Cholesterol will be insignificant if low cholesterol egg mix is used.

NUTRIENTS PER SERVE

| KJ | Cal | Pro (g) | CHO (g) | Fibre (g) | T.fat (g) | S.fat (g) | Chol (mg) | Na (mg) |
|---|---|---|---|---|---|---|---|---|
| 540 | 131 | 6 | 20 | 1 | 3 | 0.7 | 50 | 118 |

NS

| KJ | Cal | CHO (g) |
|---|---|---|
| 442 | 106 | 14 |

## LEMON DELICIOUS

*3 tabsp mono/polyunsaturated margarine (60g)*
*¼ cup sugar (55g) or equivalent substitute*
*3 egg yolks or 3 tabsp low cholesterol egg mix (50g)*
*½ cup wholemeal self raising flour (70g)*
*½ cup lemon juice (125ml)*
*2 cups non fat milk (500ml)*
*3 egg whites (80g)*

- ❏ Cream margarine with the sugar.
- ❏ Separate egg whites from yolks and beat the yolks or low cholesterol egg mix into the creamed mixture.
- ❏ Stir in the flour and gradually add the lemon juice and non fat milk, mixing well.
- ❏ Beat the egg whites until stiff but not dry.
- ❏ Fold into the mixture.
- ❏ Pour into a greased 1½-litre casserole dish and place in a water bath.
- ❏ Cook in a 160°C oven for 1 hour.

**Serves 8**

*Note*
Cholesterol would be insignificant using low cholesterol egg mix.

NUTRIENTS PER SERVE

| KJ | Cal | Pro (g) | CHO (g) | Fibre (g) | T.fat (g) | S.fat (g) | Chol (mg) | Na (mg) |
|---|---|---|---|---|---|---|---|---|
| 654 | 159 | 5.5 | 15 | 1 | 8 | 1.6 | 68 | 107 |

NS

| KJ | Cal | CHO (g) |
|---|---|---|
| 556 | 135 | 9 |

## CUSTARD SAUCE

*2½ cups non fat milk (625ml)*
*2 tsp cornflour (5g)*
*1 egg or low cholesterol egg mix (50g)*
*1 tsp vanilla (5ml)*
*2 tabsp sugar (36g) or equivalent substitute*

- ❏ Measure milk. Reserve ½ cup and heat remaining 2 cups of milk in a large dish in the microwave until just below boiling.
- ❏ Mix the remaining ½ cup cold milk with cornflour, egg, vanilla and sugar.
- ❏ Slowly add to simmering milk and beat well.
- ❏ Return to microwave and cook for a further 2 or 3 minutes, stopping to give the occasional mix.
- ❏ Remove from microwave and chill.
- ❏ Serve as a sauce over puddings such as **Lemon Sponge** p111 or **Apple Cottage Pudding** p117.

**Serves 12 x ¼ cup (Total 3 cups)**

*Note*
Traditional cooking. Cook in a heavy based saucepan on stove, stirring continuously with a wooden spoon.

NUTRIENTS PER SERVE

| KJ | Cal | Pro (g) | CHO (g) | Fibre (g) | T.fat (g) | S.fat (g) | Chol (mg) | Na (mg) |
|---|---|---|---|---|---|---|---|---|
| 155 | 38 | 2.4 | 6 | 0 | 0.5 | 0.2 | 17 | 29 |

NS

| KJ | Cal | CHO (g) |
|---|---|---|
| 112 | 27 | 3 |

## BAKING RECIPES

*Oatmeal Carrot Muffins p125*
*Oatmeal Treacle Biscuits p124*
*Pumpkin Scones p121*
*Oatcakes p124*

# Baking

*Apple Muffins 127*
*Banana Date Muffins 127*
  *Soya Muffins 127*
*Banana Tea Bread 122*
  *Apple Banana Tea Bread 123*
*Bran Muffins 128*
*Carrot Cake 121*
*Choux Pastry 131*
  *Kiwi Choux Ring 131*
*Crispy Lavash Bread 125*

*Damper with Beer 130*
*Date Loaf 122*
*Dumplings 128*
  *Sweet Dumplings 129*
*Fruity Loaf 126*
*Low Fat Cereal Loaf 123*
  *Low Fat Apricot Loaf 123*
*Low Fat Fibre Pastry 131*
*Low Joule Garlic Croutons 130*
*Oatcakes 124*
*Oatmeal Carrot Muffins 125*
*Oatmeal Fruit Slice 126*

*Oatmeal Treacle Biscuits 124*
*Plain Scones 121*
  *Cheese Scones 121*
  *Savoury Scones 121*
*Potato Muffins 128*
*Pumpkin Scones 121*
*Savoury Cases 130*
*Stained Glass Window Cake 122*
*Wholemeal Crêpes 129*
  *Crêpes with Italian Seafood Sauce 129*
  *Petite Crêpes 129*

Use high fibre products when possible. Small serves of baking products add taste without significantly increasing overall kilojoules. Recipes containing oatmeal and milk will help to give a lower Glycaemic Index.

All recipes are tested using cholesterol egg mix where indicated. All analyses are done with eggs. In many cases the quantity of cholesterol from one serve is relatively insignificant.

Where possible the sugar has been reduced or honey, fruit juice or fruit has been used instead. Certain recipes containing sugar have been tested with a sugar substitute (listed in the ingredients as an alternative) and in these instances a **No Added Sugar** (NS) analysis appears below the nutritional bar.

Muffins can be made in small patty tins and are perfect for a snack. They freeze well.

Try **Apple Muffins** p127, **Banana Date Muffins** p127, **Bran Muffins** p128, **Oatmeal Carrot Muffins** p125 or **Potato Muffins** p128.
**Plain Scones** p121 may be used as a bread substitute at lunch or for afternoon tea.
**Pumpkin Scones** p121 are moist and flavoursome and are also popular.
Rather than high fat cakes with icing, try loaves such as **Date Loaf** p122, **Fruity Loaf** p126 or **Low Fat Cereal Loaf** p123.
Pastry can be made with less fat by incorporating ricotta cheese in **Low Fat Fibre Pastry** p131. Filo pastry is often a good substitute if time is short, as in **Lemon Meringue Pie** p118. **Savoury Cases** p130 and **Choux Pastry** p131 made as puffs are excellent for low fat savoury fillings when entertaining. Make extra and freeze.

## PUMPKIN SCONES

*1 tabsp mono/polyunsaturated margarine (20g)*
*1/4 cup sugar (55g) or equivalent substitute*
*1 tabsp hot water (20ml)*
*1 egg or low cholesterol egg mix (50g)*
*1 heaped cup cold sieved pumpkin (170g)*
*2 cups wholemeal self raising flour (280g)*

- Blend margarine and sugar with hot water.
- Beat in egg and pumpkin.
- Stir in flour and mix until no dry areas are left.
- If pumpkin is dry, add a little more water to give a drop consistency.
- Using two spoons, drop mixture onto a greased biscuit tray.
- Bake in a 180°C oven for 10 to 12 minutes.
- Scones may be frozen and reheated in a oven or microwave oven.

**Serves 20 scones**

*Note*
These freeze beautifully and reheat for afternoon teas, school lunches etc.

NUTRIENTS PER SERVE

| KJ | Cal | Pro (g) | CHO (g) | Fibre (g) | T.fat (g) | S.fat (g) | Chol (mg) | Na (mg) |
|---|---|---|---|---|---|---|---|---|
| 269 | 65 | 2 | 11 | 2 | 1 | 0.3 | 9 | 96 |

NS

| KJ | Cal | CHO (g) |
|---|---|---|
| 229 | 56 | 8 |

## PLAIN SCONES

*1 cup wholemeal self raising flour (140g)*
*1 cup white self raising flour (130g)*
*1/4 cup mono/polyunsaturated margarine (65g)*
*2/3 cup non fat milk (165ml)*

- Blend flours together in a bowl.
- Cut in margarine using two knives until size of small peas.
- Stir in milk with fork, only adding to dry areas.
- Form into a smooth ball.
- Knead 2 to 3 times on a lightly floured board.
- Roll out 1 1/2cm thick.
- Using a 5cm biscuit cutter, cut into 20 scones.
- Place on an ungreased baking sheet and brush with non fat milk.
- Bake in a 200°C oven for 12 minutes.

**Serves 20**

*Variation*
**Cheese Scones** Add 1/2 cup finely grated cheese (60g) to the flour mixture.
**Savoury Scones** Add 1/2 tsp dried mixed herbs, 1/2 tsp dry mustard and 60g finely chopped lean ham to the dry ingredients.

NUTRIENTS PER SERVE

| KJ | Cal | Pro (g) | CHO (g) | Fibre (g) | T.fat (g) | S.fat (g) | Chol (mg) | Na (mg) |
|---|---|---|---|---|---|---|---|---|
| 286 | 69 | 2 | 9 | 1 | 3 | 0.5 | 0.3 | 95 |

Cakes and desserts are acceptable in controlled quantities but we should limit the consumption of sugar and fat as they can have a negative effect on health. Small serves are recommended.

## CARROT CAKE

*1/3 cup mono/polyunsaturated oil (85ml)*
*1/2 cup honey (125ml) or 1/2 cup brown sugar (90g) or equivalent substitute*
*2 eggs or low cholesterol egg mix (100g)*
*1/2 cup non fat milk (125ml)*
*1 tsp cinnamon*
*1/4 tsp ground cloves*
*1/2 tsp nutmeg*
*1 cup self raising wholemeal flour (140g)*
*1 cup self raising white flour (130g)*
*1 cup sultanas (170g)*
*2 medium finely grated carrots (200g)*

- Beat oil, honey, eggs and milk together.
- Fold cinnamon, cloves, nutmeg, flours, sultanas and grated carrot together.
- Mix dry into wet ingredients until just moistened.
- Place in a greased and lined square 20cm tin or a 30 cm ringed tin.
- Bake in a 180°C oven for 45 to 50 minutes. A skewer should come out clean when done.
- Allow to cool for 10 minutes then turn out onto a wire rack to cool.

**Serves 40 small slices**

NUTRIENTS PER SERVE

| KJ | Cal | Pro (g) | CHO (g) | Fibre (g) | T.fat (g) | S.fat (g) | Chol (mg) | Na (mg) |
|---|---|---|---|---|---|---|---|---|
| 286 | 68 | 1 | 10 | 0.8 | 3 | 0.4 | 9 | 55 |

NS

| KJ | Cal | CHO (g) |
|---|---|---|
| 249 | 60 | 8 |

## STAINED GLASS WINDOW CAKE

*Glacé red, green or yellow cherries (350g)*
*Glacé pineapple (100g)*
*Dried apricots (250g)*
*Whole peeled almonds (125g)*
*Whole pecans (125g)*
*Pitted dates (150g)*
*Sultanas (150g)*
*½ cup brandy (125ml)*
*½ cup sugar (110g) equivalent substitute*
*1 cup plain wholemeal flour (140g)*
*1 tsp baking powder (2.8g)*
*3 eggs or low cholesterol egg mix (150g)*
*1 tsp vanilla essence*

- Soak fruit and nuts in brandy overnight or by heating on **Low** in the microwave for 1 hour.
- Mix sugar, flour and baking powder together and sieve over fruit.
- Beat eggs and vanilla until frothy.
- Pour eggs over fruit mixture and stir well.
- Place in 10cm x 20cm loaf tin that has been lined with foil and sprayed with oil.
- Bake in 150°C - 165°C oven for 1½ to 2 hours.
- Cover with foil after the first 30 minutes.
- When cold remove foil and wrap in fresh foil for 2 days.
- Cut thinly into 20 slices, then each in half.
- This is not too sweet as sugar has been reduced and dried apricot has been added.
- Before serving this may be glazed with sugar, gelatine and water.

**Serves 40 slices**

NUTRIENTS PER SERVE

| KJ | Cal | Pro (g) | CHO (g) | Fibre (g) | T.fat (g) | S.fat (g) | Chol (mg) | Na (mg) |
|---|---|---|---|---|---|---|---|---|
| 667 | 161 | 3 | 18 | 2.3 | 8 | 1.1 | 14 | 19 |

NS

| KJ | Cal | CHO (g) |
|---|---|---|
| 628 | 151 | 16 |

**Note** NS = No Added Sugar

Substitute low cholesterol egg mix for eggs in baking and significantly reduce cholesterol. Wherever it has been recommended, it has been tested with that recipe.

## DATE LOAF

*¾ cup or 20 medium finely chopped dates (100g)*
*1 cup coarsely chopped pecans or walnuts (100g)*
*½ cup sugar (110g) or equivalent substitute*
*2 tabsp mono/polyunsaturated margarine (40g)*
*1 tsp bicarbonate of soda (2g)*
*1 cup boiling water (250ml)*
*2 eggs or low cholesterol egg mix (100g)*
*1½ cups plain wholemeal flour (210g)*
*1 tsp vanilla*

- Blend dates and nuts in a food processor or chop until fine.
- Place in a bowl with sugar, margarine and bicarbonate of soda.
- Pour over boiling water
- Stir in eggs, flour and vanilla.
- Place in a greased 10cm x 20cm loaf tin.
- Bake at 165°C for 50 to 60 minutes.

**Serves 40 slices**

*Note*
**Date Loaf** and **Banana Tea Bread** can be successfully doubled and frozen.

NUTRIENTS PER SERVE

| KJ | Cal | Pro (g) | CHO (g) | Fibre (g) | T.fat (g) | S.fat (g) | Chol (mg) | Na (mg) |
|---|---|---|---|---|---|---|---|---|
| 251 | 61 | 1.4 | 7 | 1 | 3 | 0.3 | 9 | 12 |

NS

| KJ | Cal | CHO (g) |
|---|---|---|
| 211 | 51 | 5 |

## BANANA TEA BREAD

*1¾ cups wholemeal self raising flour (245g)*
*¼ tsp bicarbonate of soda (0.5g)*
*2 eggs or low cholesterol egg mix (100g)*
*1 cup mashed banana (300g)*
*¼ cup mono/polyunsaturated oil (65ml)*
*2 tabsp honey (40ml)*
*¼ cup chopped walnuts or pecans (30g)*

- Mix flour and bicarbonate of soda together.
- Beat eggs with mashed banana, oil, honey and nuts.
- Stir liquid quickly and lightly into dry ingredients until whole mixture is just moistened.
- Line a 20cm x 10cm loaf tin with non-stick baking paper or greased parchment paper.
- Spoon mixture into loaf tin.

*Banana Tea Bread*
*Date Loaf*
*Fruity Loaf*

- Bake in 180°C oven for 40 minutes until golden brown with cracks across the middle.
- Serve plain or with a light spread. Cut loaf in 20 slices then each slice in half to equal 40 pieces. These are small serves.

**Serves 40 x 15g slices**

*Variation*

**Apple Banana Tea Bread** Substitute half apple for banana and replace nuts with sultanas.

NUTRIENTS PER SERVE

| KJ | Cal | Pro (g) | CHO (g) | Fibre (g) | T.fat (g) | S.fat (g) | Chol (mg) | Na (mg) |
|---|---|---|---|---|---|---|---|---|
| 217 | 52 | 1 | 6 | 0.9 | 3 | 0.3 | 9 | 45 |

## LOW FAT CEREAL LOAF

*1/2 cup skim milk powder (50g)*
*1/2 cup sugar (110g) or sugar substitute*
*1/2 cup sultanas (85g)*
*3 crushed Weet Bix™ or Vita Brits™ (45g)*
*1 tsp vanilla (5ml)*
*1 cup boiling water (250ml)*
*1 cup wholemeal self raising flour (140g)*
*1 tsp cinnamon*
*1 tsp baking powder (2.5g)*

- Mix skim milk powder, sugar, sultanas and crushed Weet-Bix™ and vanilla together.
- Add boiling water.
- Mix flour, cinnamon and baking powder together.
- Fold dry ingredients into mixture until just moistened.
- Place in a greased 10cm x 20cm loaf tin.
- Bake in 180°C oven for 35 - 40 minutes.

**Serves 20 slices**

*Variation*

**Low Fat Apricot Loaf** Substitute 1/2 cup finely chopped apricots for sultanas.

*Note*

For a lighter loaf substitute 50% white flour for all whole meal.

NUTRIENTS PER SERVE

| KJ | Cal | Pro (g) | CHO (g) | Fibre (g) | T.fat (g) | S.fat (g) | Chol (mg) | Na (mg) |
|---|---|---|---|---|---|---|---|---|
| 293 | 71 | 2 | 15 | 1.2 | 0.2 | 0.04 | 8 | 48 |

NS

| KJ | Cal | CHO (g) |
|---|---|---|
| 215 | 52 | 10 |

## BAKING RECIPES

## OATMEAL TREACLE BISCUITS

1³/4 cups wholemeal plain flour (240g)
1/2 tsp bicarbonate of soda
1 tsp cinnamon
1 cup melted mono/polyunsaturated margarine (250ml)
1 tabsp treacle (25g)
1 egg or low cholesterol egg mix (50g)
1/2 cup sugar (110g) or equivalent substitute
1/4 cup non fat milk (65ml)
2 cups quick cooking oatmeal (200g)
1 cup sultanas (170g)

❑ Mix flour, bicarbonate of soda and cinnamon together.
❑ Mix melted margarine and treacle together.
❑ Beat margarine mixture into flour mixture with egg and sugar.
❑ Mix in milk, oatmeal and sultanas.
❑ Using two teaspoons, drop walnut sized mounds onto a greased tray.
❑ Bake in a 180°C oven for 12 minutes.

**Serves 72 biscuits**

*Note*
They will be soft when cooked but will harden upon cooling.

NUTRIENTS PER SERVE

| KJ | Cal | Pro (g) | CHO (g) | Fibre (g) | T.fat (g) | S.fat (g) | Chol (mg) | Na (mg) |
|---|---|---|---|---|---|---|---|---|
| 249 | 60 | 0.9 | 7 | 0.7 | 3 | 0.5 | 3 | 38 |

NS

| KJ | Cal | CHO (g) |
|---|---|---|
| 227 | 55 | 6 |

## OATCAKES

1¹/2 cup traditional oatmeal (150g)
1¹/2 cups plain wholemeal flour (210g)
1/4 cup sugar (55g) or equivalent substitute
1/2 tsp bicarbonate of soda (1g)
1/2 cup mono/polyunsaturated margarine (125g)
1/4 - 1/3 cup of iced water (65 - 85ml)

❑ Combine oatmeal, flour, sugar and bicarbonate of soda in a mixing bowl.
❑ Cut margarine into flour mixture until the size of peas.
❑ Add ice water until it will stick together while pressing with a fork.
❑ Roll out 1/2cm thick on slightly floured board.
❑ Using a 5cm to 6cm biscuit cutter, cut into rounds.
❑ Place on greased baking sheet.
❑ Bake in a 180°C oven for 12 to 15 minutes, until crisp and golden.
❑ Remove and place on rack to cool.
❑ Store in an airtight container.
❑ Serve by themselves with small spread of margarine or with low fat cheese. They are an excellent savoury biscuit.

**Serves 36 biscuits**

*Handy Hint*
Roll between two sheets of non-stick baking paper and this makes it much easier, creates less mess and uses less flour.

NUTRIENTS PER SERVE

| KJ | Cal | Pro (g) | CHO (g) | Fibre (g) | T.fat (g) | S.fat (g) | Chol (mg) | Na (mg) |
|---|---|---|---|---|---|---|---|---|
| 265 | 64 | 1 | 7 | 0.9 | 3.4 | 0.5 | 0 | 6 |

NS

| KJ | Cal | CHO (g) |
|---|---|---|
| 242 | 59 | 6 |

*Oatcakes*
*Oatmeal Treacle Biscuits*
*Oatmeal Carrot Muffins*

## CRISPY LAVASH BREAD

*2 tsp lemon juice (10ml)*
*2 tsp Worcestershire sauce (10ml)*
*2 tsp olive oil (10ml)*
*3 Lavash bread (240g)*

- Mix lemon juice, Worcestershire sauce and oil together for marinade.
- Brush Lavash bread on both sides with marinade.
- Cut into 2cm squares using a sharp knife.
- Place on an oven tray and bake at 180°C for about 12 minute or until crisp.
- Use in a dip or with a spread.
- Allow ½ Lavash bread per serve.

**Serves 6**

*Note*
You may substitute wholemeal Lebanese bread. Serve with **Chilli Beans** p48 or **Lentil Sauce** p105 or **Hommos** p39.

NUTRIENTS PER SERVE

| KJ | Cal | Pro (g) | CHO (g) | Fibre (g) | T.fat (g) | S.fat (g) | Chol (mg) | Na (mg) |
|---|---|---|---|---|---|---|---|---|
| 569 | 125 | 3.7 | 21 | 1.6 | 3 | 0.35 | 0.03 | 218 |

## OATMEAL CARROT MUFFINS

*½ cup non fat natural yoghurt (125ml)*
*½ cup non fat milk (125ml)*
*1 cup traditional oatmeal (100g)*
*½ medium grated carrot (50g)*
*⅓ cup well packed brown sugar (60g) or equivalent substitute*
*¼ cup olive oil (65ml)*
*1 lightly beaten egg or low cholesterol egg mix (50g)*
*2 tabsp fresh or 100% orange juice (40ml)*
*1 cup wholemeal self raising flour (140g)*
*3 tsp baking powder (8g)*
*½ tsp bicarbonate of soda (1g)*
*½ cup sultanas (85g)*

- Mix yoghurt and milk with oatmeal in a microwave dish.
- Microwave on **High** for 2 minutes or until oatmeal has softened.
- Remove and allow to cool for a couple of minutes.
- Mix carrot and brown sugar into yoghurt mix.
- Mix oil, beaten egg and orange juice together.
- Add to yoghurt mixture.
- Mix flour, baking powder, bicarbonate of soda and sultanas together.
- Fold into wet mixture until no dry areas are left. Do not overmix.
- Place in small greased or non-stick patty tins.
- Bake in 180°C oven for 20 to 25 minutes.
- Delicious hot and freeze well.
- To reheat place in microwave for 1 to 2 minutes depending on number.

**Serves 24 small muffins**

*Note*
Make 12 medium size muffins but double the nutrient analysis per muffin.
This recipe is low in fat and fast absorbing sugars and very suitable for diabetes and cholesterol. If you are watching your weight have it with salad for lunch instead of the bread.

NUTRIENTS PER SERVE

| KJ | Cal | Pro (g) | CHO (g) | Fibre (g) | T.fat (g) | S.fat (g) | Chol (mg) | Na (mg) |
|---|---|---|---|---|---|---|---|---|
| 348 | 84 | 2 | 11 | 1 | 3 | 0.5 | 8 | 96 |

NS

| KJ | Cal | CHO (g) |
|---|---|---|
| 314 | 76 | 9 |

**Note** NS = No Added Sugar

## OATMEAL FRUIT SLICE

1/4 cup sultanas (40g)
20 finely chopped apricots (65g)
1/4 cup sunflower seeds (38g)
2 cups traditional oatmeal (200g)
1 cup wholemeal self raising flour (140g)
1/4 cup sugar (55g) or equivalent substitute
1/4 cup honey (65ml)
1/4 cup mono/polyunsaturated oil (65ml)
1 egg or low cholesterol egg mix (50g)
1/2 cup non fat milk (125ml)

- Mix sultanas, apricots, sunflower seeds, oatmeal, flour and sugar together in a large bowl.
- Blend honey, oil, egg and milk together in a small bowl.
- Add the wet ingredients into the dry ingredients and mix until well blended.
- Spread in a 28cm by 18cm lamington size tin which has been lined with baking paper or lightly greased. Press firmly.
- Bake in 180°C oven for 30 minutes or until firm to the touch.
- Remove from oven, leave for 10 minutes and then cut into 30 pieces.
- Store in an airtight container.

**Serves 30 pieces**

NUTRIENTS PER SERVE

| KJ | Cal | Pro (g) | CHO (g) | Fibre (g) | T.fat (g) | S.fat (g) | Chol (mg) | Na (mg) |
|---|---|---|---|---|---|---|---|---|
| 366 | 88 | 2 | 12 | 1 | 4 | 0.5 | 6 | 37 |

NS

| KJ | Cal | CHO (g) |
|---|---|---|
| 325 | 78 | 10 |

## FRUITY LOAF

25 dried apricots (150g)
10 dried figs (150g)
10 dried prunes (50g)
5 dried pears, halved (100g)
Dried apple rings (50g)
2 cups water (500ml)
1 large banana (200g)
1 cup of wholemeal self raising flour (140g)
1/2 cup almond meal (50g)
1/4 tsp cinnamon
1 tsp fine orange zest

- Place 500g mixed dried fruits in a saucepan with water. Bring to boil, cover and simmer for 5 mins.

- Remove from heat and cool for 15 minutes.
- Remove half of the apricots from the pan using tongs and blend or mash to a purée with the cooking liquid and the banana. Place in a large mixing bowl.
- Add flour, almond meal, cinnamon and orange zest to mashed fruit.
- Carefully stir in remaining stewed fruit.
- Spoon cake mixture into a greased 20cm long loaf tin and bake in 180°C oven for approximately 40 to 50 minutes.
- Allow to cool before removing from tin and placing on a cake rack.

**Serves 24 slices**

*Note*
This moist cake is fruity with a generous amount of dried fruit but no added fat or sugar. Vary the mixed fruit but make sure the total equals 500g. Orange zest is the finely grated outer rind of an orange.

NUTRIENTS PER SERVE

| KJ | Cal | Pro (g) | CHO (g) | Fibre (g) | T.fat (g) | S.fat (g) | Chol (mg) | Na (mg) |
|---|---|---|---|---|---|---|---|---|
| 291 | 70 | 2 | 13 | 3 | 1 | 0.09 | 0 | 44 |

## BANANA DATE MUFFINS

2 cups wholemeal self raising flour (280g)
1/2 tsp bicarbonate of soda (1g)
3 medium mashed bananas (300g)
20 medium finely chopped dates (100g)
1/2 cup orange juice (125ml)
1 egg or low cholesterol egg mix (50g)
2 tabsp honey (40ml)
2 tabsp olive oil (40ml)

- Mix flour and bicarbonate of soda together.
- Blend banana and dates in a kitchen whiz or mash and chop finely.
- Mix together banana, dates, orange juice, egg, honey and oil.
- Add wet to dry ingredients, mixing only until dampened.
- Place in well-greased small patty tins.
- Bake at 180°C for 15 to 17 minutes.
- Serve warm or reheat in microwave.

**Serves 24 small muffins**

*Variation*
**Soya Muffins** Substitute 1 cup (80g) soya flour for 1 cup self raising flour and add 2 tsp baking powder.

*Handy Hint*
Honey is easy to pour and measure if heated for a moment in the microwave to soften. By placing it in a cup which has previously had oil, it doesn't stick, making it easy to add to the wet ingredients without loss of honey.

NUTRIENTS PER SERVE

| KJ | Cal | Pro (g) | CHO (g) | Fibre (g) | T.fat (g) | S.fat (g) | Chol (mg) | Na (mg) |
|---|---|---|---|---|---|---|---|---|
| 341 | 82 | 2 | 14 | 2 | 2 | 0.3 | 8 | 87 |

## APPLE MUFFINS

3 medium cored and chopped apples with skin (300g)
2 tsp lemon juice (10ml)
2 cups wholemeal self raising flour (280g)
1/4 cup sugar (55g) or equivalent substitute
1 tsp cinnamon
1/2 tsp nutmeg
1 tabsp mono/polyunsaturated oil (20ml)
2 eggs or low cholesterol egg mix (100g)
1 cup non fat milk (250ml)
2 tsp sugar (10g)
1 tsp cinnamon

- Toss apple in lemon juice.
- Mix flour, sugar, cinnamon, nutmeg and apple together in a bowl.
- Beat oil, eggs and milk together.
- Fold into dry mixture.
- Place in greased patty tins.
- Bake at 180°C for 25 - 30 minutes.
- Mix sugar and remaining cinnamon together and sprinkle on top of hot muffins.

**Serves 24**

*Note*
This recipe will make 24 small or 12 medium muffins. When using standard muffin tins, double the nutrient analysis. One muffin will then have 554 kJ and 22g of carbohydrate. The large muffins are good for those with high energy needs who are not overweight.

NUTRIENTS PER SERVE

| KJ | Cal | Pro (g) | CHO (g) | Fibre (g) | T.fat (g) | S.fat (g) | Chol (mg) | Na (mg) |
|---|---|---|---|---|---|---|---|---|
| 277 | 67 | 2 | 11 | 2 | 2 | 0.3 | 16 | 87 |

NS

| KJ | Cal | CHO (g) |
|---|---|---|
| 244 | 59 | 9 |

## BRAN MUFFINS

*1½ cups natural unprocessed bran (75g)*
*1¼ cup whole meal flour (170g)*
*¼ cup sugar (55g) or equivalent substitute*
*3 tsp baking powder (6g)*
*½ tsp bicarbonate of soda (1g)*
*½ cup sultanas (85g)*
*1 egg or low cholesterol egg mix (50g)*
*¼ cup mono/polyunsaturated oil (65g)*
*2 tabsp treacle (40ml)*
*1 medium peeled, cored and chopped apple (100g)*
*½ cup non fat natural yoghurt (125ml)*
*½ cup non fat milk (125ml)*

❑ Mix bran, flour, sugar, baking powder, bicarbonate of soda and sultanas together.
❑ Blend egg, oil, treacle and apple in food processor or mixing bowl.
❑ Add yoghurt and milk to wet ingredients.
❑ Mix wet into dry ingredients until just moistened. Do not overmix.
❑ Place in greased small patty tins or use paper liners.
❑ Bake in 200°C oven for 20 to 25 minutes.
❑ They freeze beautifully. Reheat in microwave for 2 minutes on **Medium**.

**Serves 24 small muffins**

*Note*
This recipe will make 12 standard muffins but double the nutrients per serve.

*Handy Hint*
If you like less crusty muffins bake at 180°C for slightly longer. You may use self raising flour but reduce the baking powder to 1½ tsp.

NUTRIENTS PER SERVE

| KJ | Cal | Pro (g) | CHO (g) | Fibre (g) | T.fat (g) | S.fat (g) | Chol (mg) | Na (mg) |
|---|---|---|---|---|---|---|---|---|
| 349 | 84 | 2 | 12 | 2.5 | 3 | 0.4 | 8 | 49 |

NS

| KJ | Cal | CHO (g) |
|---|---|---|
| 316 | 76 | 10 |

Muffins are made in small patty tins. If standard muffin tins are used, double the nutritional analysis. Yield is then 12 muffins.

## POTATO MUFFINS

*2 medium cooked and mashed potatoes (200g)*
*2 eggs or low cholesterol egg mix (100g)*
*1 cup non fat milk (250ml)*
*¾ cup grated less than 10% fat cheese (90g)*
*¼ cup finely chopped spring onion (5g)*
*2 cups wholemeal self raising flour (280g)*
*1 tsp baking powder (2.8g)*

❑ Add prepared cooled potato to eggs, milk, cheese and onion and beat well.
❑ Fold in flour and baking powder until just moist.
❑ Place in 12 medium greased muffin tins.
❑ Bake in 180°C oven for 30 - 35 minutes.

**Serves 12 muffins**

NUTRIENTS PER SERVE

| KJ | Cal | Pro (g) | CHO (g) | Fibre (g) | T.fat (g) | S.fat (g) | Chol (mg) | Na (mg) |
|---|---|---|---|---|---|---|---|---|
| 460 | 111 | 7 | 16 | 3 | 2 | 0.5 | 35 | 240 |

## DUMPLINGS

*½ cup wholemeal self raising flour (70g)*
*½ cup white self raising flour (65g)*
*1 tabsp mixed fresh herbs or 1 tsp dry*
*⅔ cup non fat milk (165ml)*
*1 tabsp mono/polyunsaturated oil (20ml)*

❑ Mix together flours and herbs.
❑ Make a well in flour, add milk and oil until the mixture is thin enough to drop from a spoon dipped in water on to meat.

*Dumplings*

*Crêpes with Italian Seafood Sauce*

- Makes four to six dumplings.
- Cook uncovered at 220°C for 20 minutes.

**Serves 4**

## Variation
**Sweet Dumplings** Omit herbs, add a little sugar or equivalent substitute and serve with fresh fruit sauce. Golden syrup is traditional but very high in sugar. Cook in greased bowl in saucepan of water.

## Handy Hint
Drop dumpling mixture onto bubbling meat which is exposed rather than in gravy. This will allow the underside to cook better. Use on top of any stew. These dumplings are quick, easy and low fat. Make **Lamb Shank and Dumpling Ragout** p74.

NUTRIENTS PER SERVE

| KJ | Cal | Pro (g) | CHO (g) | Fibre (g) | T.fat (g) | S.fat (g) | Chol (mg) | Na (mg) |
|---|---|---|---|---|---|---|---|---|
| 692 | 168 | 5 | 23 | 3 | 6 | 0.7 | 1 | 137 |

# WHOLEMEAL CRÊPES

*1 cup plain wholemeal flour (140g)*
*3 eggs or low cholesterol egg mix (150g)*
*2 tabsp mono/polyunsaturated margarine (40g)*
*1½ cups non fat milk (375ml)*

- Place wholemeal flour in a mixing bowl.
- Beat in eggs one at a time.
- Mix melted margarine and milk together.
- Add to flour mixture and beat well.
- Refrigerate for 2 hours before using.
- Lightly grease crêpe pan and heat.
- Place ¼ cup of mixture in hot pan and tilt pan to evenly distribute. When it is dry on top, flip over.
- Leave 1 minute more and then remove and keep warm.
- Stack succeeding crêpes.
- Crêpes may be stacked, covered and refrigerated or frozen for later use.

**Serves 12 crêpes**

## Variations
**Petite Crêpes** Place 1½ tabsp of mixture in crêpe pan at a time. (Yield 24 Crêpes).
or
**Crêpes** with **Italian Seafood Sauce** p104. Prepare crêpes and **Italian Seafood Sauce** p104. Roll up crêpes and pour over sauce. Allow 3 crêpes per person.

## Note
Serve with salmon sauce or fresh asparagus sauce as an entrée or main meal.
Prepare **Savoury Stuffed Crêpes** p38. Crêpes as a dessert with sugar or equivalent substitute and lemon are delicious.

## Healthy Note
The use of wholemeal flour increases fibre content.

NUTRIENTS PER SERVE

| KJ | Cal | Pro (g) | CHO (g) | Fibre (g) | T.fat (g) | S.fat (g) | Chol (mg) | Na (mg) |
|---|---|---|---|---|---|---|---|---|
| 349 | 85 | 4 | 7 | 1 | 4 | 0.8 | 48 | 31 |

## DAMPER WITH BEER

*1 cup white self raising flour (130g)*
*1 cup wholemeal self raising flour (140g)*
*2 tabsp of fresh mixed herbs or 1 tsp dried*
*¼ cup mono/polyunsaturated margarine (65g)*
*⅔ cup light flat beer (165ml)*
*Non fat milk*

- Mix flours and herbs together.
- Cut or rub in margarine to form a coarse meal.
- Stir in beer to form a soft dough.
- Place on a floured board and knead for 2 to 3 minutes.
- Form into a smooth round ball and place on greased baking sheet.
- Brush with milk and slash the top into 12 portions.
- Bake at 200°C for 10 minutes and reduce heat to 180°C and bake for a further 40 minutes or until it sounds hollow on the bottom.

**Serves 12**

*Variation*
Substitute milk for beer if desired.

*Note*
The alcohol will evaporate during cooking.

NUTRIENTS PER SERVE

| KJ | Cal | Pro (g) | CHO (g) | Fibre (g) | T.fat (g) | S.fat (g) | Chol (mg) | Na (mg) |
|---|---|---|---|---|---|---|---|---|
| 471 | 114 | 2.5 | 14 | 1.7 | 5 | 0.8 | 0 | 153 |

## LOW JOULE GARLIC CROUTONS

*2 crushed cloves garlic (6g)*
*1 tsp mono/polyunsaturated oil (5ml)*
*2 slices cubed wholegrain bread (50g)*

- Stir-fry garlic in oil in non stick fry pan for 2 minutes.
- Add cubed bread and toss until crisp.
- Use in **Low Joule Caesar Salad** p101 and soups.

**Serves 6**

NUTRIENTS PER SERVE

| KJ | Cal | Pro (g) | CHO (g) | Fibre (g) | T.fat (g) | S.fat (g) | Chol (mg) | Na (mg) |
|---|---|---|---|---|---|---|---|---|
| 115 | 28 | 0.9 | 4 | 0.6 | 1 | 0.2 | 0 | 39 |

*Damper with Beer*

## SAVOURY CASES

*24 slices of multigrain bread (480g)*
*Mono/polyunsaturated vegetable spray*

- Cut the crusts from multigrain bread and discard.
- Roll bread flat with a rolling pin.
- Spray with oil.
- Press into patty tins. Corners will protrude.
- Bake in a 180°C oven for 20 minutes or until crisp and golden brown.

**Serves 24 savoury cases**

*Note*
10g of fat is allowed in the analysis for spraying with oil.
These may be used with any sort of filling you desire such as **Savoury Corn Spread** p32 or an asparagus or salmon filling prepared using **Low Fat White Sauce** p108 as a base.

NUTRIENTS PER SERVE

| KJ | Cal | Pro (g) | CHO (g) | Fibre (g) | T.fat (g) | S.fat (g) | Chol (mg) | Na (mg) |
|---|---|---|---|---|---|---|---|---|
| 209 | 51 | 2 | 8 | 1 | 1.0 | 0.2 | 0 | 94 |

## LOW FAT FIBRE PASTRY

**Ingredients for 2 cups pastry**
2 cups of wholemeal flour (280g)
1/3 cup of firm mono/polyunsaturated margarine (85g)
1/3 cup ricotta cheese (85g)
1/2 cup iced water (125ml)

**Ingredients for 1 1/2 cups pastry**
1 1/2 cups of wholemeal flour (210g)
1/4 cup of firm mono/polyunsaturated margarine (65g)
1/4 cup ricotta cheese (65g)
1/3 cup iced water (85ml)

**Ingredients for 1 cup pastry**
1 cup of wholemeal flour (140g)
2 tabsp of firm mono/polyunsaturated margarine (40g)
2 tabsp ricotta cheese (40g)
1/4 cup iced water (65ml)

- Measure flour and place in a bowl.
- Cut firm margarine into flour until the size of peas.
- Stir in ricotta cheese.
- Stir water into dry parts of pastry until it sticks together.
- Make into a firm ball, knead and roll to fit a pie dish or oblong tin.
- Use in recipes as desired.

**Serves 1, 1 1/2 or 2 cups pastry**

*Note*
You may substitute part self raising flour or white flour for a lighter pastry.
1 cup flour = sufficient pastry for 1 pie shell.
1 1/2 cups flour = sufficient pastry for lining a 28cm x 18cm lamington size tin.
2 cups flour = sufficient pastry for a 2 crusted pie.

NUTRIENTS PER 1 CUP PASTRY

| KJ | Cal | Pro (g) | CHO (g) | Fibre (g) | T.fat (g) | S.fat (g) | Chol (mg) | Na (mg) |
|---|---|---|---|---|---|---|---|---|
| 3086 | 748 | 21 | 74 | 16 | 40 | 8 | 17 | 81 |

## CHOUX PASTRY

1 cup boiling water (250ml)
1/2 cup mono/polyunsaturated margarine (125g)
1 cup plain flour (130g)
4 eggs (200g)

- Heat water and margarine to a rolling boil in heavy based saucepan.
- Add flour all at once, beat vigorously over low heat until mixture leaves the side of the pan and forms a ball.
- Thoroughly beat eggs in one at a time.
- Drop by spoonfuls onto an ungreased baking tray to form 24 mounds, 5cm apart or pipe in one large ring.
- Bake in a 200°C oven for 40 to 45 minutes or until puffed, golden and dry.
- Remove from oven and cut a slit in side of each puff.
- Return to a slow oven for about 10 minutes to dry and crisp.
- These may be served as individual savouries for a party with asparagus or salmon type fillings or for dessert with sweetened cream or **Ricotta Cream** p114

**Serves 24 Choux Puffs**

*Variation*
**Kiwi Choux Ring** Pipe and bake one large ring. Split in half horizontally and remove any sticky dough. Fill ring with **Custard Sauce** 119, **Ricotta Cream** p114 or sweetened cream and fresh fruit such as strawberries, kiwi fruit or peaches. Sieve icing sugar on top and serve.

*Handy Hint*
Thoroughly beating after the addition of each egg yields a smooth glossy dough which is the secret of good choux pastry.

NUTRIENTS PER SERVE

| KJ | Cal | Pro (g) | CHO (g) | Fibre (g) | T.fat (g) | S.fat (g) | Chol (mg) | Na (mg) |
|---|---|---|---|---|---|---|---|---|
| 287 | 70 | 2 | 4 | 0.2 | 5 | 0.9 | 31 | 11 |

**CHARTS AND TABLES**

# HEALTHY FOOD CHOICES BASED ON GLYCAEMIC INDEX
### Try to eat one from the BEST GROUP every meal or at least 2 times a day

|  | BEST | GOOD | FAIR |
|---|---|---|---|
| **DAIRY FOODS** | Milk - Skimmed<br>Custard (made with skim milk and custard powder).<br>Ice Cream - low fat<br>Yoghurt - low fat/diet | Whole Milk<br>Hilo<br>Reduced fat 1% milk<br>Icecream |  |
| **BREAKFAST CEREALS** | Kelloggs All-Bran<br>Psyllium<br>Rice Bran<br>Porridge - Traditional<br>Oat Bran | Mini Wheats/Shredded Wheat, Sultana Bran<br>Muesli - untoasted<br>Kelloggs Spec.K, Sustain<br>Porridge Quick or Minute oats, Vitabrits<br>Cream of Wheat | Kelloggs Cornflakes<br>Kelloggs Rice Bubbles<br>Puffed Wheat<br>Nutrigrain |
| **GRAINS/PASTA** | Bulgur, Wheat<br>Noodles - wheat flour regular or instant<br>Pasta - ravioli - meat<br>Spaghetti - all types<br>Barley | Buckwheat<br>Rice - brown, white, long grain, Basmati, Mahatma<br>Taco shells<br>Cous Cous,<br>Cornmeal, Polenta | Rice - Calrose, Instant<br>Sunbrown quick<br>Millet, Tapioca<br>Rice, Pasta |
| **BREAD** | Pumpernickel, Oatbran<br>Mixed grain bread - e.g. Kibblewheat, barley and oats | Crumpet, Pita bread<br>Wholemeal or rye bread<br>White high fibre bread<br>Fruit loaf | Gluten Free Bread<br>Bagel or Baguette, white<br>White bread<br>Bread Stuffing |
| **CRACKERS / CRISPBREADS** |  | Jatz<br>Ryvita<br>Shredded wheatmeal<br>Breton wheat crackers | Kavli<br>Rice Cakes<br>Puffed Crispbread<br>Sao, Watercracker |
| **SWEET BISCUITS** |  | Shredded Wheatmeal | Morning Coffee,<br>Milk Arrowroot, Granita,<br>Oatmeal Cookies |
| **LEGUMES** | Beans - Lima, Pinto, Baked, Butter, Soya, Haricot, Kidney<br>Lentils/green, red, Split peas, Chick peas |  | Broad Beans |
| **VEGETABLES** | Peas - green<br>Sweet corn, Taro<br>Sweet potato | Potato - all kinds<br>Yam, Carrot<br>Beetroot, Swede | Parsnips |
| **FRUITS** | Apple - raw<br>Apricot - dried<br>Cherries, Grapefruit<br>Grapes, Orange<br>Peach - natural juice, fresh<br>Pear - canned, natural juice<br>Plum<br>Banana under ripe | Banana - ripe<br>Kiwi Fruit, Mango<br>Paw Paw, Pineapple<br>Raisins, Sultanas<br>Rockmelon<br>Apricots fresh and canned<br>Vitari | Watermelon |
| **BEVERAGES** | Apple, Grapefruit, Pineapple Juice | Orange Juice |  |
| **CONVENIENCE & SNACK FOODS** | Fish Fingers<br>Soup - lentil - tomato | Popcorn - plain | Peanuts |
| **SUGARS** | Fructose, Lactose | Sucrose, Honey | Glucose, Maltose |

(The chart has been adapted from material published by Dr Jenny Brand)

# MINI FAT COUNTER TABLE

Many people feel that counting fat is the best way of losing weight. It definitely has an advantage of reducing the amount of fat which has more that twice the kilojoules per weight of protein and carbohydrate. Counting fat is not magical. If you have a slow metabolism, if you eat more than you are burning up, you can still put on weight on a very low fat intake.

1 gram of fat provides 37 Kilojoules (9 Calories). Fat should provide no more than 30% of our total Kilojoule (KJ) intake.

    On a 4200 KJ (1000 Cal) diet we should have no more than 35g fat daily.
    On a 5000 KJ (1200 Cal) diet we should have no more than 40g fat daily.
    On a 6300 KJ (1500 Cal) diet we should have no more than 50g fat daily.

The following chart shows the approximate fat and energy content of various foods and drinks. Low fat foods generally have the lowest energy values.

| FOOD | SERVING SIZE | FAT (grams) |
|---|---|---|
| **Milk** | | |
| Non fat milk | 1 cup (250ml) | 0 |
| 1% fat milk (Light Start/Soy Light) | 1 cup (250ml) | 2.5 |
| 2% fat milk (hilo) | 1 cup (250ml) | 5 |
| Full cream milk | 1 cup (250ml) | 10 |
| Soy milk | 1 cup (250ml) | 8.5 |
| Flavoured milk, reduced fat | 1 cup (250ml) | 4.5 |
| **Yoghurt** | | |
| Plain/flavoured yoghurt | 200g | 7 |
| Natural non fat yoghurt, diet | 200g | 0.5 |
| **Ice cream** | | |
| Vanilla / flavoured (10% fat) | 1 scoop (50g) | 5 |
| Reduced fat ice cream (5% fat) e.g. lite, fruccio | 1 scoop (50g) | 3 |
| **Cheese** | | |
| Regular (fully / semi-matured, etc) | 20g | 7 |
| Light cheese (25% reduced fat) | 20g (1 slice) | 5 |
| 90% fat free slices | 20g (1 slice) | 2 |
| Ricotta (10% fat) | 1 tablespoon (20g) | 2 |
| Cottage cheese - creamed | 1 tablespoon (20g) | 1.5 |
| **Meat / Fish / Chicken** | | |
| Lean meat eg trimmed beef, pork, veal, skinless chicken, fish. | 30g trim | 3 |
| Medium fat meat e.g. mince, rib eye bacon. | 30g | 5.5 |
| High fat meat eg hamburger mince, rib roast, pork ribs, lamb shoulder, duck, sausage/ frankfurts, processed meat. | 30g | 8 |
| **Eggs - Whole egg** | 1x50g | 5.5 |
| Egg white | 1 | negligible |
| Egg yolk | 1 | 5.5 |
| Almonds, cashews, hazelnuts, peanuts, pecans, walnuts, etc. | 30g | 16 |
| Peanut paste | 1 tablespoon (25g) | 13 |
| Seeds (sunflower, sesame) | 1 tablespoon (15g) | 8 |
| **Legumes** | | |
| Baked beans, kidney beans, soya beans, etc | ¾ cup cooked, ¼ cup dry | 1 |
| **Tofu** | 100g block | 4 |
| **Fruit** | | |
| Avocado | ½ (100g) | 15 |
| Olives | 3 (25g) | 2.5 |
| All other fruit | 1 | 0 |
| **Vegetables** | | |
| All vegetables (raw or cooked without fat) | ½ cup | 0 |
| Roast Potato | 2 medium halves | 2.5 |

# ALCOHOL, ENERGY AND CARBOHYDRATE (CHO) CHART

**Content of Beverages (Average Figures)**   1 Middie = 285ml   Nip = 30ml   1 Can/Stubby = 375ml

| BEVERAGE | VOLUME (ml) | ALCOHOL (g) | STANDARD DRINKS | ENERGY (Kj) | ENERGY Calories | CHO (g) |
|---|---|---|---|---|---|---|
| **BEER** | | | | | | |
| **FULL STRENGTH** 4 - 6% ALC / VOL eg. Red Back Original, V.B., Fosters, Swan Lager / Draught, Emu Export / Bitter | 375 | 15 | 1.5 | 630 | 150 | 11 |
| Hahn Longbrew / Carlton D-Ale / Diamond Draft | 375 | 15 | 1.5 | 480 | 115 | 5 |
| **REDUCED - ALCOHOL** 2 - 4% ALC / VOL - Swan Gold / Fosters Light / Red Back Light | 375 | 10 | 1 | 460 | 110 | 8 |
| Tooheys Blue | 375 | 8 | 0.8 | 545 | 130 | 17 |
| 303 Ice Gold / Carlton Light (3.25%) / Fosters Light Ice | 375 | 12 | 1.2 | 500 | 120 | 11 |
| **LOW - ALCOHOL** < 1% ALC / VOL eg. Swan Light | 375 | 3 | 0.3 | 315 | 75 | 12.5 |
| **WINE** 10 - 14% ALC / VOL, White or Red | | | | | | |
| Sweet - eg. Moselle, Sauterne | 120 | 10 | 1 | 355 | 85 | 3.5 |
| Dry - e.g. Chablis, Riesling | 120 | 10 | 1 | 315 | 75 | 1.0 |
| Claret | 120 | 10 | 1 | 335 | 80 | 0 |
| Rose | 120 | 10 | 1 | 335 | 80 | 2.5 |
| Champagne | 120 | 10 | 1 | 335 | 80 | 1.5 |
| **FORTIFIED WINE** eg. Sherry, Port, Vermouth, Sweet | 60 | 10 | 1 | 380 | 90 | 7 |
| Dry Sherry, Vermouth | 60 | 10 | 1 | 290 | 70 | 1 |
| **REDUCED ALCOHOL WINE** (4 - 6% ALC / VOL) eg. Coolabah Lite | | | | | | |
| - Dry White | 120 | 5 | .5 | 202 | 48 | 2.6 |
| - Fruity White | 120 | 5 | .5 | 270 | 64 | 6.6 |
| **NON ALCOHOLIC WINE** eg. Maison White | 120 | 0 | 0 | 285 | 68 | 15.6 |
| **WINE COOLERS** (Approx 3.5% ALC / VOL) eg. Coolabah Tropical | 150 | 3.5 | 0.3 | 355 | 85 | 14.5 |
| **SPIRITS** eg. Whisky, Brandy, Rum, Gin, Vodka | 30 | 10 | 1 | 275 | 65 | 0 |
| **STOUT** (Average) 7% ALC / VOL | 375 | 20 | 2 | 840 | 200 | 14-18 |
| **ALCOHOLIC SODA** - eg. Sub Zero (5.5% ALC / VOL) | 330 | 15 | 1.5 | 735 | 175 | 20 |
| **LIQUEUR -** 40% ALC / VOL e.g. Drambuie, Cointreau | 30 | 10 | 1 | 420 | 100 | 15 |
| **CIDER (Alcoholic) -** 4.7% ALC / VOL - e.g. Strongbow - Sweet | 375 | 15 | 1.5 | 820 | 195 | 25 |
| - Dry | 375 | 15 | 1.5 | 585 | 140 | 11 |
| **CIDER (Non Alcoholic)** | 375 | 0 | 0 | 670 | 160 | 40 |

# CARBOHYDRATE, KILOJOULE & CALORIE CONTENT OF COMMON FOODS

|  |  |  | CHO | kJ | CALS |
|---|---|---|---|---|---|
| **MILK AND MILK PRODUCTS** | | | | | |
| Whole, fluid | 2 tabsp | 40ml | 2 | 610 | 26 |
| | 1 cup | 250ml | 12 | 700 | 167 |
| Skim/non-fat, fluid | 2 tabsp | 40ml | 2 | 60 | 14 |
| | 1 cup | 250ml | 12 | 365 | 88 |
| Condensed, whole, sweetened | 1 tabsp | 28ml | 16 | 285 | 70 |
| Condensed, Skim | 1 tabsp | 20ml | 13 | 240 | 57 |
| Evaporated, unsweetened | 1 tabsp | 20ml | 2 | 125 | 30 |
|   Lowfat | 1 tabsp | 20ml | 1 | 75 | 18 |
|   Skim Carnation | 1 tabsp | 20ml | 2 | 80 | 19 |
| Flavoured Milks, average | 1 ctn | 300ml | 24 | 890 | 200 |
| Powdered Instant, Fullcream | 4 tabsp | 30g | 10 | 590 | 140 |
| Powdered, Flavoured | | | | | |
| Skim/non fat powdered | 4 tabsp | 30g | 10 | 445 | 106 |
| **MILK BEVERAGES** | | | | | |
| Milo, Ovaltine, Aktavite, Quik | 1 tabsp | 10g | 14 | 340 | 80 |
| Cocoa, Drinking Chocolate | 1 tabsp | 8g | 5 | 340 | 80 |
| Malted Milk | 1 tabsp | 12g | | 340 | 80 |
| **YOGHURTS** | | | | | |
| Plain/Natural, full fat | 200g ctn | | 13 | 670 | 160 |
| Nonfat/Skim | 200g ctn | | 13 | 500 | 120 |
| Fruit flavoured, low fat | 200g ctn | | 25 | 690 | 165 |
| Diet, fruit yoghurt | 200g ctn | | 13 | 545 | 130 |
| **ICE CREAM** | | | | | |
| Plain, flavoured, average | 1 scoop | 50g | 11 | 375 | 90 |
| Weight Watchers | 1 ctn | 145g | 20 | 406 | 97 |
| Confection, Vitari | 1 scoop | 100ml | 16 | 250 | 60 |
| **CHEESE** | | | | | |
| Cheddar Types | 1 slice | 30g | | 500 | 120 |
| Creamed Cheese | 1 tabsp | 25g | | 350 | 84 |
| Cottage Cheese, skim | 2 tabsp | 40g | | 155 | 37 |
|   creamed, flavoured | ¼ cup | 70g | | 230 | 55 |
| Ricotta Cheese, low fat 9% | 1 tabsp | 20g | | 100 | 24 |
| **MEATS (cooked weights)** | | | | | |
| Beef: Rump Steak | lean, grilled | 100g | 0 | 800 | 190 |
| Lamb/Mutton/Veal | average, lean | 100g | 0 | 730 | 175 |
| Pork, lean only | lean only | 100g | 0 | 420 | 100 |
| Bacon, grilled | 1 rasher (50g raw) | 30g | 0 | 405 | 97 |
| Sausages, meat (thin) | 1 sausage - raw | 50g | 2 | 545 | 130 |
| Liver/Kidney floured & fried | | 100g | 2 | 1005 | 240 |
| **COLD MEATS** | | | | | |
| Polony/Devon | 1 thick slice | 30g | 4 | 290 | 70 |
| Ham, leg | 2 slices | 50g | 0 | 200 | 48 |
|   sandwich | 2 slices | 50g | 0 | 245 | 59 |
| **FISH** | | | | | |
| Average, grilled | 1 medium serve | 120g | 0 | 504 | 120 |
|   fried | 1 medium serve | 120g | 0 | 882 | 210 |
|   battered & fried | 1 medium serve | 150g | 20 | 1739 | 412 |
| Canned: Sardines in oil | | 30g | 0 | 252 | 60 |
|   Tuna in oil, drained | | 30g | 0 | 260 | 62 |
|   in brine, drained | | 30g | 0 | 144 | 34 |
|   Salmon, drained | | 30g | 0 | 170 | 40 |
| Fish Fingers, average, grilled | 1 finger | 25g | 4 | 210 | 50 |
|   fried | 1 finger | 25g | 4 | 400 | 100 |
| **POULTRY/CHICKEN** | | | | | |
| Chicken baked leg rotisseried no skin | ¼ large | | 0 | 1050 | 250 |
| Duck roasted - meat only | 100g | | 0 | 790 | 190 |
| Turkey - roasted light meat | 100g | | 0 | 545 | 130 |
| **EGGS** | | | | | |
| Large (55g) size | 1 boiled | 53g | 0.5 | 335 | 80 |
| Scrambled 1 egg+1 tabsp milk+1 tsp fat | | | 1 | 520 | 125 |
| Ready Eggs | 1 sachet | 100g | 0 | 670 | 160 |

## CHARTS AND TABLES

|  |  |  | CHO | kJ | CALS |
|---|---|---|---|---|---|
| **BEANS/TOFU/LENTILS** |  |  |  |  |  |
| Beans cooked, kidney, mixed or baked | 1/2 cup | 100g | 15 | 393 | 95 |
| Lentils cooked | 1/2 cup | 100g | 7 | 280 | 67 |
| Soya beans, Tofu | 1/2 cup | 100g | 2.5 | 383 | 92 |
| **FRUITS, FRESH** |  |  |  |  |  |
| Apple - Fresh | 1 medium | 150g | 18 | 270 | 65 |
| Apple | 1 small | 100g | 12 | 190 | 45 |
| Apricots | 2 medium | 80g | 6 | 120 | 30 |
| Avocado Pear, flesh only | 1/2 medium | 80g | 5 | 532 | 127 |
| Banana | 1 medium | 150g | 30 | 365 | 87 |
| Cherries | 10 medium | 60g | 10 | 150 | 40 |
| Figs | 2 medium | 100g | 8 | 170 | 40 |
| Grapefruit | 1/2 medium (4" dm) | 100g | 5 | 85 | 20 |
| Grapes 1 small bunch | 20 medium | 120g | 18 | 315 | 75 |
| Kiwi Fruit | 1 medium | 100g | 10 | 165 | 40 |
| Lemon | 1 medium | 150g | 7 | 95 | 23 |
| Mandarins | 1 large/2 small | 180g | 14 | 220 | 53 |
| Mangoes | 1 medium | 240g | 28 | 425 | 102 |
| Nectarines | 1 medium | 90g | 6 | 135 | 32 |
| Orange | 1 small | 150g | 12 | 185 | 44 |
| Passionfruit | 1 small | 50g | 3 | 40 | 10 |
| Pawpaw | 1/2 small | 200g | 14 | 165 | 40 |
| Peach | 1 medium | 115g | 7 | 167 | 40 |
| Pear | 1 medium | 150g | 18 | 290 | 69 |
| Plum | 1 medium | 100g | 8 | 140 | 33 |
| Pineapple - flesh only | 1 slice | 85g | 7 | 140 | 33 |
| Rockmelon | 1/2 small/flesh only | 200g | 9 | 295 | 70 |
| Strawberries | 6 medium/3 large | 55g | 2 | 45 | 10 |
| Tomatoes | 1 small | 100g | 3 | 55 | 13 |
| Watermelon - flesh only | 1/2 slice | 200g | 20 | 195 | 45 |
| **STEWED/CANNED FRUIT** |  |  |  |  |  |
| Average sweetened | 1/2 cup | 125ml | 24 | 315 | 75 |
| In water | 1/2 cup | 125ml | 18 | 155 | 36 |
| **DRIED FRUIT** |  |  |  |  |  |
| Average all types |  | 30g | 20 | 335 | 80 |
| **FRUIT JUICE** |  |  |  |  |  |
| Average sweetened | 1 glass | 200ml | 20 | 305 | 73 |
| Unsweetened | 1 glass | 200ml | 17 | 295 | 70 |
| Tomato Juice average | 1 glass | 250ml | 9 | 200 | 47 |
| **VEGETABLES** |  |  |  |  |  |
| Asparagus | 3 medium spears | 60g | 2 | 40 | 10 |
| Beans French/Runner raw | 1/2 cup | 60g | 2 | 54 | 13 |
| Lima, boiled | 1/2 cup | 70g | 10 | 60 | 14 |
| Broad, boiled | 1/2 cup | 85g | 3 | 145 | 35 |
| Baked Beans | 1/4 cup | 60g | 13 | 270 | 65 |
| Bean Sprouts | 1 cup | 100g | 2 | 125 | 30 |
| Beetroot boiled | 2 slices | 30g | 2 | 55 | 13 |
| Broccoli boiled | 1/2 cup | 60g | 2 | 44 | 11 |
| Brussel Sprouts boiled | 1/2 cup | 70g | 1 | 57 | 13 |
| Cabbage raw shredded | 1/2 cup | 40g | 1 | 30 | 7 |
| Capsicum raw | 1 medium | 140g | 4 | 105 | 25 |
| Carrot raw | 1 small | 100g | 4 | 95 | 23 |
| Cauliflower cooked | 1/2 cup | 100g | 2 | 85 | 20 |
| Celery raw | 1 piece 15cm | 30g | 1 | 15 | 4 |
| Choko cooked | 1/2 cup | 70g | 3 | 60 | 14 |
| Corn boiled | 1/2 cup kernels | 60g | 10 | 210 | 50 |
| Cucumber | 4 - 5 slices | 30g | 1 | 15 | 3 |
| Eggplant baked | 2 slices, 1cm thick | 60g | 2 | 40 | 10 |
| Lettuce | 3 leaves | 30g | 1 | 17 | 4 |
| Mushrooms fresh | 1/2 cup | 60g | 1 | 60 | 15 |
| Olives | 3 medium | 18g | 1 | 30 | 6 |
| Onion raw | 1/2 cup | 60g | 3 | 65 | 15 |
| Parsnip cooked | 1/2 cup | 75g | 7.5 | 156 | 38 |
| Peas fresh cooked | 1/2 cup | 80g | 5 | 168 | 40 |
| Potato cooked | 1 small | 60g | 7.7 | 158 | 38 |
| Pumpkin boiled, mashed | 1 scoop | 50g | 4 | 105 | 25 |
| Radish | 1 small | 20g | 0 | 10 | 2 |
| Silverbeet boiled | 1/2 cup | 100g | 1 | 55 | 13 |

## CHARTS AND TABLES

|  |  |  | CHO | kJ | CALS |
|---|---|---|---|---|---|
| Spinach boiled | ½ cup | 100g | 1 | 65 | 16 |
| Turnip cooked | ½ cup | 120g | 5 | 107 | 25 |
| Zucchini cooked | ½ cup sliced | 75g | 1.5 | 50 | 12 |
| **TOMATO PRODUCTS** | | | | | |
| Tomato Sauce average | 1 tabsp | 20g | 5.5 | 110 | 26 |
| Tomato Purée | ⅓ cup | 100g | 7 | 125 | 30 |
| Tomato Paste | ⅓ cup | 100g | 17 | 300 | 70 |
| Tomato Supreme | ⅓ cup | 100g | 7 | 259 | 60 |
| Whole Peeled Tomatoes | ½ cup | 125g | 5 | 105 | 25 |
| **FLOUR/PASTA/RICE** | | | | | |
| Flour wheat rye average | 1 tabsp | 10g | 7.5 | 150 | 37 |
|  | ½ cup | 65g | 48 | 990 | 235 |
|  | 1 cup | 125g | 92 | 1890 | 450 |
| Cornflour Arrowroot | 1 tabsp | 10g | 7.5 | 150 | 37 |
| Custard Powder | 3 tabsp | 30g | 23 | 470 | 112 |
| Barley, cooked | ½ cup | 90g | 30 | 405 | 97 |
| Rice average all types cooked | ½ cup | 80g | 20 | 390 | 92 |
| Spaghetti/Pasta cooked | 1 cup | 150g | 37 | 840 | 200 |
| Breadcrumbs | ¼ cup | 30g | 17 | 330 | 80 |
| Polenta/Corn Meal (dry) | 1 cup | 150g | 103 | 2070 | 492 |
| Cous Cous - raw | ½ cup | 85g | 43 | 807 | 192 |
| **BREAKFAST CEREALS** | | | | | |
| Cornflakes, Rice Bubbles | ⅔ cup | 30g | 25 | 480 | 114 |
| Puffed Wheat | ⅔ cup | 30g | 25 | 480 | 114 |
| Special K | ⅔ cup | 30g | 20 | 480 | 114 |
| All Bran | ⅓ cup | 30g | 22 | 475 | 113 |
| Bran Flakes | ⅔ cup | 30g | 22 | 480 | 114 |
| Weet-Bix, Vita Brits, Lite Bix | 1 biscuit | 15g | 10 | 215 | 52 |
| Shredded Wheat 1 biscuit | 1 biscuit | 25g | 10 | 375 | 90 |
| Porridge/Rolled Oats: Dry | ¼ cup | 30g | 19 | 420 | 100 |
| Cooked | ¾ cup | 170g | 19 | 420 | 100 |
| High Sugar Content: | | | | | |
| Honey Smacks, Fruit Loops, | | | | | |
| Sugar Frosties, Coco Pops | | 30g | 25 | 505 | 120 |
| Nutrigrain | | 30g | 20 | 485 | 114 |
| Muesli average | | 30g | 22 | 470 | 115 |
| Toasted/Dried | | 30g | 27 | 570 | 140 |
| **SUPPLEMENTS** | | | | | |
| Lecithin granules | 1 tabsp | 12g | 10 | 420 | 100 |
| Wheat Germ | 1 tabsp | 10g | 2 | 125 | 30 |
| Psyllium Husks | 1 tabsp | 6g | 1 | 40 | 10 |
| **BREAD & ROLLS** | | | | | |
| White sliced thin | 1 slice | 28g | 14 | 275 | 66 |
| Wholemeal/grain | 1 slice | 30g | 13 | 260 | 62 |
| Roll Sandwich | 1 only | 65g | 26 | 650 | 155 |
| Roll Horseshoe large | 1 only | 60g | 25 | 585 | 140 |
| Crumpet | 1 only | 50g | 20 | 355 | 85 |
| Pita Bread | 1 piece | 50g | 25 | 580 | 140 |
| Lavash Bread | 1 piece | 60g | 28 | 750 | 175 |
| **BISCUITS/CRISPBREADS** | (per biscuit) | | | | |
| Crispbreads average e.g. Ryvita | | | 7 | 160 | 40 |
| Crackers: Savoury Shapes, | 1 biscuit | | 2.5 | 80 | 19 |
| Premium Wheat, Toasts Ritz Snaps, | | | | | |
| Jatz/Plaza/Salada | | | | | |
| Sesame, Wheat, | | | 5 | 125 | 30 |
| Sao, Saltine | 1 biscuit | | 5.5 | 130 | 31 |
| Rice Cakes | 1 cake | | 8 | 201 | 48 |
| **SUGAR/HONEY/JAM** | | | | | |
| Jam regular | 2 tsp | 12g | 4 | 135 | 30 |
| Diabetic | 2 tsp | 15g | 2.4 | 15 | 4 |
| NB Sorbitol counted as Carbohydrate | | | | | |
| Marmalade | 2 tsp | 12g | 4 | 135 | 30 |
| Honey | 2 tsp | 12g | 10 | 150 | 33 |
| Molasses light | 1 tabsp | 24g | 18 | 250 | 60 |
| Glucose/Glucodin average | 2 tsp | 10g | 10 | 170 | 40 |
| Sugar - Refined | 1 tsp | 5g | 5 | 85 | 20 |
|  | 1 tabsp | 20g | 20 | 335 | 80 |
|  | ½ cup | 125g | 110 | 2100 | 500 |

## CHARTS AND TABLES

|  |  |  | CHO | kJ | CALS |
|---|---|---|---|---|---|
| Castor sugar | ½ cup | 110g | 125 | 1850 | 440 |
| Icing/Brown | ½ cup | 70g | 85 | 1105 | 265 |
| **SPREADS** | | | | | |
| Vegemite, Promite, Marmite | ½ tsp | 3g | 0.2 | 15 | 4 |
| Lemon Spread | 2 tsp | 12g | 6 | 150 | 36 |
| Peanut Paste/Butter | 1 tabsp | 20g | 4 | 525 | 125 |
| Meat Paste | 2 tabsp | 10g | Negl | 85 | 20 |
| Fish Paste | 2 tabsp | 10g | Negl | 70 | 17 |
| **CAKE INGREDIENTS** | | | | | |
| Coconut dessicated | 1 tabsp | 5g | 1 | 196 | 47 |
|  | ¼ cup | 25g | 5 | 665 | 157 |
| Glacé cherries | 30 cherries | 100g | 67 | 1090 | 267 |
| Marzipan average | ½ roll | 100g | 55 | 1680 | 410 |
| Mixed Fruits/Peel average | ½ cup | 85g | 55 | 952 | 226 |
| **PASTRY** | | | | | |
| Flaky Puff | ½ sheet | 70g | 30 | 1360 | 325 |
| Shortcrust | ½ sheet | 100g | 35 | 1590 | 360 |
| Filo | 1 sheet | 12g | 8.4 | 175 | 41 |
| **DESSERTS/JELLIES** | | | | | |
| Custard Powder - dry | 3 tabsp | 30g | 25 | 420 | 100 |
| Custard sweetened baked with cereal | ½ cup | 125ml | 27 | 460 | 110 |
| Baked with egg | ½ cup | 125ml | 13 | 215 | 512 |
| Jelly sweetened | ½ cup | 120ml | 26 | 375 | 90 |
| Diabetic Low Cal | 1 serve | 120ml | 0 | 40 | 10 |
| Creamed Rice average | ½ carton | 100g | 16 | 441 | 105 |
| Chocolate Mousse | 1 carton | 85g | 20 | 660 | 158 |
| **SWEET BISCUITS** | | | | | |
| Morning Coffee | | | | | |
| Milk Arrowroot, Milk coffee | 1 biscuit | | 5 | 110 | 25 |
| Shortbread average | 1 biscuit | | 6 | 150 | 35 |
| Chocolate Biscuits average all types | 1 biscuit | | 9 | 300 | 70 |
| Cream Centre Biscuits averall all types | 1 biscuit | | 10 | 360 | 85 |
| **SNACKS/SEEDS/NUTS** | | | | | |
| Potato Crisps | 1 small bag | 25g | 12 | 525 | 125 |
| Cheezels Twisties | 1 small bag | 25g | 15 | 525 | 125 |
| Popcorn unpopped | 1 tabsp | 20g | 10 | 305 | 72 |
| popped plain | 1 cup | 7g | 4 | 115 | 28 |
| Peanuts/Almonds shelled roasted | 2 tabsp | 30g | 3 | 755 | 180 |
| Cashew Nuts | 15 nuts | 30g | 5 | 755 | 180 |
| Macadamia Nuts | 7 medium | 30g | 1 | 840 | 200 |
| Walnuts | 15 halves | 30g | 1 | 775 | 185 |
| Seeds: Sunflower/Pumpkin/Sesame | ¼ cup | 30g | 1 | 710 | 170 |
| **CAKES** | | | | | |
| Plain no icing | 1 piece | 60g | 20 | 940 | 225 |
| Fruit Cake, rich | 1 slice | 50g | 27 | 795 | 190 |
| Sponge plain | | 30g | 20 | 378 | 90 |
| Swiss Roll 1.5cm/½" thick | 1 slice | 40g | 23 | 500 | 120 |
| Lamington | 1 only (medium) | 80g | 38 | 710 | 170 |
| Cheesecake | 1 serve | 120g | 23 | 1670 | 400 |
| Pancakes plain | 1 (10cm/4" diam) | 50g | 18 | 505 | 120 |
| Apple Pie | 1 serve | 140g | 50 | 1385 | 330 |
| Doughnut | 1 average | 70g | 35 | 1045 | 250 |
| Jam Tart | 1 tart | 35g | 22 | 590 | 140 |
| Chocolate Eclair | 1 eclair | 60g | 24 | 945 | 225 |
| Meringue shell only | 1 (8cm/3" diam) | 15g | 13 | 21 | 50 |
| **BUNS** | | | | | |
| Sweet bun buttered | 1 medium bun | 90g | 40 | 1050 | 250 |
| Cream Bun | 1 bun | 100g | 45 | 1200 | 285 |
| Cinnamon Bun buttered | 1 bun | 120g | 45 | 1155 | 275 |
| **SCONES** | | | | | |
| Plain | 1 scone | 30g | 16 | 440 | 105 |
| Sultana | 1 scone | 35g | 22 | 545 | 130 |
| **SALAD DRESSINGS** | | | | | |
| Italian Dressing (25% oil) | 1 tabsp | 20g | 2 | 160 | 38 |
| French Dressing (50% oil) | 1 tabsp | 20g | 1 | 210 | 50 |
| Mayonnaise average, regular | 1 tabsp | 25g | 5 | 350 | 84 |
| Coleslaw Dressing Light | 1 tabsp | 20g | 6 | 45 | 10 |
| Salad Magic, no oil | 1 tabsp | 20g | 0 | 30 | 7 |

## CHARTS AND TABLES

|  |  |  | CHO | kJ | CALS |
|---|---|---|---|---|---|
| **SAUCES/GRAVY** |  |  |  |  |  |
| Apple Sauce | 2 tabsp | 40g | 10 | 225 | 60 |
| Chutney fruit | 1 tabsp | 25g | 11 | 185 | 45 |
| Low Joule Chutney | 1 tabsp | 25g | 3 | 50 | 12 |
| Gravy mix dry | 1 tabsp | 25g | 15 | 315 | 75 |
| White Sauce average | 2 tabsp | 45g | 7 | 295 | 70 |
| Mint Sauce average | 1 tabsp | 20g | 5 | 85 | 20 |
| Mustard | 1 tsp | 5g | 1 | 25 | 6 |
| Pickles Sweet Mustard | 1 tabsp | 20g | 5 | 85 | 20 |
| Diabetic | 1 tabsp | 20g | 1 | 35 | 8 |
| Soy Sauce | 1 tabsp | 20g | 1.5 | 45 | 10 |
| Vinegar | 1 tabsp | 20g | 0.5 | 10 | 3 |
| Worcestershire Sauce | 1 tabsp | 20g | 4 | 85 | 20 |
| **SOUPS** |  |  |  |  |  |
| Chicken Noodle, 1 pkt reconstitued | 1 cup | 250ml | 7.5 | 205 | 48 |
| French Onion, 1 pkt reconstitued | 1 cup | 250ml | 7.5 | 145 | 34 |
| Cream of Chicken, condensed | diluted | 250ml | 14 | 575 | 137 |
| Tomato canned | diluted | 250ml | 15 | 315 | 75 |
| Pea & Ham canned | diluted | 250ml | 20 | 450 | 108 |
| Stock cube average | 1 cube | 8g | 2 | 130 | 31 |
| **CONFECTIONERY** |  |  |  |  |  |
| Chocolate Nut Milk average |  | 30g | 19 | 670 | 160 |
| Diabetic Chocolate |  | 30g | 13 | 650 | 155 |
| Carob Chocolate |  | 30g | 20 | 650 | 155 |
| Kit Kat | 2 wafers | 20g | 14 | 435 | 104 |
| Boiled Lollies average | 1 lollie |  | 4 | 25 | 8 |
| Chewing gum - regular | 1 stick |  | 1 | 25 | 6 |
| - sugar free |  |  | 0 | 15 | 3 |
| - e.g. Jols |  |  | 2 | 35 | 8 |
| Diabetic Pastilles | 1 pastille |  | 0 | 5 | 1 |
| Toffee mixed | 1 toffee | 5g | 4 | 85 | 20 |
| **BEVERAGES - SOFT DRINKS/CORDIALS** |  |  |  |  |  |
| Coke, Lemonade, etc average | 1 glass | 200ml | 20 | 340 | 82 |
| Tonic Water, Dry Ginger Ale | 1 can | 375ml | 34 | 565 | 135 |
| Soda Water | 1 glass | 200ml | 0 | 0 | 0 |
| Cordial average 1 glass diluted 1:4 | 1 glass | 200ml | 18 | 290 | 70 |
| No Added Sugar Soft |  |  |  |  |  |
| Drinks/Cordials: average | 1 glass | 200ml | 1.5 | 20 | 5 |
| **ALCOHOLIC DRINKS** |  |  |  |  |  |
| (See Alcohol Chart p134) |  |  |  |  |  |
| **TAKE-AWAY FOODS** |  |  |  |  |  |
| Meat Pie | average, 1 pie | 175g | 25 | 1880 | 450 |
| Hamburger | medium | 150g | 43 | 1670 | 400 |
| Pizza | average, ¼ large | 150g | 54 | 2175 | 570 |
| Chicken, crumbed, fried | ¼ chicken | 130g | 8 | 1800 | 430 |
| Chicken, rotisseried, no stuffing | ¼ chicken | 120g | 0 | 1260 | 300 |
| Hot Dog, in medium roll | 1 only |  | 20 | 1170 | 280 |
| Chiko Roll, fried | 1 roll | 160g | 44 | 1550 | 370 |
| **FATS/OILS** |  |  |  |  |  |
| Butter, Margarine (all types) | 1 tsp | 5g | 0 | 150 | 35 |
|  | 2 tabsp | 40g | 0 | 1210 | 220 |
| Oils, all edible types |  |  |  |  |  |
| (includes polyunsaturated oils) | 2 tabsp | 40ml | 0 | 1470 | 352 |
| Cream: Sour Light (18% fat) | 1 tabsp | 20g | 0.5 | 160 | 38 |
| Reduced (25% fat) | 1 tabsp | 20g | 0.5 | 210 | 50 |
| Thickened (35% fat) | 1 tabsp | 20g | 0.5 | 280 | 67 |
| Whipping (40% fat) | 1 tabsp heaped | 30g | 0.5 | 440 | 105 |

# RECIPE NUTRITIONAL ANALYSIS SUMMARY

| Recipe Index | Page No | KJ | Cal | CHO | Fat | NS (CHO) |
|---|---|---|---|---|---|---|
| **Breakfast** | | | | | | |
| French Toast | 31 | 487 | 118 | 15 | 3 | |
| Fruit Smoothie | 33 | 858 | 206 | 41 | .3 | |
| Oatmeal Apple Porridge (1 cup) | 32 | 537 | 129 | 23 | 2 | |
| Savoury Baked Beans (½ cup serve) | 33 | 439 | 106 | 17 | 2 | |
| Savoury Corn Spread (¼ cup) | 32 | 320 | 77 | 13 | 2 | |
| Strawberry Fruit Spread (1 tabsp) | 32 | 44 | 10 | 2 | 0.02 | |
| Untoasted Muesli (¼ cup) | 32 | 506 | 122 | 13 | 6 | |
| **Luncheon** | | | | | | |
| Luncheon and Sandwich Ideas | 34 | | | | | |
| Sandwich Ingredients Chart | 36 | | | | | |
| **First Course, Dips & Accompaniments** | | | | | | |
| Avocado Salmon Mousse | 41 | 841 | 202 | 12 | 12 | |
| Bruschetta | 40 | 638 | 154 | 17 | 6.5 | |
| Hommos | 39 | 140 | 34 | 2 | 2 | |
| Mediterranean Spread | 40 | 107 | 26 | 0.35 | 2.6 | |
| Mexican Dip | 38 | 214 | 51 | 3 | 2.4 | |
| Red Capsicum Dip | 38 | 32 | 8 | 1 | 0.1 | |
| Savoury Meat Balls | 41 | 122 | 37 | 1.4 | 2 | |
| Savoury Stuffed Crêpes | 38 | 672 | 163 | 10 | 11 | |
| Seafood Avocado Dip | 41 | 399 | 97 | 4 | 7.3 | |
| Spinach Dip | 37 | 536 | 129 | 22 | 1.7 | |
| Spring Rolls | 40 | 112 | 27 | 3 | 0.3 | |
| Yoghurt Cheese | 39 | 93 | 22 | 2.4 | 0.08 | |
| **Soups Light Soups** | | | | | | |
| Cauliflower Soup | 42 | 184 | 44 | 5 | 0.6 | |
|    Choko Soup | 43 | | | | | |
|    Zucchini Soup | 43 | | | | | |
|    Broccoli Soup | 43 | | | | | |
|    'CCC' Soup | 43 | | | | | |
| Eggplant Soup | 43 | 271 | 64 | 5 | 3 | |
| Leek and Pear Soup | 44 | 285 | 68 | 9 | 2 | |
|    Two Tone Soup | 44 | | | | | |
| Pumpkin and Ginger Soup | 44 | 395 | 95 | 12 | 2 | |
| **Substantial Soups** | | | | | | |
| Clam Chowder | 45 | 655 | 158 | 15 | 4 | |
| Laksa | 46 | 919 | 221 | 34 | 4.5 | |
|    Seafood Laksa | 46 | | | | | |
|    Vegetarian Laksa | 46 | | | | | |
| Lombok Fish Soup | 45 | 316 | 75 | 5 | 2.3 | |
| Red Lentil Soup | 46 | 839 | 201 | 26 | 3 | |
| West Meets East Soup | 45 | 662 | 160 | 21 | 2.5 | |

NOTE: NS = NO ADDED SUGAR

## CHARTS AND TABLES

| Main Meal Meat Alternatives | Page No | KJ | Cal | CHO | Fat | NS (CHO) |
|---|---|---|---|---|---|---|
| **Beans Dishes** | | | | | | |
| Chilli Beans | 48 | 652 | 156 | 20 | 4 | |
| Kidney Bean Rice Medley | 48 | 962 | 229 | 45 | 4 | |
| Lentil Bean Goulash | 49 | 838 | 201 | 27 | 3.3 | |
| Lentil Bean Pie | 49 | 1318 | 318 | 35 | 12 | |
| Red Lentil Bean Capsicum Stew | 50 | 789 | 189 | 26 | 3 | |
| | | | | | | |
| **Soya Bean Dishes** | | | | | | |
| Asparagus and Tofu Stir Fry | 50 | 933 | 225 | 7 | 16 | |
| Marinade Baked Tofu | 50 | 209 | 50 | 4 | 2 | |
| Soya Bean Patties | 51 | 265 | 64 | 6 | 3.6 | |
| Tofu Vegetable Stir Fry | 51 | 472 | 113 | 8 | 4.5 | |
| | | | | | | |
| **Egg/Cheese Dishes** | | | | | | |
| Baked Frittata | 52 | 1032 | 249 | 27 | 8.5 | |
| Broccoli Soufflé | 52 | 731 | 176 | 9 | 10 | |
| Cheesy Pumpkin Ricotta Bake | 54 | 958 | 231 | 17 | 10 | |
| Ham and Bocconcini Cheese Bagel | 55 | 1482 | 357 | 39 | 9 | |
|     Salmon Bagels | 55 | | | | | |
| Quiche | 54 | 973 | 234 | 15 | 8 | |
| Spinach Pinenut Roulade | 53 | 1242 | 300 | 10 | 20 | |
|     Creamy Corn Roulade | 53 | | | | | |
| Zucchini Slice | 55 | 1247 | 301 | 17 | 17 | |
| | | | | | | |
| **Pasta and Grain Dishes** | | | | | | |
| Chick Peas With Tomato & Macaroni | 56 | 840 | 202 | 35 | 3 | |
| Gnocchi | 58 | 1207 | 291 | 29 | 11.5 | |
| Macaroni Cheese | 56 | 992 | 239 | 25 | 8.2 | |
| Paella | 57 | 1732 | 418 | 44 | 4.5 | |
| Pasta Verde Primavera | 58 | 697 | 168 | 29 | 1.5 | |
| Pasta With Low Fat Pesto Sauce | 56 | 1217 | 294 | 37 | 10 | |
| Polenta Pie | 58 | 845 | 204 | 25 | 6 | |
| Vegetable Lasagne | 59 | 1126 | 271 | 36 | 6 | |
| Vegetable Pasta | 55 | 1209 | 290 | 47 | 3 | |
| | | | | | | |
| **Main Vegetable Dishes** | | | | | | |
| Baked Ratatouille | 60 | 438 | 104 | 5 | 4 | |
| Mediterranean Pie | 61 | 1123 | 270 | 23 | 10 | |
| Vegetable Curry | 61 | 363 | 87 | 10 | 3.6 | |
| Vegetable Parcels - 2 Parcels Per Serve | 60 | 850 | 203 | 37 | 2 | |
| Vegetable Savoury | 60 | 769 | 185 | 10 | 9 | |
| | | | | | | |
| **Chicken** | | | | | | |
| Apricot Chicken Breast In Filo | 64 | 1953 | 472 | 22 | 3 | |
|     Chicken and Asparagus in Filo | 64 | | | | | |
| Chicken Dhal Curry | 65 | 1366 | 326 | 24 | 7.3 | |
| Chicken Ginger Kebabs | 65 | 690 | 164 | 5 | 3 | |
| Grilled Tandoori Chicken | 66 | 728 | 173 | 1.4 | 5.5 | |
| Chicken With Barbecue Sauce | 63 | 1422 | 341 | 21 | 10 | |
| Hungarian Chicken | 62 | 1005 | 240 | 12 | 6 | |
| Satay Chicken Kebabs | 63 | 1643 | 397 | 6 | 8 | |
| Sherried Mushroom Chicken | 63 | 1246 | 297 | 18 | 8 | |
| Turkey Breasts In Marinade Sauce | 66 | 291 | 71 | 2 | 5 | |

NOTE: NS = NO ADDED SUGAR

## CHARTS AND TABLES

| Beef | Page No | KJ | Cal | CHO | Fat | NS (CHO) |
|---|---|---|---|---|---|---|
| Beef Curry | 68 | 1115 | 266 | 10 | 12 | |
| Beef Stroganoff | 68 | 1236 | 296 | 8.4 | 12 | |
| Chilli Con Carne | 71 | 874 | 275 | 18 | 8.3 | |
| Cabbage Rolls | 69 | 1128 | 324 | 40 | 7 | |
| Cornish Pasties | 70 | 1066 | 257 | 25 | 10.4 | |
| Lasagne | 68 | 1089 | 284 | 30 | 8 | |
| Meat Balls With Sauce | 72 | 862 | 206 | 15 | 7 | |
| Moussaka | 71 | 820 | 197 | 10 | 12 | |
| Savoury Mince | 70 | 564 | 188 | 8.3 | 7.5 | |
|    Shepherds Pie | 70 | | | | | |
| Spaghetti Bolognaise | 70 | 1302 | 347 | 49 | 6.7 | |
| Steak Diane | 72 | 766 | 182 | 10 | 4 | |
| Steak With Green Capsicum | 72 | 1338 | 320 | 12 | 16.6 | |
| **Lamb** | | | | | | |
| Lamb Kebabs | 73 | 622 | 147 | 2 | 3 | |
| Lamb and Mushroom Curry | 74 | 801 | 191 | 7 | 6 | |
| Lamb Shank and Dumpling Ragout | 74 | 1405 | 337 | 26 | 9 | |
|    Lamb Shank Pie | 74 | | | | | |
| Tropical Crown Lamb Roast | 73 | 1381 | 331 | 8 | 16.5 | |
| **Pork** | | | | | | |
| Barbecue Spare Ribs | 76 | 1969 | 475 | 19 | 24 | |
| Pork Tenderloin Teriyaki | 75 | 555 | 132 | 3 | 1 | |
| Spicy Pork Medallions | 75 | 712 | 169 | 0.3 | 4 | |
| Sweet and Sour Pork | 76 | 1138 | 272 | 20 | 7 | |
| **Fish And Seafood** | | | | | | |
| Suggestions For Cooking Fish | | | | | | |
|    Microwave | 77 | | | | | |
|    Steamed | 77 | | | | | |
|    Mornay Sauce | 77 | | | | | |
|    Grilled | 77 | | | | | |
|    Baked Fish Fillets | 77 | | | | | |
|    Baked Whole Fish | 77 | | | | | |
|    Barbecue Fish Fillet | 78 | | | | | |
|    Pan-fried Fish | 78 | | | | | |
|    Fish in Filo | 78 | | | | | |
|    Fish Pie | 78 | | | | | |
|    Fish Cakes | 78 | | | | | |
| Barramundi Almondine | 81 | 914 | 218 | 3 | 10 | |
| Chilli Mussels | 79 | 1344 | 321 | 11 | 6 | |
| Curried Fish | 80 | 1041 | 249 | 9 | 10 | |
|    Curried Prawns with Fish | 80 | | | | | |
| Dhufish With Cucumber Sauce | 82 | 781 | 186 | 3 | 7 | |
| Fish Fillet Puff | 83 | 784 | 187 | 0.3 | 8.4 | |
| Lemon Fish Rolls | 80 | 910 | 217 | 8 | 10 | |
| Pan-fried Fish With Fresh Tomato Salsa | 78 | 794 | 190 | 8.5 | 5 | |
| Salmon Steaks | 78 | 1229 | 295 | 0.6 | 20 | |
| Schnapper Fillets Julienne | 83 | 928 | 221 | 8 | 5 | |
| Stir Fry Scallops | 79 | 898 | 215 | 9.3 | 8 | |
| Tuna Hot Pot | 82 | 1362 | 327 | 27 | 8 | |

NOTE: NS = NO ADDED SUGAR

# CHARTS AND TABLES

| Vegetable and Grains | Page No | KJ | Cal | CHO | Fat | NS (CHO) |
|---|---|---|---|---|---|---|
| **Low Joule Low Carbohydrate Vegetables** | | | | | | |
| Asparagus | 84 | | | | | |
|     Asparagus with Cheese Sauce | 84 | | | | | |
|     Asparagus with Lemon Sauce | 84 | | | | | |
|     Asparagus Soufflé | 84 | | | | | |
|     Marinated Asparagus Salad | 84 | | | | | |
|     Savoury Cases with Asparagus | 84 | | | | | |
|     Cocktail Puffs with Asparagus | 85 | | | | | |
|     Asparagus Rolls | 85 | | | | | |
| Beans | 85 | | | | | |
|     Green Beans and Cherry Tomatoes | 85 | | | | | |
|     Green Bean Bundles | 85 | | | | | |
| Broccoli | 85 | | | | | |
|     Cheesy Broccoli | 85 | | | | | |
|     Lemon Broccoli | 85 | | | | | |
| Brussel Sprouts | 85 | | | | | |
|     Brussels Sprouts with Baby Corn | 85 | | | | | |
|     Lemon Brussel Sprouts | 85 | | | | | |
|     Seasoned Brussel Sprout Salad | 85 | | | | | |
| Cabbage | 86 | | | | | |
|     Sweet and Sour Red Cabbage | 86 | | | | | |
|     Cabbage and Bacon | 86 | | | | | |
| Capsicum | 86 | | | | | |
| Peeled Capsicum | 86 | 52 | 13 | 2 | 0.1 | |
| Cauliflower | 86 | | | | | |
|     Cauliflower Cheese | 86 | | | | | |
|     Baked Cauliflower Cheese | 86 | | | | | |
|     Mustard Tarragon Cauliflower | 87 | | | | | |
| Eggplant | 87 | | | | | |
| Grilled Eggplant | 88 | 158 | 38 | 2 | 3 | |
|     Stuffed Eggplant | 87 | | | | | |
| Globe Artichokes | 87 | | | | | |
| Stuffed Artichokes | 87 | 403 | 96 | 7 | 3 | |
| Pumpkin | 88 | | | | | |
| Spinach | 88 | | | | | |
|     Spinach Triangles | 88 | | | | | |
| Savoury Spinach | 88 | 138 | 33 | 1.3 | 1.5 | |
| Tomatoes | 89 | | | | | |
| Sun Dried Tomatoes | 89 | 109 | 26 | 0.8 | 2.4 | |
| Zucchini | 90 | | | | | |
|     Savoury Tomato Zucchini | 90 | | | | | |

NOTE: NS = NO ADDED SUGAR

## CHARTS AND TABLES

| High Joule High Carbohydrate | Page No | KJ | Cal | CHO | Fat | NS (CHO) |
|---|---|---|---|---|---|---|
| **Vegetables and Grains** | | | | | | |
| Cous Cous | 90 | 332 | 80 | 15 | 1 | |
|    Fruity Cous Cous | 91 | | | | | |
| Noodles | 91 | | | | | |
| Pasta | 91 | | | | | |
| Peas | 92 | | | | | |
| Polenta | 92 | | | | | |
| Grilled Fine Polenta | 92 | 311 | 75 | 16 | .4 | |
| Rich Coarse Polenta | 92 | 580 | 141 | 21 | 3 | |
| Potato | 93 | | | | | |
|    Baked Potato | 93 | | | | | |
|    Stuffed Baked Potato | 93 | | | | | |
| Armadillo Potatoes | 93 | 209 | 50 | 7 | .6 | |
| Crunchy Cajun Chips | 94 | 345 | 83 | 13.6 | 1.5 | |
| Scalloped Potatoes | 93 | 400 | 97 | 12 | 3 | |
| Rice | 94 | | | | | |
| Sunflower Rice | 94 | 630 | 153 | 20 | 6 | |
|    Steamed Rice | 94 | | | | | |
| | | | | | | |
| **Salads and Dressings** | | | | | | |
| **Dressings** | | | | | | |
| Balsamic French Dressing | 95 | 317 | 77 | 0.7 | 8 | |
| Cider Vinegar Dressing | 95 | 265 | 65 | 7 | 4 | 0.08 |
| Creamy Mustard Dressing | 96 | 96 | 23 | 3 | 0.5 | |
| Honey Orange Dressing | 96 | 289 | 70 | 5 | 5.5 | |
| Horseradish Dressing | 96 | 174 | 42 | 4 | 2 | |
| Low Joule Caesar Salad Dressing | 97 | 220 | 53 | 3 | 3.5 | |
| Mustard Herb Dressing | 97 | 134 | 32 | 1.5 | 0.5 | |
| Spicy Cream Dressing | 96 | 93 | 22 | 3.5 | 0.4 | |
| Thai Dressing | 97 | 198 | 49 | 10 | 0.1 | |
| Tomato Yoghurt Dressing | 97 | 134 | 32 | 2 | 3 | |
| **Salads** | | | | | | |
| **Main Meal Salads** | | | | | | |
| Asian Salad | 98 | 877 | 209 | 3.3 | 7.2 | |
| Macaroni Bean Salad | 99 | 481 | 116 | 17 | 3 | |
| Mango Chicken Salad | 99 | 1827 | 441 | 11 | 9 | |
| Rare Roast Beef Salad | 98 | 763 | 182 | 8 | 6 | |
| Thai Fish Salad | 100 | 1500 | 361 | 31 | 11 | |
|    Thai Chicken Salad | 100 | | | | | |
| **Side Salads** | | | | | | |
| Salad Maker Chart | 103 | | | | | |
| Chinese Mixed Vegetable Salad | 102 | 512 | 124 | 11.4 | 7 | |
| German Potato Salad | 100 | 452 | 109 | 20 | 0.7 | |
| Low Joule Caesar Salad | 101 | 358 | 86 | 7 | 4 | |
| Red Cabbage Salad | 101 | 531 | 128 | 9.5 | 9 | |
| Roast Vegetable Salad | 101 | 387 | 93 | 13.5 | 2.5 | |
| Spinach Tomato Salad | 100 | 515 | 125 | 5 | 10 | |
| Tropical Sicilian Salad | 102 | 553 | 133 | 4 | 9 | |

NOTE: NS = NO ADDED SUGAR

## CHARTS AND TABLES

| Sauces | Page No | KJ | Cal | CHO | Fat | NS (CHO) |
|---|---|---|---|---|---|---|
| Bechamel Sauce   ¼ Cup Serves | 106 | 414 | 99 | 7 | 7 | |
| Cheese Sauce   ¼ Cup Serves | 108 | 253 | 61 | 4.4 | 3 | |
| Fresh Tomato Basil Salsa | | | | | | |
| ¼ Cup Serves | 106 | 59 | 14 | 2.5 | 0.1 | |
| Fresh Tomato Savoury Sauce | | | | | | |
| ½ Cup Serves | 105 | 133 | 32 | 4 | 1.4 | |
|     Cooked Tomato Savoury | 105 | | | | | |
| Italian Pasta Sauce   ½ Cup Serves | 104 | 196 | 47 | 6 | 1.2 | |
|     Italian Seafood Sauce | 104 | | | | | |
| Lentil Sauce   ⅔ Cup Serves | 105 | 233 | 56 | 7.4 | 1 | |
| Low Fat Pesto   ¼ Cup Serves | 105 | 474 | 115 | 2 | 8.6 | |
| Low Fat White Sauce   ¼ Cup Serves | 108 | 203 | 49 | 4 | 1.7 | |
| Plum Sauce   1 tbsp Serves | 106 | 102 | 25 | 6 | 0.03 | |
| Seafood Sauce   1 tbsp Serves | 107 | 87 | 21 | 4 | 0.4 | |
| Spaghetti Sauce   ½ Cup Serves | 104 | 1004 | 240 | 9 | 10.4 | |
| Sweet & Sour Sauce   ⅔ Cup Serves | 106 | 345 | 83 | 16 | 1.4 | |
| Yoghurt Sauce   1 tbsp Serves | 108 | 50 | 12 | 1.3 | 0.05 | |
| | | | | | | |
| **Desserts** | | | | | | |
| **Cold Desserts** | | | | | | |
| Fresh Fruit Ideas | 109 | | | | | |
| Apple Orange Fool | 110 | 376 | 91 | 22 | 0.1 | 13 |
| Apricot Whip | 110 | 290 | 71 | 14 | 0.1 | 6 |
|     Apple Whip | 110 | | | | | |
|     Strawberry Whip | 110 | | | | | |
|     Raspberry Whip | 110 | | | | | |
|     Apple/Blueberry Whip | 110 | | | | | |
| Blancmange Pudding | 110 | 282 | 69 | 14 | 0.09 | 8 |
|     Apricot Blancmange Pudding | 110 | | | | | |
|     Banana Blancmange Pudding | 110 | | | | | |
|     Strawberry Blancmange Pudding | 110 | | | | | |
|     Passionfruit Blancmange Pudding | 110 | | | | | |
|     Chocolate Blancmange Pudding | 110 | | | | | |
| Burgundy Pears | 113 | 409 | 98 | 19 | 0.1 | 13 |
| Chocolate Mousse | 111 | 337 | 82 | 14 | 1.5 | 5 |
|     Strawberry Mousse | 111 | | | | | |
| Compote of Fruit | 112 | 312 | 74 | 17 | 0.1 | |
| Fresh Fruit Lemon Jelly | 112 | 465 | 113 | 23 | 0.1 | 4 |
|     Lemon Orange Jelly | 112 | | | | | |
| Gingered Rockmelon | 111 | 265 | 65 | 15 | 0.2 | 7 |
| Lemon Sponge | 111 | 299 | 73 | 14 | 0.04 | 2 |
|     Lemon Orange Sponge | 111 | | | | | |
|     Lemon Passionfruit Sponge | 111 | | | | | |
| Ricotta Cream | 114 | 165 | 40 | 3 | 2 | |
| Spanish Cream | 116 | 318 | 77 | 11 | 1 | 4 |
| Strawberry Pie | 114 | 573 | 139 | 13.5 | 6.6 | |
| Strawberry Whirl | 113 | 406 | 98 | 15 | 2 | 4 |
|     Banana Whirl | 113 | | | | | |
|     Passionfruit Whirl | 113 | | | | | |
|     Raspberry Whirl | 113 | | | | | |
| Summer Pudding | 116 | 423 | 102 | 21.5 | 0.6 | 14 |
| Tulip Fruits | 115 | 804 | 192 | 30 | 7 | 14 |

NOTE:   NS = NO ADDED SUGAR

## CHARTS AND TABLES

| Hot Desserts | Page No | KJ | Cal | CHO | Fat | NS (CHO) |
|---|---|---|---|---|---|---|
| Apple Cottage Pudding | 117 | 390 | 94 | 16 | 2 | 13 |
|    Apricot Cottage Pudding | 117 | | | | | |
|    Peach Cottage Pudding | 117 | | | | | |
|    Rhubarb Cottage Pudding | 117 | | | | | |
|    Rhubarb Apple Cottage Pudding | 117 | | | | | |
| Bread Pudding | 119 | 540 | 131 | 20 | 3 | 14 |
| Custard Sauce | 119 | 155 | 38 | 6 | 0.5 | 3 |
| Lemon Delicious | 119 | 654 | 159 | 15 | 8 | 9 |
| Lemon Meringue Pie | 118 | 809 | 197 | 34 | 4.5 | 16 |
| **Baking** | | | | | | |
| Apple Muffins | 127 | 277 | 67 | 11 | 2 | 9 |
| Banana Date Muffins | 127 | 341 | 82 | 14 | 2 | |
|    Soya Muffins | 127 | | | | | |
| Banana Tea Bread | 122 | 217 | 52 | 6 | 3 | |
|    Apple Banana Tea Bread | 123 | | | | | |
| Bran Muffins | 128 | 349 | 84 | 12 | 3 | 10 |
| Carrot Cake | 121 | 286 | 68 | 10 | 3 | 8 |
| Choux Pastry - variation Kiwi Choux Ring | 131 | 287 | 70 | 4 | 5 | |
|    Kiwi Choux Ring | 131 | | | | | |
| Crispy Lavash Bread | 125 | 569 | 125 | 21 | 3 | |
| Damper With Beer | 130 | 471 | 114 | 14 | 5 | |
| Date Loaf | 122 | 251 | 61 | 7 | 3 | 5 |
| Dumplings | 128 | 692 | 168 | 23 | 6 | |
|    Sweet Dumplings | 129 | | | | | |
| Fruity Loaf | 126 | 291 | 70 | 13 | 1 | |
| Low Fat Cereal Loaf | 123 | 293 | 71 | 15 | 0.2 | 10 |
|    Low Fat Apricot Loaf | 123 | | | | | |
| Low Fat Fibre Pastry 1 Cup | 131 | 3086 | 748 | 74 | 40 | |
| Low Joule Garlic Croutons | 130 | 115 | 28 | 4 | 1 | |
| Oatcakes | 124 | 265 | 64 | 7 | 3.4 | 6 |
| Oatmeal Carrot Muffins | 125 | 348 | 84 | 11 | 3 | 9 |
| Oatmeal Fruit Slice | 126 | 366 | 88 | 12 | 4 | 10 |
| Oatmeal Treacle Biscuits | 124 | 249 | 60 | 7 | 3 | 6 |
| Plain Scones | 121 | 286 | 69 | 9 | 3 | |
|    Cheese Scones | 121 | | | | | |
|    Savoury Scones | 121 | | | | | |
| Potato Muffins | 128 | 460 | 111 | 16 | 2 | |
| Pumpkin Scones | 121 | 269 | 65 | 11 | 1 | 8 |
| Savoury Cases | 130 | 209 | 51 | 8 | 1 | |
| Stained Glass Window Cake | 122 | 667 | 161 | 18 | 8 | 16 |
| Wholemeal Crêpes | 129 | 349 | 85 | 7 | 4 | |
|    Crêpes with Italian Seafood Sauce | 129 | | | | | |
|    Petite Crêpes | 129 | | | | | |

NOTE: NS = NO ADDED SUGAR

# Handy Abbreviation and Measurement Guide

### MICROWAVE SELECTION CHART

| This Book | Category | Number | Watts | Percentage |
|---|---|---|---|---|
| **High** | Full power | 9 | 650 | Full power |
|  | High Heat | 8 | 620 | 100% |
| **Medium High** | Roast | 7 | 550 | 80% |
|  | Bake | 6 | 470 | 70% |
| **Medium** | Medium | 5 | 400 | 50% |
| **Low** | Defrost | 3 | 300 | 30% |
| **Warm** | Low | 1 | 150 | 10% |

### OVEN TEMPERATURES - Fan Forced Temperatures used in this book

| Oven Guide | C° Gas or Electricity Fan Forced | C° Electricity No Fan |
|---|---|---|
| **Keep Warm** | 80 | 80 |
| **Slow** | 150 | 150-160 |
| **Moderately Slow** | 160 | 160-170 |
| **Moderately Hot** | 190 | 200-210 |
| **Hot** | 200 | 210-220 |
| **Very Hot** | 220 | 230-250 |

### LENGTH

| Centimetres (cm) | Inches |
|---|---|
| 2.5 | 1 |
| 23 | 9 |
| 25 | 10 |
| 30 | 12 |

### ANALYSIS ABBREVIATIONS

| Kilojoules | Kj |
|---|---|
| Calories | Cal |
| Protein - grams (g) | Pro |
| Carbohydrate - grams (g) | CHO |
| Total Fat - grams (g) | T. fat |
| Saturated Fat - grams (g) | S. fat |
| Cholesterol - milligrams (mg) | Chol |
| Sodium - milligrams (mg) | Na |

### ABBREVIATIONS

| **tabsp** | tablespoon |
|---|---|
| **tsp** | teaspoon |
| **g** | gram |
| **kg** | kilograms |
| **ml** | millilitres |
| **p** | page |
| **C** | Centigrade |
| **bold** | recipe or information in book |

# INDEX

Abbreviation & Measurement Guide,147
Adapt Your Cooking recipes,14
Alcohol,11
Alcohol, Energy, CHO Chart,134
Analysis, Recipes explained,30
Almondine Barramundi,81
Apple
    Banana Tea Bread,123
    Blueberry Whip,110
    Cottage Pudding,117
    Cottage Pudding, Rhubarb,117
    Muffins,127
    Orange Fool,110
    Porridge, Oatmeal,32
    Whip,110
Apricot
    Blancmange Pudding,110
    Chicken Breast in Filo,64
    Cottage Pudding,117
    Loaf, Low Fat,123
    Whip,110
Armadillo Potatoes,93
Artificial sweeteners,11
Asian Salad (Hot or Cold),98
Asparagus,84
    Cocktail Puffs wit ,85
    in Filo, Chicken &,64
    Rolls,85
    & Tofu Stir Fry,50
    with Cheese Sauce,84
    with Lemon Sauce,84
    Savoury Cases with,84
    Soufflé,84
    Salad, Marinated,84
Artichokes, Globe,87
    Stuffed,87
Avocado
    Dip, Seafood,41
    Mango Chicken Salad,99
    Salmon Mousse,41
Baby Corn, Brussel Sprouts with,85
Bacon, Cabbage &,86
Bagel
    Ham & Bocconcini Cheese,55
    Salmon,55
Bake(d)
    Beans, Savoury,33
    Cauliflower Cheese,86
    Cheesy Pumpkin Ricotta,54
    Fish Fillets,77
    Frittata,52
    Potato,93
    Potato, Stuffed,93
    Ratatouille,60
    Tofu, Marinade,50
    Whole Fish,77
Balanced Meal Plan, Energy
        Requirements,18
Balsamic French Dressing,95
    Spinach Tomato Salad,100
Banana
    Blancmange Pudding,110
    Date Muffins,127
    Tea Bread,122
    Tea Bread, Apple,123
    Whirl,113
Barbecue
    Fish Fillet,78
    Menu,27
    Sauce, Chicken with ,63

Spare Ribs,76
Barramundi
    Almondine,81
    Pan-fried Fish with Fresh Tomato
        Salsa,78
Basil
    Low Fat Pesto Sauce,105
    Pasta with low Fat Pesto
        Sauce,56
    Salsa, Fresh Tomato,106
Bean(s)
    & Cherry Tomatoes, Green,85
    Bundles, Green,85
    Capsicum Stew, Red Lentil,50
    Chilli,48
    Chilli Con Carne,71
    Goulash Lentil,49
    Pie, Lentil,49
    Rice Medley, Kidney,48
    Salad, Macaroni,99
    Savoury Baked,33
    Soya Bean Patties,51
    West Meets East Soup,45
Bechamel Sauce,106
Beef (see Mince & Steak)
    Asian Salad (Hot or Cold),98
    Curry,68
    Salad, Rare Roast,98
    Stroganoff,68
Beer, Damper with,130
Biscuit(s)
    Oatcakes,124
    Oatmeal Treacle,124
Blancmange
    Pudding,110
    Pudding, Apricot,110
    Pudding, Banana,110
    Pudding, Chocolate,110
    Pudding, Passionfruit,110
    Pudding, Strawberry,110
Blood Fats & Diabetes,10
Blood Glucose Monitoring,9
Blueberry(ies)
    Apple Whip,110
    Whip, Apple,110
Bocconcini Cheese Bagel, Ham &,55
Bok Choy Stir Fry Scallops,79
Bolognaise, Spaghetti,70
Bran Muffins,128
Bread(s)
    Apple Banana Tea,123
    Banana Tea,122
    Cereals & Grains & Starchy Veg
        Group,17
    Crispy Lavash,125
    Pudding,119
    Spinach Dip,37
    Summer Pudding,116
Breakfast Menu,21
Broccoli,85
    Lemon,85
    Soufflé,52
    Soup,43
    Stir Fry Scallops,79
    Vegetable Savoury,60
Bruschetta,40
Brussel Sprouts,85
    Lemon,85
    Salad, Seasoned ,85
    with Baby Corn,85

Buffet Menu,27
Burgundy Pears,113
Cabbage
    & Bacon,86
    Rolls,69
    Salad, Red,101
    Sweet & Sour Red,8
Caesar Salad
    Dressing, Low Joule,97
    Low Joule,101
Cajun, Crunchy, Chips,94
Cake(s)
    Carrot,121
    Fish,78
    Stained Glass Window,122
Capsicum
    'CCC' Soup,43
    Dip, Red,38
    Peeled,86
    Steak with Green,72
    Stew, Red Lentil Bean,50
Carbohydrate, CHO,30
    Control & Diabetes,8
    Distribution,8
Carrot
    Cake,121
    Muffins, Oatmeal,125
Cases
    Savoury,130
    with Asparagus Sauce, Savoury,84
Cauliflower,86
    Cheese,86
    Cheese, Baked,86
    Mustard Tarragon,87
    Soup,42
'CCC' Soup,42
Cereal(s)
    Breads & Grains & Starchy Veg
        Group,17
    Loaf, Low Fat,123
    Oatmeal Apple Porridge,32
    Untoasted Muesli,32
Changing Insulin requirements,9
Charts & Tables,132
Chart, Healthy Food,16
Cheese/Cheesy
    Bagel, Ham & Bocconcini,55
    Baked Cauliflower,86
    Broccoli,85
    Cauliflower,86
    Macaroni,56
    Pumpkin Ricotta Bake,54
    Sauce,108
    Sauce, Asparagus with,84
    Scones,121
    Yoghurt,39
Cherry Tomatoe(s)
    Green Beans &,85
Chicken
    & Asparagus in Filo,64
    Breast in Filo, Apricot,64
    & Dahl Curry,65
    Ginger Kebabs,65
    Grilled Tandoori,66
    Hungarian,62
    Kebabs,Satay,63
    Salad, Mango,99
    Salad, Thai,100
    Sherried Mushroom,63
    with Barbecue Sauce,63

# INDEX

Chick Peas
    Hommos,39
    with Tomato & Macaroni,56
Chilli
    Beans,48
    Con Carne,71
    Mussels,79
Chinese Mixed Vegetable Salad,102
Chocolate
    Blancmange Pudding,110
    Mousse,111
Choko Soup,43
Cholesterol,30
    Fat Lower,14
Choux
    Pastry,131
    Ring, Kiwi,131
Christmas Menu,27
Cider Vinegar Dressing,95
    Chinese Mixed Vegetable
        Salad,102
Clam Chowder,45
Cocktail
    Party Menu,28
    Puffs with Asparagus,84
Common Foods
    KJ, Calories Chart,135
Con Carni, Chilli,71
Cooked Tomato Savoury,105
Corn
    Roulade, Creamy,53
    Spread, Savoury,32
    with Brussel Sprouts,Baby,85
Cornish Pasties,70
Cottage
    Pudding, Apple,117
    Pudding, Apricot,117
    Pudding, Peach,117
    Pudding, Rhubarb,117
    Pudding, Rhubarb Apple,117
Cous Cous,91
    Fruity,91
Cream
    Dressing, Spicy,96
    Ricotta,114
    Spanish,116
Creamy
    Corn Roulade,53
    German Potato Salad,100
    Mustard Dressing,96
Crêpes
    Petite,129
    Savoury Stuffed,38
    Wholemeal,129
    with Italian Seafood Sauce,129
Crispy Lavash Bread,125
Croutons,Low Joule Garlic,130
Crudits,30
Crunchy Cajun Chips,94
Cucumber Sauce, Dhufish with,82
Curried
    Fish,80
    Prawns with Fish,80
Curry
    Beef,68
    Chicken & Dahl,65
    Lamb & Mushroom,74
    Vegetable,61
Custard Sauce,119

Dahl Curry, Chicken &,65
Damper with Beer,130
Date
    Loaf,122
    Muffins, Banana,127
Delicious, Lemon,119
Dhufish with Cucumber Sauce,82
Diabetes
    & Control,8
    Australia,13
Diane, Steak,72
Diet
    & Blood Sugar Control,9
    & Diabetes,8
Dietary Guidelines,13
Dinner Menu
    High Carbohydrate,26
    Low Carbohydrate,25
    Special,28
    Vegetarian,22
Dip
    Mexican,38
    Red Capsicum,38
    Seafood Avocado,41
    Spinach,37
Distribution of Carbohydrate,8
Dressing
    Balsamic French,95
    Cider Vinegar,95
    Creamy Mustard,96
    Honey Orange,96
    Horse Radish,96
    Low Joule Caesar Salad,97
    Mustard Herb,97
    Spicy Cream,96
    Thai,97
    Tomato Yoghurt,97
Dumpling(s),128
    Ragout, Lamb Shank &,74
    Sweet,129
East Soup, West Meets,45
Eggplant
    Grilled,87
    Moussaka,71
    Soup,43
    Stuffed,87
Energy Requirements, Balanced Meal
    Plan,18
Exercise & Diabetes & Physical
    Activity,10
Fat,30
    & Cholesterol Lower,14
    Counter Tables, Mini 133
Fibre
    Increase,14
    Pastry, Low Fat,131
Fillet(s)
    Julienne, Schnapper,83
    Puff, Fish,83
Filo
    Apricot Chicken in,64
    Chicken and Asparagus in,64
    Fish in,78
Fish
    Baked Whole,77
    Barramundi Almondine,81
    Cakes,78
    Curried,80
    Curried Prawns with,80
    Dhufish with Cucumber Sauce,82

Fillet, Barbecue,78
Fillet Puff,83
Fillets, Baked,77
    Grilled,77
    in Filo,78
    Microwave,77
    Mornay Sauce,77
    Pan-fried,78
    Pie,78
    Rolls, Lemon ,80
    Salad, Thai,100
    Salmon Steak,78
    Schnapper Fillets Julienne,83
    Soup, Lombok,45
    Steamed,77
    Tuna Hot Pot,82
    with Fresh Tomato Salsa,
        Pan-fried,78
Food
    Groups,16
    Chart, Healthy,16
Fool, Apple Orange,110
French
    Dressing, Balsamic ,95
    Toast,31
Fresh
    Fruit Ideas,109
    Fruit Lemon Jelly,112
    Tomato Basil Salsa,106
    Tomato Salsa, Pan-fried Fish
        with,78
    Tomato Savoury Sauce,105
Frittata, Baked,52
Fruit(s),109
    Compote of,112
    Groups,17
    Lemon Jelly, Fresh,112
    Slice, Oatmeal,126
    Smoothie,33
    Spread, Strawberry,32
    Tulip,115
Fruit, Mixed
    Summer Pudding,116
    Tulip Fruits,115
Fruity
    Cous Cous,91
    Loaf,126
Garlic Croutons, Low Joule,130
German Potato Salad,100
Gestational Diabetes,8
Ginger
    Kebabs, Chicken,65
    Soup, Pumpkin and,44
Gingered Rockmelon,111
Globe Artichokes,87
    Stuffed,87
Glycaemic Index (GI),8,12
    Chart,132
Gnocchi,58
Goulash,Lentil Bean,49
Grains, Breads, Starchy Veg Group,17
Grilled
    Eggplant,87
    Fine Polenta,92
    Fish,77
    Tandoori Chicken,66
Ham
    and Bocconcini Cheese Bagel,55
Healthy Food Chart,16
Herb Dressing, Mustard,97

# INDEX

Home Blood Glucose Monitoring,9
Hommos,39
Honey Orange Dressing,96
    Red Cabbage Salad,96
Horseradish Dressing,96
    Rare Roast Beef Salad,98
Hot Pot, Tuna,82
Hungarian Chicken,62
Impaired Glucose Tolerance,8
Indulgences,17
Insulin
    Dependent Diabetes Melitus,8
    Requirements,9
Italian Pasta Sauce,104
    Meat Balls in Sauce,72
Italian Seafood Sauce,129
    with Crêpes,129
Jelly
    Fresh Fruit Lemon,112
    Lemon Orange,112
Julienne,30
    Schnapper Fillets,83
Kebabs
    Chicken & Ginger,65
    Lamb,73
    Satay Chicken,63
Kidney Bean Rice Medley,48
Kiwi Choux Ring,131
Laksa
    Seafood,46
    Vegetarian,46
Lamb
    Kebabs,73
    & Mushroom Curry,74
    Shank & Dumpling Ragout,74
    Shank Pie,74
    Roast,Tropical Crown ,73
Lasagne,68
    Vegetable,59
Lavash Bread, Crispy,125
Leek & Pear Soup,44
Lemon
    Broccoli,85
    Brussel Sprouts,85
    Delicious,119
    Fish Rolls,80
    Jelly, Fresh Fruit,112
    Meringue Pie,118
    Orange Jelly,112
    Orange Sponge,111
    Passionfruit Sponge,111
    Sauce, Asparagus with,84
    Sponge,111
Lentil
    Bean Capsicum Stew, Red,50
    Bean Goulash,49
    Bean Pie,49
    Sauce,105
    Soup, Red,46
Lombok Fish Soup,45
Loaf
    Date,122
    Fruity,126
    Low Fat Apricot,123
    Low Fat Cereal,123
Low Fat
    Apricot Loaf,123
    Cereal Loaf,123
    Fibre Pastry,131
    Pesto Sauce,105

Pesto Sauce, Pasta with,56
    Vegetable Group,17
Low Joule
    Caesar Salad,101
    Caesar Salad Dressing,97
    Garlic Croutons,130
Lunch Menu
    High Carbohydrate, 24
    Low Carbohydrate,23
    Special,27
    Vegetarian,22
Macaroni
    Bean Salad,99
    Cheese,56
    Chick Peas with Tomato,56
Mango Chicken Salad,99
Marinade Sauce, Turkey Breast in a,66
Marinated
    Asparagus Salad,84
    Baked Tofu,50
Meal Planning,8
Measurement, Abbreviation Guide,147
Meat
    & Meat Alternativies Group,17
    Balls with Sauce,72
Medallions, Spicy Pork,75
Mediterranean
    Pie,61
    Spread,40
Medley, Kidney Bean Rice,48
Menu
    4200 KJ,18
    5000 KJ,19
    8,400 KJ,20
    Barbecue,27
    Breakfast,21
    Buffet,27
    Christmas,27
    Cocktail Party,28
    Dinner,25,26
    Dinner Party,28
    Lunch,23,24
    Special,
    Vegetarian,22
Meringue Pie, Lemon,118
Mexican Dip,38
Microwave Fish,77
Milk & Milk Products,17
Mince
    Cabbage Rolls,69
    Chilli Con Carne,71
    Cornish Pasties,70
    Lamb Kebabs,73
    Lasagne,68
    Meat Balls in Sauce,72
    Moussaka,71
    Savoury,70
    Savoury Meatballs,41
    Shepherds Pie,70
    Spaghetti Bologanise,70
    Spaghetti Sauce,104
Mixed Vegetables(s)
    Creamy Corn Roulade,53
    Salad, Chinese,102
    West Meets East Soup,45
Monitoring, Blood Glucose,9
Mornay Sauce, Fish in,77
Moussaka,71
Mousse
    Avocado Salmon,41

    Chocolate Mousse,111
    Strawberry,111
Muesli, Untoasted,32
Muffins
    Apple,127
    Banana Date,127
    Bran,128
    Oatmeal Carrot,125
    Potato,128
    Soya,127
Mushroom(s)
    Chicken,Sherried,63
    Curry, Lamb & ,74
Mussels, Chilli,79
Mustard
    Dressing, Creamy,96
    Herb Dressing,97
    Tarragon Cauliflower,87
Non Insulin Dependent Diabetes
    Mellitus,8
Noodles,91
Oatmeal
    Apple Porridge,32
    Carrot Muffins,125
    Fruit Slice,126
    Oatcakes,124
    Treacle Biscuits,124
Orange
    Dressing, Honey,96
    Fool, Apple,110
    Jelly, Lemon.112
    Sponge, Lemon,111
Paella,57
Pan-fried
    Fish,78
    Fish with Fresh Tomato Salsa,78
Parcel, Vegetable,60
Passionfruit
    Blancmange Pudding,110
    Sponge, Lemon,111
    Whirl,113
Pasta
    Sauce, Italian,104
    Vegetable,55
    Verde Primavera,58
    with Low Fat Pesto Sauce,56
Pasties, Cornish,70
Pastry
    Choux,131
    Low Fat Fibre,131
Patties, Soya Bean,51
Peach Cottage Pudding,117
Pear(s)
    Burgundy,113
    Soup, Leek &,44
Peas,92
Peeled Capsicum, 86
Pesto
    Sauce, Low Fat,105
    Sauce, Pasta with Low Fat,56
Petite Crêpes,129
Physical Activity, Exercise & Diabetes,10
Pie
    Fish,78
    Lamb Shank,74
    Lemon Meringue,118
    Lentil Bean,49
    Mediterranean,61
    Polenta,58
    Shepherds ,70

# INDEX

Strawberry, 114
Pinenut Roulade, Spinach, 53
Plain Scones, 121
Plum Sauce, 106
Polenta, 92
    Grilled Fine, 92
    Rich Coarse, 92
    Pie, 58
Pork
    Asian Salad (Hot or Cold), 98
    Barbecue Spare Ribs, 76
    Medallions, Spicy, 75
    Sweet and Sour, 7
    Tenderloin Teriyaki, 75
Porridge, Oatmeal Apple, 32
Potato(es), 93
    Armadillo, 93
    Baked, 93
    Crunchy Cajun Chips, 94
    Muffins, 128
    Salad, German, 100
    Scalloped, 93
    Stuffed Baked, 93
Prawns with Fish, Curried, 80
Primavera, Pasta Verde, 58
Pudding
    Apple Cottage, 117
    Apricot Blancmange, 110
    Apricot Cottage, 117
    Banana Blancmange, 110
    Blancmange, 110
    Bread, 119
    Chocolate Blancmange, 110
    Passionfruit Blancmange, 110
    Peach Cottage, 117
    Rhubarb Apple Cottage, 117
    Rhubarb Cottage, 117
    Strawberry Blancmange, 110
    Summer, 116
Puffs
    Fish Fillet, 83
    with Asparagus, Cocktail, 85
Pumpkin, 88
    & Ginger Soup, 44
    Ricotta Bake, Cheesy, 54
    Scones, 121
Quiche, 54
Ragout, Lamb Shank & Dumpling, 74
Raspberry
    Whip, 110
    Whirl, 113
Ratatouille, Baked, 60
Recipe
    Analysis Explained, 30
    Nutritional Analysis Summary, 140
Red
    Cabbage Salad, 101
    Capsicum Dip, 38
    Lentil Bean Capsicum Stew, 56
Rhubarb
    Apple Cottage Pudding, 117
    Cottage Pudding, 117
Rice, 94
    Medley, Kidney Bean, 48
    Steamed, 94
    Sunflower, 94
Ricotta
    Bake, Cheesy Pumpkin, 54
    Cream, 114
Ring, Kiwi Choux, 131

Roast
    Beef Salad, Rare, 98
    Tropical Crown Lamb, 73
    Vegetable Salad, 101
Rockmelon, Gingered, 111
Rolls
    Asparagus, 85
    Cabbage, 69
    Lemon Fish, 80
    Spring, 40
Roulade
    Creamy Corn, 53
    Spinach Pinenut, 53
Salad, Main Meal
    (Hot or Cold), Asian, 98
    Macaroni Bean, 99
    Mango Chicken, 99
    Rare Roast Beef, 9
    Thai Chicken, 100
    Thai Fish, 100
Salad Maker Chart, 103
Salad, Side
    Chinese Mixed Vegetable, 102
    German Potato, 100
    Low Joule Caesar, 101
    Marinated Asparagus, 84
    Red Cabbage, 101
    Roast Vegetable, 101
    Seasoned Brussel Sprout, 85
    Spinach Tomato, 100
    Tropical Sicilian, 102
Salmon
    Mousse, Avocado, 41
    Steak, 78
Salsa
    Fresh Tomato Basil, 106
    Mexican Dip, 38
    Pan-fried Fish with Fresh Tomato, 78
Satay Chicken Kebabs, 63
Sauce
    Asparagus with Cheese, 84
    Asparagus with Lemon, 84
    Bechamel, 106
    Cheese, 108
    Chicken with Barbecue, 63
    Cooked Tomato Savoury, 105
    Custard, 119
    Fish in Mornay, 77
    Fresh Tomato Basil Salsa, 106
    Fresh Tomato Savoury, 105
    Italian Pasta, 104
    Italian Seafood, 104
    Lentil, 105
    Low Fat Pesto, 105
    Low Fat White, 108
    Meat Balls with, 72
    Pasta with Low Fat Pesto, 56
    Plum, 106
    Savoury Cases with Asparagus, 84
    Seafood, 107
    Spaghetti, 104
    Sweet and Sour, 106
    Turkey Breast in a Marinade, 66
    Yoghurt, 108
Savoury
    Baked Beans, 33
    Cases, 130
    Cases with Asparagus Sauce, 84
    Cooked Tomato, 105

    Corn Spread, 32
    Meat Balls, 41
    Mince, 70
    Sauce, Fresh Tomato, 105
    Scones, 121
    Stuffed Crêpes, 38
    Vegetable, 60
Scalloped Potatoes, 93
Schnapper Fillets Julienne, 83
Scones
    Cheese, 121
    Plain, 121
    Pumpkin, 121
    Savoury, 121
Seafood (see fish)
    Avocado Dip, 41
    Chilli Mussels, 79
    Laksa, 46
    Paella, 57
    Sauce, 107
    Stir Fry Scallops, 79
Seasoned Brussel Sprout Salad, 85
Shank
    & Dumpling Ragout, Lamb, 74
    Pie, Lamb, 74
Shepherds Pie, 70
Sherried Mushroom Chicken, 63
Sicilian Salad, Tropical, 102
Slice
    Oatmeal Fruit, 126
    Zucchini, 55
Smoked Salmon Bagels, 55
Smoothie, 33
Snacks Between Meals, 8
Sodium (Na)
    Salt Lower, 14
    Explained, 30
    Sodium, Low Stock Powder, 30
Soufflé
    Asparagus, 84
    Broccoli, 52
Soup
    Broccoli, 43
    Cauliflower, 42
    'CCC', 43
    Choko, 43
    Clam Chowder, 45
    Eggplant, 43
    Laska, 46
    Leek & Pear, 44
    Lombok Fish, 45
    Pumpkin & Ginger, 44
    Red Lentil, 46
    Seafood Laksa, 46
    Two Tone, 44
    West Meets East, 45
    Zucchini, 43
Soya Beans Patties, 51
Spaghetti
    Bolognaise, 70
    Sauce, 104
Spaghetti Sauce
    Lasagne, 68
    Spaghetti Bolognaise, 70
Spanish Cream, 116
Spicy
    Cream Dressing, 96
    Pork Medallions, 75
Spinach, 88
    Dip, 37

# INDEX

Pinenut Roulade, 53
Savoury, 88
Tomato Salad, 100
Triangles, 88
Spare Ribs, Barbecue, 76
Sponge
    Lemon, 111
    Lemon Orange, 111
    Lemon Passionfruit, 111
Spread
    Hommos, 39
    Mediterranean, 40
    Savoury Corn, 32
    Strawberry Fruit, 32
    Yoghurt Cheese, 39
Spring Rolls, 40
Stained Glass Window Cake, 122
Starchy Veg & Breads & Cereals & Grains, Group, 17
Steak
    Diane, 72
    Salmon, 78
    Sweet & Sour Pork, with Green Capsicum, 72
Steamed
    Fish, 77
    Rice, 94
Stew, Red Lentil Bean Capsicum, 50
Stir Fry
    Asparagus and Tofu, 50
    Scallops, 79
    Tofu & Vegetable, 51
Stock Powder, Low Sodium, 30
Strawberry
    Blancmange Pudding, 110
    Fruit Spread, 32
    Mousse, 111
    Pie, 114
    Whip, 110
    Whirl, 113
Stroganoff, Beef, 68
Stuffed
    Artichokes
    Baked Potato, 93
    Crêpes, Savoury, 38
    Eggplant, 87
Sugar
    Lower, 14
    Substitutes, 12
Summer Pudding, 116
Sunflower (Seeds),
    Rice, 94

Sweet and Sour
    Pork, 76
    Red Cabbage, 86
    Sauce, 104
Tandoori Chicken, Grilled, 66
Tarragon Cauliflower, Mustard, 87
Tea Bread
    Apple Banana, 123
    Banana, 122
Teriyaki, Pork Tenderloin, 75
Thai
    Chicken Salad, 100
    Dressing, 97
    Fish Salad, 100
Toast, French, 31
Tofu
    & Vegetable Stir Fry, 51
    Marinate Baked, 50
    Stir Fry, Asparagus &, 50
Tolerance, Impaired Glucose, 8
Tomato(es), 89
    & Macaroni, Chick Peas with, 56
    Basil Salsa, Fresh, 106
    Green Bean & Cherry, 85
    Salad, Spinach, 100
    Salsa, Pan-fried Fish with Fresh, 78
    Savoury Cooked, 105
    Savoury Sauce, Fresh, 105
    Sundried, 89
Tomato Yoghurt Dressing, 97
    Macaroni Bean Salad, 99
Topside
    Beef Stroganoff, 68
    Rare Roast Beef Salad, 98
Treacle
    Biscuits, Oatmeal, 124
Tropical
    Crown Lamb Roast, 73
    Sicilian Salad, 102
Tulip Fruits, 115
Tuna Hot Pot, 82
Turkey Breasts in a Marinade Sauce, 66
Two Tone Soup, 44
Type
    I Diabetes, 8
    II Diabetes, 8
Untoasted Muesli, 32
Vegetable(s) see individual Vegetables
    Asian Salad (Hot or Cold), 98
    Cornish Pasties, 70
    Curry, 61
    Group, Low Joule, 17

Hungarian Chicken, 62
Lasagne, 59
Mediterranean Pie, 61
Parcels, 60
Pasta, 55
Pasta Verde Primavera, 58
Polenta Pie
Salad, Chinese Mixed, 102
Salad, Roast, 101
Savoury, 60
Schnapper Fillets Julienne, 83
Starchy Veg, Bread & Cereal & Grains, Group, 17
Stir Fry Scallops, 79
Stir Fry Tofu, 51
Sweet and Sour Pork, 76
Vegetarian
    Eating, 11
    Laksa, 46
    Menu, 22
Verde Primavera, Pasta, 38
Vingear Dressing, Cider, 95
Water, 17
Weight Control & Diabetes, 9
West Meets East Soup, 45
Whip
    Apricot, 110
    Apple, 110
    Apple Blueberry, 110
    Raspberry, 110
    Strawberry, 110
Whirl
    Banana, 113
    Passionfruit, 113
    Raspberry, 113
    Strawberry, 113
White
    Sauce, Low Fat, 108
    Sauce, Mustard Tarragon, 87
Wholemeal Crêpes, 129
Yoghurt
    Cheese, 39
    Dressing, Tomato, 97
    Sauce, 108
Yoghurt Sauce, 108
    Lamb Kebabs, 73
Zest, 30
Zucchini, 90
    Savoury Tomato, 90
    Slice, 55
    Soup, 49